The Milli Vanilli Condition

Essays on Culture in the New Millennium

Eduardo Espina

English Translation by Travis Sorenson

The Milli Vanilli Condition

Essays on Culture in the New Millennium

Eduardo Espina

English Translation by Travis Sorenson

ARTE PÚBLICO PRESS
HOUSTON, TEXAS

The Milli Vanilli Condition: Essays on Culture in the New Millennium is made possible through grants from the City of Houston through the Houston Arts Alliance and the National Endowment for the Arts. We are grateful for their support.

Piñata Books are full of surprises!

Arte Público Press
University of Houston
4902 Gulf Fwy, Bldg 19, Rm 100
Houston, Texas 77204-2004

Cover design by John-Michael Perkins
Cover photo by Eloísa Pérez-Lozano

Espina, Eduardo.
   [Essays. Selections. English]
   The Milli Vanilli Condition : essays on culture in the new millenium / by Eduardo Espina ; English translation by Travis Sorenson.
      p   cm
   ISBN 978-1-55885-811-4 (alk. paper)
   I. Sorenson, Travis. II. Title.
PQ7798.15.S585A2 2015
864'.64—dc23
                                                          2015003059
                                                          CIP

∞ The paper used in this publication meets the requirements of the American National Standard for Information Sciences—Permanence of Paper for Printed Library Materials, ANSI Z39.48-1984.

Printed in the United States of America

12 11 10 9 8 7 6 5 4 3 2 1

To Adriana, who, after having been unjustly deported for six years, was told by the immigration official at Miami International Airport as he stamped her passport, "Welcome home, ma'am."

Table of Contents

Oh

Virginia Woolf (*Mrs Dalloway*)

PROLOGUE
A CENTURY IN THE NEXT CENTURY

FEW TIMES IN HISTORY has the art of pretending enjoyed so much continuity and led to so few consequences as during the hinge-like period between the end of the 20th century and the beginning of the next, or the one in which we currently find ourselves. In the journey between *yes* (or perhaps *no*) and something else, there emerged a landscape of events and effects without precedents. We were just beginning to get a glimpse of what the future could be (and it will no longer be what it once was), when, with the turn of the century and millennium, there arose an oasis of mirages, though in truth the symptoms of this reality—characterized by its unique peculiarities—were already more than a decade old. They arrived like a gust of wind, and some fled the scene in the same fashion, at the speed of a blinking eye. It is history as *blitzkrieg*.

If one were to establish a precise date as to when this scenario of pretending began, it would have to be during the last few months of 1989, the end of a decade and the beginning of another (and of another history). It is a history that at times has been clouded and that at other times has been excessively bright, so much so that its magnitude has yet to be appreciated in totality. We still are not able to see very well. In a short period of time, we went from darkness to a blinding light. We still do not know if the light at the end of the tunnel is the way out or if it is that of an oncoming train.

3

On November 9, 1989, television images projected a scene that was real and whose effects were special, both in the short and the long term. It was a very particular date: with the fall of the Berlin Wall there also appeared to come crashing down the concept of the bipolar world that for years had structured modern reality. It was a concept conceived in accordance with the Manichaeistic notion of cause and effect. Under these circumstances one ideology was crumbling as another was being consolidated (or at least that was the impression). There was nothing gradual about the situation, and it gave rise to a phrase as spurious as it is doubtful: "global village." That is where we had arrived. Without knowing if we were still part of the same world, though supposing that we were, we imagined ourselves to be a committed part of some unanimous deal, even though small- and large-scale differences continued to appear. One of the first effects of the global village was the standardization of tastes and trends. MTV and remote control for all. We learned to share boredom with extreme ease.

The redeeming task of the superficial, which has characterized Hollywood's movie industry during the aforementioned historical period, soon extended to food (the universal menu was born in the form of fused food: even those who had never seen a dead fish in their lives began eating sushi), to clothing, and to the media and entertainment, as well as to the ways used to justify what was present in, or absent from, reality, including where the presence of reality was a random occurrence. It soon became clear that what was real and what was reality did not necessarily need to coincide in all regards. The effects of continuity overlapped the not always synchronic relationship between history and temporality. The coincidence set in motion an unrestricted chain of quote-unquote "avatars" that were subject to the wake of illusions that they left behind them. Not only was food "fast," but the accumulation of weak intensities was also.

Nearly a year after the global village was established with not-so-solemn scenes, a scandal added a peculiar historic note to the history of popular culture. The Wall and Communism had fallen, but the credibility of the entertainment industry was also unprotected from its effects. On November 14, 1990, Milli Vanilli, a duo from Germany (just like the fallen Wall), fell into disgrace when it was proven that other singers had sung the songs in their recordings. All the duo did was lip sync, a technique that when perfectly executed merely requires an image to match it.

In this case the technique was used by two black men with long hair (one born in New York and the other in Paris) who had seduced, above all, the female public by presenting an image of exotic masculine beauty (ideal for a record cover). And these men also happened to be able to give a striking performance for the approximately three minutes that a video clip lasts. The desired reality was accepted as "real," even though it took place in front of a pretentious set that enabled the duo to sell 14 million records in a short period of time and win a Grammy in the category of "Best New Artist." Without having planned it, Milli Vanilli had established a new identity: that of the contemporary figure prone to the unverifiable, to not being demonstrable.

The duo, as a vocal presence, was totally nonexistent; they did not even sing the choruses. They were merely the physical intermediary of a reality that remained veiled. Borrowed voices were directly responsible for their success. This pair of imposters had so completely accepted their real condition within a virtual category that when they were discovered they denied the accusations, not so much to hide the truth, but rather because they were possessed by the fiction they were portraying. Even they were seduced by their own deceit; they became prisoners of their karaoke. Finally, the expanding infinite came to an end and Milli Vanilli was stripped of its Grammy (the first and only time that such a thing had occurred in the history of the award:

they had to return it), thus becoming a parodic performance of its past actions. Before they had not sung, and after they were left with nothing to say. The truth was learned, and it coincided with a sign that anticipated the endgame: the duo's most popular song was "Girl You Know It's True." The fiction of the nearly perfect act of pretending was already a truth that had been sung beforehand.

One of the group's members, Rob Pilatus, died, depressed, at age 33, on April 3, 1998, the victim of an overdose of drugs and alcohol. His death came a short time after he was interviewed on the television program *Behind the Music*, where he spoke sadly of the deceit of which he had been a part. He never managed to adapt to the sudden death of his 15 minutes of fame, and he was forced to reap what he had sown. Returning to reality was not a part of his plans. He even felt deprived of the memories of his short-lived glory. The other, Fab Morvan (with a name akin to that of a comic book villain, like Lex Luthor), in order to convince himself that he continued to be a real person, tried to strike up a career as a soloist, but it never got off the ground. He later worked as a disc jockey. He continued living the music of others.

The "Milli Vanilli practice"—a true vampirization of the microphone—has been replicated with only minimal variation by other music groups invented through marketing strategies. These groups use the voices of others to accompany gymnastic movements and embellish a pleasing look, like giftwrap on an empty box. This healthy sense of artificiality, which the West at time stigmatizes, is looked at favorably in several parts of the planet. In India, lip-syncing work is a prosperous and respected industry. No one sees it as an unforgivable trick. Unknown singers record songs that are later performed in movies and on music videos by famous stars (the same practice is repeated ad nauseam on YouTube). The secret of success lies in preserving the anonymity that will be baptized in the process of adoption.

It is plagiarism deliberately authorized by the person being plagiarized: the original singers record the songs without knowing
who will perform them later (without singing them). In the
country of tandoori chicken, Milli Vanilli would not have had
to return its award. We must place blame on the West for the
duo's complete disgrace.

Epitomizing anomalous situations, other examples of "Millivanillization" arrived on the scene with appearances that dif-
fered from reality, bringing with them the noise of specific
avatars to which thought is not always able to respond with
irony. Performance was turned into the height of transvestism,
displaying an affinity with the pathetic and non-demonstrable:
lips move easily when there are no real words to interrupt them.
In a context that is even more fictitious, the lip-syncing of reality has reached levels at which nothing ever seems to be totally complete. Suddenly, a variety of events entered the scene of
reality once it was stripped of gravity and consequences,
demonstrating that the innocence of expectations is definitively lost, no matter how much nothing ever seems to be definitive
in this era of recycling.

It is the usury of ridiculousness turned into an avatar. Its
network of results provided that which was being reported with
an absence of verification. We wonder about what is there,
being shown with portent: is it or is it not real? In this doubt
regarding transpiring events, the erosion of borders (what
before was chaos is now order and vice versa) corresponds to
the way of understanding a reality that is less and less understandable. The trail leads to the deleted referent and the stag-
ing of neglected meanings. No one pays any heed, and that is
the point: the reading of the immediate scene focuses on specific distractions.

It is for this reason that truth, beyond the appearance of the
phenomenon, remains inaccessible, since of all its appearances
(a constellation marked by fleetingness and movement), the

main one is the one that is taken as such: a truth in a state of fiction. So many centuries later, Plato's cavern has been reconfigured: the shadow casts a body, but it no longer occurs the other way around. In a state of simulation one can be perfect. Or nearly so. This is the perception that is projected. But it does not so much have to do with a blurring (or with its protective container) of that which is pertinent to credibility (whether it be that of an event or a person), as it does the condition of the staunch unflappability of the mechanisms that are in play. From sheer dint of repetition, a lie easily becomes accepted truth, a spoken image of everything, at the halfway point between concealment and evidence.

In current times ("current" turns out to be more current that speaking of post-modern, post-industrial, post-contemporary, or post-everything, because current does not necessarily mean a new historic temporality: today there is too much *post* and very little posterity), replication of the truth favors a style defined by the insistence of purposes. The serial falsification of events has become entropy, a damaged *déjà vu*. In this context, the dissolving of meaning attracts and pushes one toward what seems to be reality after, always after, it has been. The truth of events, moving further and further away until disappearing, occupies a significant area of doubtful thickness. In the present social body —which is telegoverned by the media, by the globalization of oligophrenia, and by disinterest in everything that is not degradable—the ephemeral located within arm's length emerges as the only infinite that is possible to be represented. In a universe of lesser meaning, marked by the transitory nature of judgments and values (nothing is forever, and this is not meant to be, either), the truth remains within reach of sudden images and words, in the event that it is able to exist in such a manner, including after having been examined and refuted.

Voluntary reason, which is becoming more and more unrepresentable despite the supposed perceptive rigor imposed (vir-

tually) by computer science, continues to depend on confusion
to be able to differentiate itself from the specificities and behaviors that, like a rapid galactic wake, it leaves behind: it is living
in the authenticity of the rearview mirror. Faced with an
absence of morals (to the story) and certainties (the Renaissance of man attempted to invent such things and ended up
being Modern), the interpretation of everything rests on the
least common mirage: on the inexplicability of a copy. The few
existing rules regarding the representation of events in history
confront man with distrust. He is informed but continues without knowing.

Everything has random significance; in the path to the creation of reason the absence of truth is excluded *a priori*. Everything has to be popular, pop culture, since the missing certainty ends up entertaining and, for the future good of show
business, generating good ratings. Disciplined functionality in
the service of one of these aspects found in television its greatest intermediary. Television, in its eagerness to intervene in history, with and without fictitious mitigating factors, causes precisely that which it does not seek: an exhaustive fiction of
example. For this reason, the ambition of truth as an objective
of security ceased to be a mission of closeness and, rather, leads
to the contrary: it causes spectators to intervene in the passivity of events, as if they were neighbors involved in that which
they are not, or recently, in the very near past, ceased to be. Just
as in Babel, confusion is the speech of the social body: "And
they said, Go to, let us build us a city, and a tower, whose top
may reach unto heaven; and let us make us a name, lest we be
scattered abroad upon the face of the whole earth."

Just as with the polyglottic tower, opposition to dispersion
has led to its acceleration. And yet, the chaos lies elsewhere. It
is the disinterest and weakening of the centers of attention. For
television, the best way to abolish conformism and apathy is
through the establishment of indifference—which is also con-

formist—regarding the model plan, which casts a pall on the perception of possible events and destabilizes the caution of reason, the governability of phenomena. It makes one believe that understanding works, even if in reality there is nothing to understand, since even the language that attempts to represent events has become residual. The "illusion of truth" is what fascinates.

Just as Romantic writers were attracted by Orientalism, today the exotic also attracts. Life is a reality show where the most in vogue *modus vivendi* can be exercised. What prevails is all that which is "beyond": beyond order, beyond understanding, and even beyond chaos itself. There arises an inconvenient order that, for the purpose of being inhabited, resists being repaired. Nothing in the meantime is indispensable, as confidence in interpretation has been crushed—in the objective distance that it creates—by way of the immediate confession of events, which have ceased to have value. They are a non-neutral objective of the medium that presents them as an epiphenomenon of a disillusioned truth, like an illusion of lucidity and synthesis. Information speaks of its social libido and leaves it unprotected; it demonstrates its rational lack of inhibition in order to enter, without a plan, into the essential matter. In the end what triumphs is an excessive mirage of antinomical events outside of the script, and something even lesser triumphs: nothingness wrapped up as a gift. No other era before has exercised rapid forgetfulness as quickly as this one.

Broadly speaking, the state of deception which, like a stampede, filled the two most recent decades of history has to do with the use of the truth as nonsense. In the triumphant era of late capitalism, or "fierce" capitalism, as John Paul II called it (even popes exercise instantaneous politology), a reverse communism has been born. Added to the ideological debacle derived from news referring to the world's political changes has been the collapse of cultural meanings. All attempts to reorder the unpredictable reality of events have ended in failure. In the business of imaginary certainties, everything is reduced time and time again to a high tide of unconvincing signs: the phenomenon is worth more than its referent. We live between the chip and the lip-sync, *a priori* and *a posteriori*. Why "the truth?" And, if so, how long will it be valid?

In this way, the avatar has become, before and after being corroborated, a suspicion impossible to resolve. Is that which inhospitably entered into daily reality so that it might stay longer "real" or not? And what about "that" which takes place without having a place in reality: has it already happened, or will it happen soon, or is it the previous and perverse sum of its attempts? We are witnessing a carnivalization of hypotheses turned into random truths by their repetition, by detours that favor the permanent postponement of understanding. Almost beforehand, the field of operations of contemporary history became a broad and random map minimally salvaged by the lack of remorse that shows its sparse conclusions: even if the hypotheses of truth fail, or cannot be demonstrated, the validity of their continuity is never put to the test. This continuity transcends itself so as to then establish itself as a fetish in search of an authentic referent rather than its own ends. In a series of completely unrestricted aspects, where everything is within reach, it became easy to turn suspicion into evidence. Events came to situate themselves there, in between that which might be and that which still has not come to be.

From a perspective whose only conclusions barely allow themselves to be observed—the difference is in the avatar and not in its end—there emerge certain coincidences of era which in the end define the place where we are, giving it its own rank among similar phenomena. The word *phenomenon*, "an observable fact or event; an exceptional, unusual, or abnormal person, thing, or occurrence," accompanies the other, *avatar*: "a variant phase or version of a continuing basic entity" (Webster). In this expanding parenthesis between the avatar and the phenomenon move the essays of this volume. They range from the private to the subjective without attempting to find objective definitions, or definitions of objects, not even when they can be found. Rooted in the very interest of the "Millivanillization" of reality—due to a shift from the virtuous to the virtual, and from the fatuous to the fast—the essays of this book cover a precise time period (the post 9-11 era) and then leave it when it begins to become the past, because current times are not contemporary; they became something else. Their essence lacks the fidelity of history.

G.K. Chesterton once said that reality is like anything else. Today's reality, one that has spun out of control, does not resemble any earlier one, even though this is surely the way in which history readjusts when one era arrives to succeed another. Life today is no longer understood as if it were a series of permanent ideals, but rather as an arbitrary bundle of events and inserted presences that appear and reappear, seeking some sign which, from its ephemeral condition, might interpret the enigma of these days when they change their physiognomy. The reality from which topics and themes come, that variation of space where an exchange of empirical abstractions is carried out, desires to not appear like any prior one, and it achieves this objective. A reparation of certainties coincides with a non-reality postponed for another occasion. What survive are happenings indifferent to memory, even if they are associated with the change of memories. Progress of planetary proportions is verified, progress toward the outside and the digressional, toward a peculiarity capable of ceasing to exist at any moment and which even before its disappearance managed to free itself from nostalgias, even if it cannot escape them, since the era exhibits its desires for the future by evoking precise times from the past.

If we accept as valid the phrase by Théophile Gautier, "There is nothing more beautiful than that which is good for nothing," then the effects of this period of history have been beautiful. They *are* beautiful. The union of the phenomenon and the avatar has led to a non-specific history whose abstractive will transforms everything into something else, even into the sign of a possible aesthetics. In most cases, the beauty of events lies in the shortage of consequences that does not require much to continue existing. What are the consequences of a reality in bits, an embryonic reality whose pride lies in lacking resemblances, in being alone precisely in the place where things flow behind history's back? It is defined by a lack of desire for permanence. This reality, which is centrifugal and centripetal at the same time, cannot be entered—not to mention exited—with a self-reliant perspective.

In an era as strange as the current one (strange because it is indefinable)—all eras have been weird and strange, but this one is even more so—words have the luxury of saying whatever they want to. The indecisive neutrality of empiric reality has allowed them to do this. Everything undergoes such a rapid transformation that when language shows up to say something, no matter how important or unimportant it might be the things that there were to say have ceased to be the same. They have changed in place and meaning. Life has become implanted in pure becoming. In short, it is the world trying to feel less alone through the company of a mob of effects. How can one describe the history of fleetingness? How can one write about it? Is it possible? Nothing is impossible for language, not even getting inside events after they have passed by.

The era is also strange for another reason: never before had memory been so devalued (which accounts for the surge of nostalgia, of a retro-futurism). At least in reality, where events supposedly occur, few young people feel obligated to know what happened before they arrived in the world, even if not much time has passed between their birth and the present. History is a discipline of study on its way to extinction. "It doesn't interest me; all that happened *so long ago*." That is what a teenager told me not *so long ago* when I asked him if he wanted me to give him a very good book on the history of World War II for his birthday. Yes, all of that happened *so long ago*. It actually happened just last century, but it is a century that is of less and less interest to those born during its death throes. It is a century with two X's that, despite its horrors and great moments, its inventions and its holocausts, runs the risk of being forgotten sooner than previously thought. That is how far we have come, or gone.

Therefore, just as the present circumstances lead one to suppose, perhaps history is only able to be scrutinized through a careful reading of its fragments, of the isolated behaviors stemming from it, of the splinters of events that appear to be real, in short, of certain specific dates that have managed to survive better than others the general lack of attention. Distraction dominates, and we are moving in this distraction toward a place we do not yet know and do not dare to imagine (science fiction is also a devalued genre). History, at once chronology and continuity of successive events, is an entity that grows less and less understandable all the time, since nowadays the chain of causes and effects does not operate in accordance with a foreseeable logic, if it ever had one.

When in daily reality absolute banality triumphs, and even worse in a process of omnipresence and of usurping popular synonymities such as "celebrity," "cool," and "instant reality," the learning of unrememberance has gained speed, motivated by the accelerated perspective with which we look at the world with us inside. Even if the data of reality cause one to think of a universal lifestyle characterized by a rather unfortunate order (randomness is never deliberate), we move in an era of improvisation. The creative resource used in jazz has become something like an unconsciously collective method to fragment the central motives of reality, in the event that such motives remain. In times when monopolistic devices of excessively peremptory use such as Facebook, Twitter, WhatsApp, etc., control expectations and forms of communication, the question might well be asked, "What can one think and write about so that the ideas generated by reality are not completely obsolete tomorrow?"

Are there indisputable realities, which will retain their permanence even when they have lost it? What differentiating linguistic energy emerges from the era, with its secrets and plots? What themes might be able to vanquish disinterest, and at the maximum velocity that everything has, to then disappear even from its initial form? On Internet portals, such as Yahoo!, for example, news remains prominently featured on the information menu for no longer than two hours, at which time another immediately comes to replace it, without necessarily being either more or less important than the previous one. The sense of expiration has radicalized the perception of the present, or rather of the very instant in which things occur. The emergence of the imperceptible has ceased to coincide with the changing reality of events, which, in this asymmetry, end up losing memory and analysis. There is no time to remember or interpret the referent to be considered. The tendency has reached such an extreme that the suppression of illusions of posterity seems to be intentional.

Perhaps, just as this collection of essays somehow seems to suggest, a good way to approach the reality of events from recent history—not the only way or the most valid—is to focus on certain moments of subjectivity, exclusively those in which there prevails an approximate and lasting idea of reality (with the world inside). Therefore, getting inside information from recent history is only possible through an enthusiastic reading of what happens when we coincide with history. It is a reading, it should be noted, which has not lost its enthusiasm for certain goings-on from the "current" past, from which memory has also not been able to detach itself. It is an "imperfect" past determined to survive on its own and in whose echoes can be heard voices from a time that still has not completely passed into yesterday. Seen in retrospect, the beginnings of centuries have served well to better understand what came after, in the following decades, as if reality always had the need to look back in an attempt to know how things were when they still belonged to the present and interpretations and predictions could be made.

So then, this book brings together essays about the present time, one that coincided with the end of one century and the beginning of another, a hinge period in which a little bit of everything has happened and which today seems to have passed by. Or maybe not completely; it has perhaps passed by incompletely, and what the following pages have preserved is merely a handful of events and reality, with their specificities of currentness, and which through the intermediation of language seek to be saved from forgetfulness, at least as long as forgetfulness has nothing to say to the contrary. To try to present these things through a superficial interpreted synthesis of its effects and consequences would be to fall into the contradiction noted above. It would mean imposing exhaustive explanations on a very particular moment in history, which can only be accessed through the oblique reading of certain scattered fragments of reality which, for some not necessarily rational reason, keep this history current, evoking it, adding perspectives to it, and postponing the last and definitive interpretation which can be written about it.

THE DAY AFTER THE FLAG

I WAS SLEEPING IN TEXAS on the morning of September 11, 2001. I was asleep until I awoke. Everything was the same, just as I had left it the night before, until the telephone rang. A phone call can change many things. It was my brother, Alejandro, calling me from Uruguay to tell me what had happened, although at first no one knew very well how or why it had happened. I woke up surprised, without time to remember what I had dreamt. *To sleep* and *to wake up* are rival verbs, enemy verbs. On that day many things took place that took their place in history. People spent the day watching television, since that is where reality goes first.

I had barely gotten up when I saw that the events had changed the world forever. No matter how much I changed the channel, all of them were showing the same thing. Without trying to convince anyone of anything (which that day was everything), the earlier origin was giving notice that it had been replaced by another. As always, but more than before, the world is comprised of things that have not happened yet. And that day, in such a surprising way, the world began to transform into something different. The glaring brightness of the unforeseen, which for hours without interruption had been spilling images that in another time were better, was still an unfinished work.

At about three o'clock in the afternoon, with a calm coming from the abyss, television viewers saw, for about the twelfth time, as the two Boeing 767 planes struck the outside of the sequoia-like buildings whose structures were tied to the heights. Their velocity became buried in the transparency of the windows, which were made of a glass that until that moment had been unbreakable. Through unimaginable images, humanity was learning to stop and take notice of a heroism appropriate for another, less incomplete world. History was having its debut day.

The present was changing its habits, because this time the prosperity of exceptions increased as much as it possibly could. Since the attack occurred early on a Tuesday, life soon ceased to be so simple. For centuries the world has begun on that day, a Tuesday, also chosen by eternity, even more than Friday. It is a day to be taken into account, though this time the message was different than on earlier occasions. This event had, in the incredulous sight of the world, invented a dominion, an unreal dependence with reality. It was demonstrating what it could say any time that it was so inclined.

The tremendous collapse of the towers caused a dust cloud the type of which had not been seen repeated over and over like that since the days of stagecoaches and cowboys on horses, not to mention on television during a workday. The images came in the form of a stampede. The entertainment was sudden, tragic, and various special effects like the kind used in bad Hollywood movies became instantly obsolete, because reality turned into a supreme fiction where the most unlikely things could occur, just as they did occur, that they might be rewound. It seemed as if the world was going to exit the world, even though it only began to draw attention to itself after the disaster occurred. To the eye, the effects were more effective than the causes.

While the events were still unfolding, reality paid honor to its main questions: Had a war started? Against what or whom? Was the alien invasion reported by Orson Welles on CBS radio in 1938 only now actually occurring, so many decades later? Why on this particular day? By mutual accord—though none of us knew it—we all came to be silent enemies of the same fear, of the unwanted doubts that reality was sending us without moving an inch out of its place. Even though this change of uncertainties was unnecessary, it soon became part of a set of plans that we had not thought all the way through, or even part way through.

The world spent that day glued to the inches of their television screens in stereo, speaking softly about the same topic and awaiting the arrival of the fifth attack, which was erroneously announced by the Hispanic network Univisión. The only kindness that could be seen in the stunning images was far from being a danger without consequences. They were images that replaced unequal quantities and exemplified the way they had been conceived. Around midnight—since the United States, without having left, was returning to apparent normality, or rather it was getting used to an anxiousness accompanied by panic with drowsiness—most people went to sleep. They went to sleep thinking, and thinking correctly, that the next day the world would continue moving, by car in this case (since most Americans walk but little), and that forgetfulness would begin its assiduous work, because even in unrepeatable things such as this it is relentless. Even in the case of phenomenal catastrophes, people have never completely lost the habit of forgetting, and of sleeping. Morpheus never fails. And that night the world slept. Calmness came in bed. The hygiene of chaos at last began to show its clean side.

The first thing I noticed the next day, besides the fact that the replay of the destruction of the World Trade Center could be seen commercial-free at all hours and on all channels (it was like popular songs heard over and over on the radio because people request them), was that the country had awakened covered with flags. Just as with mushrooms after the rain, they were everywhere. The era of the flag had arrived. Houses and other buildings had grown flags during the night, even though no one had watered them. Flags, flags everywhere: in the front yard and the backyard, in the bedroom, in the kitchen, in and on the car, on one neighbor's house and that of another, on the house to the east (East of Paradise Lost), and the one after that, too. One neighbor was black, the other was white, and the one in the middle was sort of brown, like a mulatto or a mixture of black and Amerindian, Hispanic. He also had a flag out. The flags were the same, even if their owners were of differing origin and skin color and had different flag poles.

During those days, unlike shares in the stock market, flags were going up but not down. There was flag inflation: there was a proliferation of these cloth semaphores for low-hanging clouds and for birds. The cirrus clouds and the sparrows were grateful. This Wall Street of sentiments involved any house or home in the Union. Not even mansions were immune from the flood of red, white, and blue emblems. I went out to scan the inhabited surroundings and determined that my house was the only one with a Uruguayan flag. It was somewhat strange, too strange for the moment. I thought about taking it down. I was afraid that someone might think it was an act of rebellion against that sudden frenzy of U.S. patriotism. I looked at it so that it would tell me what it thought about the whole thing and to know if it wanted to stay raised up there, but flags always exercise a magnificent impassivity with those who want to know their opinion. They have learned to live without saying what they think. They are secretive in their silence, which is how they display their good manners and teach lessons, because there is no better behavior than the one that defends the liberty of the heavens.

Since I was not able to decide, I opted to leave my flag in its hoisted position one more day, in other words the day following the one before it. But, now that I think about it, I actually left it up two more days, since on Thursday I had something important to do which today I do not recall what it was. I think I went to the supermarket. Since there was a rumor circulating that something even bigger than what had taken place two days before might occur, some supermarkets were having sales. They did not want the end of the world to find them with their shelves full. Another entire day passed, from the time it started until the time it ended. On television they continued showing the same documentary movie of that Tuesday wed to the apocalyptic. When I remembered to remember it was already Friday, September 14, and by then the entire block was full of American flags. They were united by a state of general nervousness. Reality lived up to the reputation of its doubts.

Suddenly, through the art of (terrorist) magic, flags came into style just like miniskirts, though the latter are more to my liking. Even though they had different flowers and were of different shapes and sizes, all the yards on the block seemed identical. They flew the same flag across the front, not a battle front but rather the home front. I even began to think that the whole world had a flag, believing it would protect them from any possible aerial threat. Flags were like vaccinations: they were good just in case. Anchored to a mast, they sustained a fixed idea. That day the flags had reason to feel the same as always. It is all the same to them.

Therefore, with such an avalanche of patriotism, having a Uruguayan flag in the midst of so many U.S. flags became an unusual act, even an exotic one. A freak flag. No one before had ever paid attention to the yard of my modest residence, which was considerably inferior in comparison to the others with regard to flowers. Nevertheless, it became a hit overnight (but especially in the afternoon). People walked or drove by and looked surprised at those light blue and white stripes with a sun suspended in the air, avoiding having to give any answers, this flag that was the tenant of a mast proud to have it attached to it. Cars stopped, and they themselves honked their horns and took an interest in knowing a little more about the visual content of that rectangle with colors different from those that the unprecedented circumstances had made so popular. During one of those days a woman took a Polaroid photo so that she would have proof of what was happening, while a man made a gesture of displeasure, as if he had seen the Nazi flag, or even— for him—a worse one: that of Mexico.

I feared for the well-being of my solitary Uruguay flag, which was surely feeling its minority status, as if inhabiting an aerial ghetto, and suffering alone—out in the elements—that sudden xenophobia dressed up as curiosity. There it was, up there all alone, with only the birds in their sonorous variety for company, and perhaps a butterfly here and there of the kind that never know what it happening, and all the better for them. I saw it, and reflected in its dismayed silk was the sign of an anguish that wanted to know right then, "Where am I? What the hell am I doing here? Is this an embassy?" In an attack of heraldic nationalism, I raised it after the game in which Uruguay defeated Peru, in Lima, as part of the elimination rounds for the upcoming World Cup of soccer in 2002, a game which had taken place a few days before the terrorist attack.

When I put it there, on a pole that looked like a toothpick, or perhaps more accurately like a Genoa sausage the length of a basketball player, it was the only flag in the calm environs of an area with people who, generally speaking, were rational folk. It was adorned by solitude. Without ever having imagined it, its presence among none-too-exotic plants and common, everyday birds attracted other flags on the same block. Mine was a pioneering flag of the flag craze. With its biased romanticism, and constantly betraying the calm, there, erect and upright, was my flag, anticipating the intentions of the air, that source of harassing wind. It was there to be, not merely to exist.

The continuous presence of people in front of my house who I did not know and did not want to know motivated me to keep the patriotic emblem right where it should be, flying in its glory with more-than-rectangular reasons. Without having set out to do so, it turned into a tourist attraction. Even though one could not take an elevator up inside it, my flag competed with the Empire State Building and the Sears Tower, the latter of which, I have been told, has undergone a name change. On Saturdays and Sundays, especially in the early afternoon, after church, people from other places came to see it. In fact, it was such a success that I even thought about opening a convenience store in the garage to sell souvenirs and postcards with (of course) the picture of my flag on them.

I further considered going into my kitchen and beginning to make blue-colored candies called "Flag," which inside would have some advice or saying, just like Chinese fortune cookies. I had even thought of a slogan: "Eat some Flag candies and then eat some more and you will no longer be the person you were before." But I immediately abandoned the idea because I realized that I would not have been able to put up with the questions from the constant stream of visitors, the same boorish people as always, who exercise the ignorance of ignorance and mistake the English-language pronunciation of Uruguay with "Are you gay?", or with Kuwait or Hawaii, or, even worse, with eBay. The blindness of Americans vis-à-vis the remainder of the educated world tends to be insulting. It treats it precisely like that: a remainder. I therefore left the flag in its well-placed position so that it could serve the principal purpose of its race: to give sight something haughty and superior to look at later. Inventing more hours than it needed, it soon became an autonomous geography.

However, I began to spy on it in order to atone in its behalf for all the intrusive looks. Never—and I bear witness of this— did I see it lose its composure, not even on the October afternoon of that year when they took three photographs in a row of it and said something about it in English, with a Texas accent, or on that morning when it had rained quite heavily and the insolent wind shook it while it was all wet, leaving it to look as though it had just gotten out of the shower. This left it refreshed and awake, but without a bathrobe. This flag, transplanted to American air, had learned to live its life as an immigrant better than the majority of undocumented immigrants. This flag had not crossed the border wet, even if it got that way on rainy days. It spent its days contemplating other flags, which also had stripes, and it said things to them which were of little importance to them. It spread rumors. One day I caught it red-handed right in the middle of a conversation with the others.

I heard it saying "Hi, cousins" to the U.S. flags. I could hear that it said this in English (that was the day I realized that my flag was bilingual). In good families there are no language barriers. They got along very well (it did not tell me this, but I could tell), with a cordiality free from nationalisms and explanations. From a distance they greeted one another in their rebellious dialect, one that does not need dictionaries or translators to make sense, because it is a dialect consisting of a sense of Zen. The wind wisps through these flags of different sizes, and it learns from memory to read their continuous history. They are the dissimilarity of themselves. From the time that a piece of fabric causes them to be born moving forward, they become accustomed to an obedience that they can continue until they wear out, even though they are not in a position to guarantee that so much demonstrated obedience will last forever.

Rising in insurgency, and sharing the same secret as coins, flags, like birds, offer a toast with the cup of a rose, a toast to the health of an aboriginal symbolism. They caress the air with borrowed kisses for reasons that the homeland instills, and then they stop to contemplate the interpretation until they simply stay there. Being able to go to their Pleistocene whenever they want, and feeling above the circumstances—let it be noted—they make their invasion a vertical one. With the answers that they themselves believed to possess, they were conceived to put metaphors to work. They learned to be made in this way. And when nothing happens in the history of the world, they find salvation by remaining still. Love might be blind, but they keep their eyes open, as long as they do not fall in love. They place their faint presence on the altar of that which cannot be postponed, speaking whatever language they so desire. In place of shouting up at the sky, they remain silent. This silence, extended to movement, does not come in exchange for anything.

Being as they are, brides to the cosmic wind, they first understand half and only later the rest. So predisposed to thinking that the past has not yet arrived, or that it will not arrive, they live their day as soon as it appears. For this reason they are always in the present, the today which is attributed to their condition. Furthermore, an intelligence assimilates them. With the optimism of skyscrapers, they learned not to confuse solitude with boredom, the solstice with any specific sun. Sustained by an engrossed transparency that is as intentional as that which it conceals, they feel like connoisseurs of words through actions. Being good at things taken one at a time and at matters dealing with the psychic when it is universal, they purposefully ignore the importance of peace in their core, of the ideas given to last through it all, given the circumstances. Who could fail to look at them when they are still there? There they are, and they do not charge a toll. It is their way of refuting the temptation to remain still.

Flags of the U.S.A. and Uruguay, what a combination for multicultural times: *Urusa* y *Usaguay*. They are up in the air, their air. When they meet, they say "U," as if they had hurt each other lovingly, as if they had stepped on one another's feet, or as if they had arrived together at a U-Haul center to rent a truck in which to move. In front of the United Nations building there are some 200 flags. Those of the United States and Uruguay are next to each other, even in typical times of rain and darkening skies before a storm. On those days they wish their universal home were under an umbrella, united in the fog when it speaks, but also in the air accustomed to living without water on top of it, down there below, together, without commotion, delivered up to the discretion of the dry wind. This was also the way they were on the block where I lived. Perhaps my Uruguayan flag is right, so tolerant and, for a time, all alone just for me. Maybe it is a cousin to the American flag and shares some kind of ancestral genealogical link with it, even if Uncle Sam is not its uncle. I always wanted to know before, but now I do not. What little I know about the two flags is there, calling attention to itself, and that is enough for me. They are the landscape of an obviousness, secure as long as they are visible. One has a sun and the other has several stars. Both depend on some galaxy. The world is crazy and they are twisting in the wind.

The flags that proliferate today seem to have a greater number of stars and stripes than before, but they have the same amount (I only said it *seemed* like they had more). All of them are the same, but none of them are completely the same, as their sizes change, but not the color or the number of stars and stripes. There are so many flags with stars that even at midday the sky is star-spangled. There are not more stars in human reality (the world is barren), but on flagpoles they abound and then some. These poles are very monogamous: they only raise one single flag on top. Has anyone ever seen a flagpole with two flags, making an exhibitionism of its colored polygamy? Such fidelity to a cause should be rewarded with something more than pure chance.

The U.S. flags of yesteryear had fewer stars because the country had fewer states. Today it has a greater number, 50, but the state of its morale has fallen to the ground. Neither men nor flags were meant to be down so low, sharing the ground, far from the heavens. The flagpole was created for the flag (the name of the inventor is not known). It is an embalmed pole. The ground is for worms, for beetles, for feet, for lost objects (those who find a coin are rewarded by being able to keep it). With their morale on the ground, the American people, and those in the rest of the world, think based on the principle of uneasiness. People are tense, nervous, more nervous than at other times in history. Before there were Attila, Hitler, Nero, and Stalin. Today there are figures with Arabic names we cannot pronounce who want to usher in a post-modern medieval era, moving us backward. How do tell them no, to take a step back, and that this can all still be fixed?

Despite the consequences, we cannot deny that this is an original threat. We live in a world saturated by paradoxes where realities, when they change, must become new once again. Expectations of originality are generated, but when this originality comes we tremble. The lyrics of the Uruguayan national anthem say "Tremble, tyrants." Nevertheless, these days tyrants are not the only ones to tremble. The recovery of enthusiasm, just as it must have been on the first day of history, is disconcerting, and it causes tremors in morale. Faced with so much novelty regarding things in the world, people's behavior stands out as nervous. Flags, on the other hand, know how to conceal their nervousness, leaving it for tomorrow, feeling like the inalterable part of some as-yet-nonexistent country. That is enough for them. They no longer want to be (and they are right) representatives of Persia, Prussia, or Tanganyika. Of the Soviet Union, of Zaire, of Czechoslovakia. Of East Germany! Of countries that, for better or worse, no longer exist. What is this! What has happened to this symbolism? Flags depend on the present to know what their argument hangs on today.

Feeling chosen by a faint light, all these flags adorn a beauty that could be considered to be complete. Beginning with the wind and moving on from there, even though they do not need to do so, flags improvise an involuntary happiness, desiring to do things that surely are not important to people, such as, for example, reciting a poem by Góngora or Walt Whitman, listening to jazz right now, playing the piano in the Methodist Church on Sundays, or putting transparency in order. Without paying any attention to the warnings of the present, they feel secure because they know they are wise in their illiteracy. All of them, with a look of not being friends with any president in particular, united in an accessible symphony; agree to modify the direction of the coming wind. Impartial air is their opium den, the indecisive target to shoot in the bull's-eye. Despite their influence over centuries, flags have been misinterpreted altogether too much. The eye has trivialized their ties, believing that they are only useful on holidays when some heroic deed is commemorated but which no one remembers during the rest of the year.

For the first time since the Civil War a century and a half ago, Americans have enemies at home. Terrorism has many countries and no single flag. Those who are threatened hide in front of the flag to protect it and face whomever it is who might come. In a time of obscurantisms, people go out and wave the gleaming stars of the flag so that at least something will shine. It is good to always have at hand a docile high point that allows itself to be raised and lowered for any reason. It is not, however, a reason for just anyone. There is also surely a war of the flags in this era just as there was one in the time of the Crusades. And does anyone know what the other flags are like, be they those of allies or foes?

Flags are so meek that in the United States there are those who burn them without encountering the slightest resistance. I met a former soldier who on a sunny Saturday lit the barbecue grill with the national flag. Certain strips of it burned before the others. Since returning from Vietnam, his hobby had been to burn stars and stripes. His flags fluttered amid the flames. Even though the U.S. Constitution does not prohibit such actions, some of the guests became very angry upon seeing this symbol of patriotism smoldering in the coals and they had some ugly words to say to the griller. There were colorful arguments around that barbecue of symbolism. But the hamburgers were tasty and did not taste at all of flagpole, and the same went for the truly delicious hotdogs, some of which were long enough that they could have held up the flag of some country, provided it was not too heavy.

Although it is but an insipid piece of cloth, any flag, no matter which one, embodies something. In that regard it resembles a bone. People instill absolute meaning into a concrete size. Flags are revered the world over. They are so important that they have their own verbs: to hoist, to unfurl, to flutter. There is even a discipline dedicated to their study: vexillology (from the Latin *vexillum*). I do not know anyone with a doctorate in that. Uruguay and the United States have striped flags. Flags with stripes look like zebras, just like those where pedestrians cross the street (as seen in the Beatles' *Abby Road* album cover); except for in this case the pedestrian is the wind, just a common, run-of-the-mill pedestrian. This attacker of light silk twirls flags as if they were an androgynous zone representing the conversion of individuals in a group.

In front of the United Nations building in New York, there are, as I have said, hundreds of flags. They are all together, having a secular party, all with the same style (not even in this does the present world demonstrate originality). Not one of them says anything, and yet people speak of the language of flags, which is silent, like that of deaf-mutes. Flags are also this way: deaf and mute like the woman in Shakira's song "Ciega sordamuda," and even unfeeling. If someone dies for them, they remain silent, and they also say nothing when someone burns them. They are, in the end, an anonymous facsimile leaving behind them immaculate ashes.

In times of unrehabilitated examples and of excessively concrete realities—hunger, environmental pollution, violence, and overpopulation—man believes, just as he did in the Middle Ages, in emblems that are intermediate between an ideal and a vague idea, with plenty of physical activity in the middle. In their inevitable fullness, which does not depend on either stripes of territories, flags enlist in the concise army of their meanings. They resist the passing of eras from the prestige of their permanent marketing. International symbols of certain examples, they are intermediaries of senses and origins. Their justification lacks a cause. With their undulating nature, these proportioned parallelograms symbolically represent a faith that, nonetheless, can be official, a mobile homeland that wards off birds and recruits looks. Man, naturally unfaithful in his love, swears allegiance to a vague identity.

Abstractions are stronger than feelings. A single flag makes more than a hundred comments or says more than a thousand words, which tend to be worth a picture: someone who visits a neighbor and sees a swastika or a hammer and sickle hanging in the living room knows what should not be said. I had a neighbor who had in his house all the flags he admired. The only one he did not have was the flag of randomness. And he had been born in one of them: in the town of Bandera (Spanish for "flag"), Texas, the world capital of cowboys.

There are all manner of flags in the world. There are too many flags. Even the gay community has one: in the middle of the rectangle there is a rainbow. It could have featured a pink teddy bear, or a violet Teletubby, but as it turn out it is multi-colored. There is much solecism regarding the way in which people feel subject to something akin to a disproportionate feeling, which, invariably, ends up being run up a flagpole or placed on a wall. After all, the symbolic fabric is no more than a size distributed in proportion. In Spanish, as had been noted, the word for "flag" is bandera, which they say comes from another word, bandoleros, "bandits" who were the first to carry banners used to mark their outrages. The word in Gothic, a Germanic tongue, was bandwa, meaning "a sign." The English word "flag" is the beginning of the word "flagellation," the work of a scourge reminiscent of bandits in their time: they were of hostile mast. The word "flag" has many synonyms: standard, pennant, emblem, oriflamme, ensign, insignia, rosette, and blazon. Just as with flowers, flags are at the mercy of that which blows them. The height of their circumstances accepts winds from any direction. When they flutter restlessly from this high point, these gallant emblems scare away the flies and butterflies that circle around them, thus creating a dazzling scene that inspires respect and beautiful phrases. Flags do not know how to be neutral.

People revere many flags at the same time: that of their country; of their state, province, or department; of their city; of their school; of their soccer team; of their favorite hotel; of their religion; and of their political party. Spaniards, who utilize *banderas*, might even revere Antonio Banderas. Cousins to the elevator, though they go up and down without occupants, flags give in to the pleasure of looking at the world from non-too-stormy heights. They are confidantes of the air and they know how to listen. In order not to leave the clouds all alone, they persevere in their waving. Their opportunism is scandalous: they blow with the first thing that arrives, be it the wind or a fan. I tend to believe quite often, as if I really believed it, that God created flags so that the wind could play. In this regards they are indeed pleasing. They please the living and the dead. For having defended the freedom and sovereignty of the nation, governments award soldiers with a folded flag that is given to the families of the deceased. They are used to pay debts.

Just as happens with politicians, flags change positions in accordance with how the wind is blowing. There are in the world, where the wind blows, companies so big that they have their own flag. Luckily not all companies have them. It would be horrible if workers' salaries depended on respect shown toward a useless piece of cloth. Very few flags have usefulness. The only ones that are truly useful are those that are placed on the beach to symbolize the liquid language of the water, that country of high tides. When I see a colored flag on the beaches of Florida indicating danger, I do not go and dive into the water. However, the green flag used to indicate that it is safe to enter the water confuses me: at some of the world's horse racing tracks they also use a green flag to note that two horses crossed the finish line at the same time. So, does this mean that two people at the beach can swim and sunbathe simultaneously?

The definition of the word "flag" in the Merriam-Webster Dictionary is deservedly stupendous: A usually rectangular piece of fabric of distinctive design that is used as a symbol (as of a nation), as a signaling device, or as a decoration." The first flags, which appeared in China 3,000 years before the time of Christ, served to differentiate armies, so that soldiers on the same side would not fight against each other. They were useful for life. And there are white ones, with their physiognomy of truce. But national banners work a lot, even when there are no wars. During peacetime, troops set about raising and lowering flags on a tall pole, as if they were the stock market of national sentiment, the visual nourishment of nationalism. Since its place is in the air, some nations gave their flag a corresponding symbol. That of the Babylonians had a dove; that of the Armenians featured a lion; and that of the Persians was adorned with an eagle (the Egyptians put an ox on theirs and for this reason needed stronger flagpoles). In short, we are faced with a zoological order that requires an interpreter to decipher its estimable symbolism, which is rarely generalized.

Modern flags carry a cosmic symbology: they bear suns, moons, and starts (and rainbows). They embody elevated values and summarize a collective soul. In their universal representation, flags symbolize and communicate a common path, but one must know how to interpret them. Not all flags carry the same meaning. A man waving a white flag on the deck of a ship that is on fire is not the same as another who is waving a checkered flag at the end of a car race. Flags must be read correctly. It is not right to shoot at someone who is carrying a white flag in his hand, nor should one be afraid of someone carrying a red flag: it could be a lifeguard.

Some Americans wear a bandana on their heads with an image of their flag; they have patriotic thoughts. The enemy wears a turban. The country is troubled by those who wear such garb. The national flag, with its stars (there is no longer room to add one more—that of Puerto Rico?), looks down on them from on high, as if it were a giraffe's head with its nation among the highest clouds (and even better if they are cirrus clouds), up there were it is unlikely that the least normal fear will reach it. Up go the flags, and up goes the value of shares in weapons factories. Flags also come down. I had to lower mine the day that I moved (it did not move a muscle to speak when it discovered what was happening). On a Thursday morning it ceased to be at the (high) level of events, although it was some two inches above average.

There are still flags scattered everywhere, including where there did not use to be any, and even on flagpoles that earlier were bereft of flags there are some U.S. flags in the process of being raised, halted at a certain distance from the next sensations. In place of its flags speaking to the wind, the heart of nations accepts exiles and transplants. On the midnight newscast a man confessed that his flag had been with flagpoles from 40 different U.S. states, going up and down them like a national mountain climber without an elevator. Nevertheless, no one would dare consider it a flag of ill repute, a promiscuous flag. In this regard, flags are pets that do what their owners tell them. If they are to be up, they go up; if they are to be down, they ask to be left alone. Their life moves between being raised and being lowered.

Flags are such homebodies that they never sleep away from home. Yards are their bedroom, the wind their pillow—twin resting places. This is how their abstract fidelity is rewarded. Twin towers or other material places full of people may fall, but flags are spared: they were born to be the remnants of something emblematically improbable and of a great diversity of things put to the test upside down. Mine, of Uruguayan lineage, says the same thing, even in the closet where I have it stored, exiled in the wardrobe next to clean winter clothes. It must be the one flag in the world, besides that of the terrorists, which would be happy if another 9-11 took place. It wants action. It does not have the blood of a white flag. It desires to get back into battle, a banner on the attack.

In 2001 my flag was young, fluttering, jealous of its safe solitude, defiant of the circumstances that it never understood very
well. Now it awaits a similar opportunity to reunite with its
cousins and swap memories, the kind which take a while to
develop. When it is on the flagpole that best suits it, which in its
case could be any and all (my Uruguayan flag's capacity of adaptation is extraordinary: it is a flagpole polygamist), things round
out nicely for it, even if its shape is rectangular. It is a rectangle
whose average amount of beauty increases in wintertime, when it
can more exactly copy the writing of those cold days. In the
frozen outdoors that have been pardoned by danger, flags do not
need to bundle up; they feel a little better naked. Isolated in the
air, they do what the air tells them. Standing on a sofa of national fanfare, they exhibit the height of vanities. They have the
name and the moment. They leave exclusivity to executioners.

These flags, the opposite of traitors, feel something of a
moral nature that compels them. All of them, high on the
world's summit, are imitated from afar by the south wind when
it is calm—there is no heroic inhabitant of the Pampas there to
help them—because they have had the temerity of coming and
living without questioning. But they are not for sale: they
learned this lesson in patriotic clauses and on hot days. As
metaphoric as that very thing that they unwittingly symbolize,
they feel the same love (or whatever it is) as shields and
emblems. Observing the war of the worlds with haughtiness,
they have been faithfully unfaithful to their birthdays. They
have received persistence as an inheritance. With all their
examples in rules and regulations, they are the spies of optimism. Soldiers die for their colors, but the latter ceased to be
brave on the day they discovered what they were. Useless, bearing forgiveness, they know that the very thing that they seek is
not above or hidden out there somewhere in some lost galaxy.
While Heraclitus read in the water all that existed, flags read

the emptiness in the wind where they bathe more than twice, being always the same in their mysteriousness.

Having a flag is like having a dog, a faithful guide: both are fetishes of a fidelity in no way illusive. Flags stoically assume the unchangeability of the feelings they represent, the summarized abstraction of the country. Despite the material of which they are made, they do not accept having their mettle called into question. Through their unavenged haughtiness, with cosmetic gestures and methods suitable for all, flags survive, invincible, any bombardment. Turned into their principal characteristic, the tribute to a veneration without attributes, they join with the air in common directions in search of common sense. It is not a mistake to attempt to learn the details of their benefits. The Uruguayan flag has them. I know this from experience. All other flags have them, also. Feminine and asexual, flags are here and there, tied to a form that bears witness as it waves. They are the CNN of universal symbolism: they have correspondents everywhere. A poet once said that God made flags so that the wind could play. Between East and West, an unexpected duet out of step, they turned flags into a harem: flags to beget flags.

When the world is least expecting it, flags will forget about their good memory, and even about their inexact striptease of values and meanings. They will be freed from the causes of their arguments. Centuries later they will be asked in their vertical and open habitation—the flagpole—what they think about this, this (oft) so-called reality, and they will say the same thing they always do: "Ah, humans, our greatest idolaters." In the midst of fields where pitched battles are fought, before and after the grateful truce; in flower-covered fields; and in fields turned into concentration camps, flags know how to accept the consequences. They are always calm, always preceding the voice of the wind. No matter where they are, they are not willing to trade their exceedingly slow peace for anything. Today the world wishes it were a flag.

THE FUTURE OF THE PAST:
THE WORLD CAPITAL OF NOSTALGIA

FIVE, 10, 20, 200, 700 YEARS have gone by since the last time that something occurred. First these things happened separately; now all of them together make up the past. They are years that represent notions, inventions, reverses, wars, vaccinations, technology, in short, a postmortem periphery of time. In this world, anniversaries abound to the point of excess, but, incredibly, they continue to be created notwithstanding. There is always some date, moment, or circumstance to thaw out and bring into the present as a commemorative thingamajig. The point is to preserve memory.

The point is to celebrate life as seen looking backward. If it is not the end of WWII then it is that of WWI, or the date that someone died who was famous and continues to be, even after death, or the year a book or record came out or a mass concert took place, or the celebration of some country's independence, which can account for many such days, since the world is full of countries (more than 200). That which is and exists in reality can easily be celebrated as an anniversary 10, 20, 30, or 100 years after having happened. Or it can be 500 years after the fact, as occurred in 1992 with the lavish revelry over the discovery of America. When the discovery of this continent hits the millennium mark, the party will surely be twice as big, since 1,000 years is 500 times two. Columbus will continue to arrive, not in America, but in memory.

Without preambles, the past prospers. It reawakens. Nostalgia is a diva, a huge hit, and an audiovisual voyeurism enshrines it. On radios around the world songs from the 1980s proliferate. Since there were many good songs during that time period we hear lots of them. In fact, the nostalgia that we feel for said decade is so acute that in 2005 a group named Bowling for Soup recorded a song called (what originality!) *1985*. In some 20 years (provided that 'memory' is not a forgotten word by then) we will feel nostalgia for this song. That is to say, there will be a sort of nostalgia for nostalgia. That year, 1985, *annus mirabilis*, was very special for music because the massive Live Aid concert was held. This was the first great international action aimed at combating the blights suffered by a forgotten Africa, one of which is AIDS.

Nevertheless, to attempt to return to those consequential days that ceased to be immediate, it is not necessary to listen to a handful of memorable songs that help rewind the senses and feelings, acts of the stimulus and of the wild abandon that are called upon to testify. All one has to do is look and see that in Africa everything continues on just as before, or worse. In other words, in that regard time remains the same as always, so miserly and autistic, favoring nostalgia for that which has not yet happened, not by a long shot.

With a different repertoire, man has always lived trying to recover a time in the past which, because it happened earlier, was allegedly better. Or this is how he imagines it. He has made this emancipated resurrection exclusive. However, this situation has become radicalized in the present day. It is a brightly shining weapon. Who these days speaks of "progress?" When does this word ever come up, other than in the dictionary? The idea of the future is disquieting. The present—an inhospitable place, a bad word—has been replaced, suspended without pay (perhaps it is responsible for its loss of prestige). It is a bonsai-like present. Today, the past enjoys more fame than before. There is an entire nostalgia industry. Its rating is on the increase. Looking at itself in the mirror of its own influence through the ages, nostalgia, through an unrecognizable trail, chooses eras and hours to revisit. Its self-reliance, exercised to the nth degree, brings about a consumer apartheid, though it does not guarantee that reality will continue to be honest. The process, it seems, is one in which there is no turning back.

The levels of reminiscence have been increasing. It is now much more than a fantasy to which it has occurred to become stylish. At this point, only a good case of Alzheimer's disease will be able to save us from dying of an overdose of nostalgia. This nostalgia that of today—the only time to take into account—confirms that time left behind has left us forever. We have been abandoned between nothingness and ignorance: we are clones of Robinson Crusoe, on an island with fewer hours that, furthermore, for our inconvenience, do not repeat themselves. These are rules that time had never heard talked about, even if, supposedly, they are part of an age in history. In this earlier era, people looked forward. The goal was never before. In 1968, Stanley Kubrick make a movie imagining a future 33 years later, *2001: Space Odyssey*. In 1983, the singer Prince recorded a song with a futuristic theme called "1999" ("tonight we're gonna party like it's 1999"), moving up to the end of the millennium. In that before from not so long ago, it made sense to imagine about tomorrow. That was the first law. In this regard, the rules of the game have changed.

To live while rewinding time, believing that the future is coming from behind and more slowly, as if it were having a hard time arriving, is the characteristic—its genome—of our time, a time concerned about highlighting the biographical importance of reality. The tendency is along those lines. The past makes believe that it is real. It is one of so many immediate excesses. Since things in the world and in the country—another world— generate greater uncertainty than before, nostalgia has become the trench in which to seek refuge and not think. Faced with so much insecurity, without any plans for comfort in sight, we force the future to take shelter in the past, one which has not yet become completely preterite, because, moving backward; it has remained in motion without being able to stop.

A century ago, in 1905, when the 20th century was just beginning, a scientist, one of the many in the modern era, ventured to say (because it began as the century of optimism): "Within 100 years we will have conquered the future." Apparently we are the future, inhabitants of a today belonging to an irreversible present. But the future, lacking visible strategies, is timid. No one dares to predict, as a century does, what realities will be possible over a period of 100 years. The future is an inaccessible moment, a time which has not put off the current today until tomorrow, if reality still exists by then. On the face of its watch, the hands move counterclockwise, a tick-tock in reverse.

Ensconced in its seat in the orchestra circle, nostalgia configures and reconfigures those pendulum-like days in which it is difficult to achieve that delicate balance between desires and memories. We live in a century which in many uses and customs is still new, but we do so with our feet anchored in the one that ended precisely when it was supposed to end. We scrutinize up and down that culmination situated between what could be again and what is gone forever. To be precise, the present (in all its interpreted imprecision) lives in parentheses, stuck between that which happened until recently and that which will perhaps come to happen one day.

This present, with its complex-ridden vagueness, is a universal feeling characterized by certain behavior and attitudes adrift. In one way or another, *tête-à-tête* with the impossibility of being repeated, the preterite is filtered through the reality of the present with images that are associated with certain earlier experiences which remain current, in a state of voluntary embalming. In this manner, we exalt these experiences, awarding their doubtful glamour with reissues.

In the midst—finally—of this turmoil of materials belonging to days and years gone by, man (meaning us) lets loose some intrinsic contradictions marked by paradox. We invoke music, clothing styles, colors, words, the sexy promise of satisfaction, and even imperfect ideas belonging to specific eras—the 1970s and 1980s, as well as the 1960s, though less so—in which, as we well know, humanity was no happier than it is today. Not only was it not happier, it was not as stable politically and emotionally. Nevertheless, we still invent, in improved fashion, that which we never were. There is a lack of answers for all the questions of *why?* that would like not to be postponed. The recuperation of the doubtful 1970s carried out by collective memory is incomprehensible. There was nothing extraordinary about that decade, not even for the feelings that have memory less demanding than reason. In many regards it was a rather disastrous decade (a very well-begun disaster).

In South America, with toppled democratic governments and thousands of disappeared persons, the "rather" part is no exaggeration, and this was also the case on other parts of the map. Many things happened in the 1970s, so many in fact that it even seems as if everything happened: the oil crisis (with prices as high as the sky, a sky often black with pollution); a war (Vietnam); high-level political corruption (Richard Nixon); terrorism (this decade made it a profession); political holocausts (the Soviet Union, China); coups and cases of disappeared persons by the dozen (South America); ideological frauds and fanatics celebrating a beast who at the time was politically *chic* (Pol Pot); and other things with visceral consequences that would be better forgotten but which still live on residually, allowing themselves to be rethought in order to be recalled and awarded with a subsequent existence. The decade of the 1980s was a little better than the one that immediately preceded it, especially in the area of music. For this reason, invoking the 1980s in the present could be justified. Radio stations that play songs from said decade prevent the utterance of anathemas against it.

Time makes its audience evident. The 21st century began influenced by people's radical tendency to live with their eyes fixed on the rearview mirror, to stretch out their adolescence as if it were chewing gum by remembering experiences and events that imagination, which by nature is more spontaneous than reflexive, sets out to improve, touching them up cosmetically so that they appear less loathsome than they were in truth (without truth). It must be noted, however, that these things have not slipped completely into the past, because in our present lives we save them from being part and parcel of a complete preterite, something that would be better to let happen. It would seem, by seeing the expansive remake of realities that can be witnessed all about, that we have gotten to the point of believing that the worn-out past might be able to save us from something. But from what? From the fears for which we lack an antidote? Whether it be one thing or the other or several things at once, what is certain is that the future of the present imposes itself up to this point as a culminating moment that we would like to stop and rewind whenever we need to. Just click and it is done. Click and the same thing returns again, though a little different, as if to say that it is first going to think about it.

Our era—which should be the future—is defined by a trend: life came to depend on the past (we depend more on it that it does on us). The examples associated with such a rewinding plan (a plan without concrete purposes) stand out in different disciplines and in specific places of a reality with many derivatives that conspire to conceal their aims. There is a channel on cable television called VH1 Classic, whose programming is comprised almost exclusively of music videos from the 1980s, with a few occasionally thrown in from the 1960s and 1970s, when the format in question lacked aesthetic attributes. Movies, meanwhile, resort to things that have already been done: recently there have been remakes of *War of the Worlds*, *Charlie and the Chocolate Factory*, *The Bad News Bears*, *The Longest Yard*, *The Love Bug* (*Her-*

bie Fully Loaded), *Carrie*, *The Great Gatsby*, and cinemagraphic versions of past television hits such as *Mission: Impossible*, *Charlie's Angels*, and *The Dukes of Hazzard*.

Asymmetrically sublimated, the trend currently in vogue deals with all formats of communication and entertainment. Among radio stations with the highest ratings are those that only play songs from the 1980s. In the field of advertising, both today and in the past (represented in the television series *Mad Men*); there are numerous commercials that employ songs from that same decade, many of them aiming to sell new cars. It is the past turned into the day after tomorrow. They are the days in between. It is an unending story. Thousands of people have also gone back to buying vinyl records, the black ones with grooves, as an intuitive way of freezing in place a time that always spins, just like LPs themselves, in the same direction. That which is retro is not anachronic, because being outside of time does not imply being out of style. And technology has made possible images that before seemed impossible. Steve McQueen, who died in November 1980, came back from the great beyond to star in a series of commercials in the 21st century for Ford Mustangs. As one can see (and hear), these are days in which nothing and no one, not even death, can prevent time from being cloned.

With the gift of the gab but without anger, past eras come together to speak and to leave us in even greater emotional solitude than before. That 1985, evoked with an exegesis of anti-currentness by Bowling for Soup's song ("Stop and bring back Springsteen, Madonna"), an uneven year in which as many important things happened as there were expectations in favor of memory, is growing ever more distant, farther and farther behind. The preterite ceased to be imperfect because, simply, it ceased to be so. It is not even the past; it is more like an echo, a house of images threatening to come crashing down. That time (which leads to the insistence on "reviving it") was the first time for something: a beginning moving forward, in stereo, the start of something predictive that makes one think of what Rainer Maria Rilke wrote in *Letters to a Young Poet*: "Dear Friend: Do you not see that everything is a beginning, and that beginning in itself is always so beautiful? Therefore, let life happen to you. Believe me: life is in the right, always." Rilke was wrong: life is not always right, and the few times that it is are precisely the ones we want to save from forgetfulness, because the past, on occasion, is better than forgetting.

In the United States, a country that built its present by paying attention only to the future, nostalgia is a successful industry. There is a feast of yesterday, of a beguiled nostalgia for a past time that, for having been in the past, appears to be better. The Beatles had already taken this into consideration and yearned: "Yesterday, all my troubles seemed so away / Yesterday, love was such an easy game to play." Retro does not recede. There is an abundance of radio stations exclusively dedicated to playing music from the past, "golden hits." On television, there have been several shows dealing with the past (*That '70s Show, I Love the 70s*, and *I Love the 80s*). And the silver screen in Hollywood periodically revisits emblematic eras (and were any of them not?), including decades from not long ago, including the 1950s, which must not be that far in the past since it can still be brought into the present, as has been done with the movies *Pleasantville, L.A. Confidential, Far from Heaven, Good Night, and Good Luck*, and *On the Road*, five recent films from that period, which is also the case with the television series *Mad Men*, about the 1960s. It would appear that in the United States novelty without warning associated with nostalgia does not seem strange, since its people live saturated by novelties.

This trend could even be considered a natural option, if one takes into account the fact that the entertainment industry is constantly in search of a new sense of fun, and that nostalgia today, paradoxically, is that which is new. It is entertaining to look back, back to an era that brings us relief, making us believe that there really was a better time. Nostalgia is, after all, a yearning. Furthermore, reality prior to 9/11/2001—a pivotal date, the AC and DC of our era, when calm was not an example of anything and contributed to nostalgia not being a complete exaggeration—is seen with instructive intensity, as an irreplaceable era, because perhaps it was just that.[1]

On October 22, 2014, Annie Lennox was interviewed on the *Charlie Rose* show in order to talk about the recent release of her new album, *Nostalgia*. The singer stressed the fact that *Nostalgia* is also being sold in a vinyl version, the same way the Eurythmics' records were produced three decades ago. For the newer generations, the use of the (in appearance) "anachronistic" sonorous product represents a challenge. They will need to train themselves in the nearly ritualistic act of placing the record on the record player's turnstile so that the music will start playing. For those who grew up with this technology, in contrast, and have missed it, it will be a trip to the childhood of melomania. They will once again feel the serene pleasure of sliding the needle into the groove and extracting sounds from the temporal indifference to which they had been condemned by the DVD, that accomplice to an automatism.

---

[1] The nostalgia train travels with extreme ease from past to present (and vice versa), and this can be seen, or rather heard and verified, in one of the current trends on the most popular U.S. radio stations in the country's top markets. On Saturdays and Sundays, radio stations in the 50 states play old recordings of the program *American Top 40* from the 1970s and 1980s. It should be noted that the majority of the stations that broadcast this program are those of contemporary hit radio or CHR, meaning that most of its programming, aside from Kasem's countdown, is dedicated exclusively to musical hits from the present. *Casey Kasem's American Top 40—The 70s and 80s* can also be heard on XM Satellite Radio, which has carried this program since 2006. The only difference between this version and the original is the greater sound fidelity: the original vinyl LPs have been digitally remastered.

The preaching of nostalgia—even if it lacks specific vocabulary and a theoretical apparatus with which to read the era in question based on its rugosity and detours—imposed a sense of habitualness on all of this that increasingly appears like a bipolarity of the temporal, of time as a spatial reality. Therefore, how does one account for this bittersweet journey—a backwards voyage in life can never be completely happy—to the beginning of what came before, when time, incredibly, was not yet a finality? This time, which does not destroy, which does not manage to become new again, is precisely that of nostalgia. It is time that still seeks virtual places, both in reality and in the mind. These are places where time can appear and even remain, even if its condition is one of permanent motion, one of being a nomadic time that hauls along with it all of its past and present histories. It is also time that cannot get out from under itself, and it continues this way in plain sight, with all its finalities, which, fortunately, are unfinished. And the act of lifting one's arm and moving one's hand in a movement toward the minimum that can be seen (the beginning of the record's groove, the description of the event in all its infamous details), is the structural gesture of a passage back to what was before, what is so dearly yearned for.

When we lower the fragile needle, we lift the curtain on an act: the music always arrives before the past. It is a moment to take great care, one in which we must have control of our hands, lest with the slightest slip we ruin the record and the needle, too. It is like the lyrics of the 1919 classic tango "Margot": "You even changed your name/Just as you changed your luck/You are no longer Margarita/Now they call you Margot." Or, like the words of another classic tango, "Madame Ivonne," from 1933: "Mamausel [Mademoiselle] Ivonne, today she is only Madam." In these tangos, the women change names, but in reality the magical act of causing the record to make music retains its enchantment with an unchangeable name. In this regard, justice has once again been done to a type of beauty that teaches us to hope, to enjoy the happenings of slowness, since the act of bringing together the needle and the groove does not accept the velocity of an impatient impetus. Billy Childish once said that what we like at age 17 is what we really like. Who, at that age, does not like to make music the only valid present and to set it in motion? Chilean vocalist Violeta Parra sang: "To be 17 again, after living a century." On the journey back in time on the magic carpet of music, making it produce such strains is part of the happiness exaggerated by the ritual that has been recovered.

So then, by activating this act beyond expectation (who would have guessed that in the second decade of the 21st century someone would be using vinyl records again?), we become part of the journey toward the instantaneousness of the long "time ago" that becomes current again so many years after having been considered outdated. All of this highlights the exceptionality of the durable amid temporal corrosion accelerated by the tendency of the times to sponsor the permanent deletion of the permanent, or which based on its own merits seemed to be. The continuity of time detained in its duration, obedient to reminiscing, bring us a dramatic conclusion; the past can change from one day to the next, but the future is affected by a similar destiny. An unusual situation stands out starkly: the present provides images of the past, and the future only exists in the memories destined to exist in a permanent present. We are collectors of dead moments that have managed to survive with dignity in a cryogenic state.

Nevertheless, the boom of nostalgia is inexplicable for a country like Uruguay—a veritable midget in population and territory—which in many fundamental ways continues even now to be anchored to the 1950s, with its glorious World Cup soccer victory over Brazil in Rio's Maracanã Stadium (and to an even earlier past). Therefore, it should long for a reality that is

more futuristic than commemorative, more unprecedented
than recycled. But it is not the case. And there is some tradition in this, because the collective disposition to feel weighed
down by the lack of enough of a past comes from earlier times.
The tango "*Tiempos viejos*" ("Old Times) composed by
Uruguayan Francisco Canaro in 1925 and recorded by another
(alleged) Uruguayan, Carlos Gardel, in 1926 (and also later by
Julio Sosa), is the epitome of nostalgia. Already by that era, as
can be heard (nostalgia was also sonorous back then), man,
placing in doubt the masculinity of his contemporaries, felt nostalgia for the women of yesteryear, that is, those of 1900, since
in the life of the lead character a quarter of a century has gone
by: "Do you remember, brother? Those were the days! / Our
men were different, more manly, / No one used coke or mor-
phine, / Guys in those days didn't use hair gel. / Do you remember, brother? Those were the days! / Twenty-five Aprils that will
not return / Twenty-five Aprils, what I wouldn't give to have
them back, / When I remember I weep."

The first meaning of the word "nostalgia" deals with the
"pain" caused by being far from one's home. In contrast, in
Uruguay—a country admirable for being incomprehensible,
including on the part of native Uruguayans—pain becomes a
cause for celebration. Nostalgia is a party, a deity with a national gene. People dance and drink in the name of this word,
which is a cousin on its mother's side to 'melancholy.' They
even say to each other: "Happy Nostalgia Day."[2] They look at
time gone by, ex-time, on a Rolex made in Paraguay, and they
make a toast, generally to the past itself. In the name of yesterday and of before, they do things today that do not have a
name. It is magical realism applied to Uruguay, to the small

---

[2]"Nostalgia Night," the celebration that has come to compete in terms of
importance with national holidays, even has its own Wikipedia entry:
http://en.wikipedia.org/wiki/Nostalgia_Night\

country of the unusual South that was born invented and which continues to be a star of its constellated invention. It is a realist south that is surreal. The Eastern Republic of Uruguay, or *República Oriental del Uruguay* (ROU), is a country—an acronymic country—of rationally odd people who collectively enjoy that which is abhorred in other places: melancholy, that ill which is an identical Siamese twin to sadness. A growing majority of Uruguayans spend their lives in the present wishing that right now it were the past, and they receive the future by warding it off, with nostalgia, so that it will seem as nearly as possible like a far-off yesterday.

No one hates the usefulness of calendars as much as Uruguayans. They believe that by breaking the clock—which is not so soft as in the painting by Salvador Dalí— they will stop time. For one night (which almost always continues on into the next day, since excessive dancing and drinking have their con-sequences), Uruguayans celebrate something that should cause instant pain, as it recalls the past with all of its instants brought together in one. They take refuge in the idyll of an unrecover-able time that certain outdated songs take upon themselves to hurriedly invoke. The great celebratory date only serves to pro-vide work for disc jockeys instead of jockeys, the latter of whom do not get their chance until the next day when an important great stakes classic race takes place at Maroñas horse track. For at least a few hours the national unemployment rate goes down. Thanks, old hits.

The heart of those born in Uruguay has been diagnosed with a sorrow that can hardly be alleviated by the enjoyable pain of memory. Therefore, the past stands out as a synonym and a symptom of a collective mental and emotional state, and because it represents something allegedly better that existed before. That is why Uruguayans feel as though they are accom-plices of a saving melancholy, because, it would seem, the past has a condition that liberates from the present. It is a past that is desired as if it were up ahead, without a burka or the need for company, equivalent to a collective loyalty to an earlier future to which one can no longer return, because perhaps it never existed as such. This excessive nature of reason when it remembers too much of the bad should be abandoned. Nevertheless, life—and not just any life, but Uruguayan life—wants to continue being the same one that it has been or imagined being. In this dimension of reality occupied by its modalities, the mask is transformed by the very thing that it covers.

"Nostalgia" is a term that comes from the Greek (*nóstos*: returning home; and *álgos*: pain, ache), a term coined on June 22, 1688 by Swiss Johannes Hofer (1669-1752) while he was writing his doctoral thesis in the field of medicine. At that time, and for more than a century afterward, this ailment was seen as a pathological condition, since in its name many have given themselves up to depression, alcoholism, drugs, and suicide. The celebration of Uruguayan nostalgia comes accompanied by several of these interesting elements, though no one commits suicide from so much partying, despite what famous Uruguayan disc jockey Henry Mullins said on the matter: "The oldies kill." Perhaps this older music does kill, but at the same time it prevents the past from being executed. To the contrary, with the support of a brigade of thousands of citizens who do not want the past to commit suicide, or even die of natural causes, be they what they might, this handful of songs continues feeding nostalgia, determined as it is to demonstrate that progress in Uruguay travels backward, far backward, toward where it once—at least once—has already been (in this country the future walks backward).

"Nostalgia," in another of its invariable synonymic variants, refers to the desire to recover a time of youthfulness (on the part of those who are no longer young), or a place that has changed: it alludes to an earlier and better mental state. This bittersweet feeling, one of temporal and spatial expatriation, appears to be an excessive piece of information for Uruguay, one of the countries in the world that changes the least, including its president, José Mujica, whom the people venerate because he drives a Volkswagen beetle from the 1970s and because he lives with a minimum of comfort, as if he were from the 19th century, or an even earlier century (at least that is the image that he projects). This static state produces ecstasy. The term is also excessive when used to refer to its capital, Montevideo, which is distinguished by *not* changing very much, and whose manner of being (to the extent possible) is always the same. It is a very Dorian Gray-like city. But this lack of satisfaction with the present hours is not something exclusively native to Uruguay. Nostalgia is the contemporary hallucination of the world at large. Each day the past has 24 hours in which to be present. It assumes the pleasure (whatever form that might take) of not giving the today of dates its free space.

What great craziness (if craziness in fact has a memory)! Uruguayans feel nostalgia for the times when they felt more nostalgia; Russians spend their days missing the Soviet years of Breznhev and Andropov because there was greater social order and lower unemployment; Americans yearn for the secure times of Ronald Reagan and Bill Clinton (and even those of Dwight Eisenhower); Iranians experience nostalgia for the early days of the fundamentalist revolution, when the Ayatollah Khomeini was a still-living idol who prayed and had a beard. The Middle East and the West are rusting away, and in the relatively recent past they find excuses to continue manufacturing doses of an artificial present. Even the "current" moment comes from earlier.

Among 20-something youth, the best-selling T-shirts are those sporting images of Marilyn Monroe, James Dean, Che Guevara, and Jimi Hendrix—a timeless iconography, mythological grandparents in a permanent state of youthfulness. It is pure cryogenics, an anniversary of adolescence. In short, it is an epidemic of irrecoverable reality, one that is ineffable in it errors. Where, then, and in what moment, does the present become the past, and when does the past begin to cease to pass? In *The World as Will and Representation*, Schopenhauer offers an answer: "The form of the appearance of the will is only the present, not the past or the future; the latter two do not exist except in the concept and by the linking of the consciousness, so far as it follows the principle of reason. No man has ever lived in the past, and none will live in the future; the present alone is the form of all life."

We are passing through a modernity that is both seminal and post-, in which everything is disposable. Nothingness may not last long, but the past persists with its influence and its suspicious interferences. And the obsession over life in the preterite goes to the extreme of being nostalgic for nostalgia. In the 1990s people yearned for the 1980s, and today we feel nostalgia for the decade that 20 years ago yearned for the one before it. It is a history that repeats itself. In the 1970s, the movies *American Graffiti* and *Grease* (*Grease 2* did not come until the early 1980s) rescued the 1950s, which is to say they made them present by presenting them as an ideal time, a haven in which it was possible to recover the childhood and adolescence of the things which happiness determines to give another chance. The main characters in *Back to the Future* also arrived at this same superlative era, in their particular case 1955, the second-to-the-last season of promise. The allegory of superimposed moments that would like to be similar had, in the nostalgic vision of that decade of Dwight Eisenhower, James Dean, and the Cold War, its asymmetric beginning, one in which the realism of reality is presented in manneristic, Rococo fashion.

With the elimination of rivalries without an expiration date, no decade possesses the exclusivity of the past. With its lesser data, the preterite has become an assiduous, visitable place. Completed time receives compliments. Nostalgia begins at the slightest opportunity, without accepting suggestions, because its predictions always go the other way. The adolescence of certain spaces lost in time—though not so lost—comes back liberated from its ungrateful moments, which is why they have been forgotten. But the occurrences of this adolescence are rescued in idyllic condition, with the childhood of the least recent events on its back. In the process of exchange and recovery, a golden age that was surely not completely golden is temporally altered, because progress in reverse undergoes a strange bath of redemption. Time became a perfect democracy in which past and present live together congenially, though one of them should not be so alive.

And the West is not alone in this: India and China, two superpowers that plan for the day after tomorrow, live in debt to nostalgia due to their thousands-year-old history. The past is repeated daily in the streets, reproducing customs that do not want to adapt completely to their today in subjunctive form and which march in equal conditions toward the future without reproaching at all the preterite, but rather having it as an accomplice of that which will happen one day, because something will always happen. Seeing this crossroads of possible pasts subsisting simultaneously, one might well wonder: Was there ever a time in which man did not suffer from nostalgia? Highly unlikely. Since Adam and Eve, humanity has lived pining for a paradise lost. Furthermore, because dissatisfaction is their normal state, human beings suffer promiscuously from their fondness for plagiarizing earlier feelings, tempted by a desire that has already been fulfilled and which, as a result, is trustworthy. Humans were born with the stigma of dispossession. The past in the form of a lost paradise represents the irreplaceable transfer to a place that is ideal for being timeless, to a time that, just as with jeans that are intentionally faded by their owners (because they look better that way), can still dress itself.

With the abolition of the present, time becomes idealized. It is benefitted by collateral effects. Memory is the generating plant of a dazzling flash in retrospect. Literature has represented these transfigured states in which memory, wanting so much to remember, must imagine how everything else was before in order to be able to keep it safe and sound. Perhaps the book most representative of the past as a replicating force of the good news that has not been able to be forgotten, including with its patina of sadness light, is *A la recherché du temps perdu*. The title of this novel by Marcel Proust was translated literally into Spanish as *A la búsqueda del tiempo perdido*. In English this would be *In Search of Lost Time*, but the actual title it received was *Remembrance of Things Past*. The past can only live— assuming this verb is the right one for the occasion—as an exclusive time in reverse, in "memory," as a sum "of things past." Otherwise it would be something akin to someone who yearns to experience adolescence having already turned 40. This would seem to be an excessive aspiration, and yet it is quite in vogue: an ego tired of eras is obligated to rejuvenate, and this is the way it looks at itself in the mirror, but not just in any mirror, rather the rear-view mirror. Postmodern dogs are nostalgic for Lassie and Rin Tin Tin.

In this game of Russian nesting dolls, of a fold inside of a fold, the utopian practice of nostalgia aspires to place one everydayness inside of another. What prevails is the romanticism of a sadness that cannot become completely sad, since absence is observed in its repetition, even if it is only with its signal on "off." With its precursor presences of reminiscence, the past exhibits properties (and priorities) that prevent it from being abandoned. But the past cannot be transformed or replaced, and therein lies its attractiveness: in times when "right now" lives in permanent mutation, yesterday is the island that resists without being flooded, a time remembered outside of duration, through moments that require the attention of the present in a retrospective state. Mnemosyne has several gifts. They are strange gifts but gifts nonetheless. This is why the conversation between memory and time ends in the conversion of said time, in its reincarnation, one that is also illusory because it is not able to accept that youth is but a retrospective offering traveling forward at top speed.

The language of the Hopi tribe in North America lacks a verbal past tense. In the by-no-means silent language of the southern Uruguayan tribe, even the future is conjugated in the past. It is part of a pact of silence. Tomorrow will be yesterday. It embodies a temporal simultaneousness defined by the prefix *pre-*. In Uruguay, the present is previous, a prequel. In a country where so many have known exile in all its iterations, many want to feel exiled in time, a time that, despite being wooed, does not impede the reinhabiting of native moments which in the beginning had no stigma attached to them. Uruguay is a place where nostalgia has quite a future. The following maxim of Winston Churchill illustrates this ardor for earlier times: "The future is unknowable, but the past should give us hope." In Uruguay, the past is destined to play that role, perhaps excessively, dispersed here, there, and everywhere, conceived in such a way that it might give whatever is asked of it.

No one in their right mind finds nostalgia attractive. Who wants to experience, as the Merriam-Webster Dictionary explains, the pain or sorrow of a "wistful or excessively sentimental yearning for return to some past period or irrecoverable condition," or of "the state of being homesick"? So then, how can there be so many people who celebrate "pain" and "sadness" with drinking and loud music? The Uruguayan reality gives off signs that are hard to comprehend, such as the radio advertisements announcing the following during the month of August: "Come and enjoy nostalgia." While the rest of the world entered a posterior period (post-industrial, postmodern, post-ideological, post-psychedelic, post-contemporary), Uruguayans continue to hold fast to a *pre-* world, a world previous to this one that ceased to be valid a long time ago. Just as in soccer, they know how to make time. In a country epitomized by John Keats' phrase "Where but to think is to be full of sorrow," all of the places dispersed in the past alleviate—without thinking too much—the sorrows of the present.

History, a poorly received gift, began a new millennium and is trying out new attempts at thought, none of which lack extenuating circumstances. Nevertheless, there are among us those who still believe that the past will be able to come back and save us at any moment. Ours is a retro country, an antique dealer's world not suited for the world. If things continue as they are now, when we reach the 22nd century we will be celebrating the 19th century, or any other one before that, and we will celebrate it not only on August 24, but rather all the days of the year, as we have up to now. Can somebody *please* put another quarter in the jukebox of sounds associated with certain images that animate the present? Music is a symbolic corrective, a reconsideration at the cost of rhythm. There are those who, upon hearing sounds that are familiar due to their repetition, believe they are restoring the mannered image of certain ways of being. To them it is a revival.

In the museum of memory, one of the five senses prevails: the past is auditory, and it is there, with familiar rhythms of exhausted brightness, that an attempt is made to deceive the arithmetic of the calendar. There has been disco music; alternative rock; punk; heavy metal; psychedelia; *porteñada* songs from the Buenos Aires of the 1970s; *cumbia*; and music from the groups Chumamwamba, Los Wawancó, and Wham!, as well as the canonic rock of Jim Morrison. There has been ideology (Che Guevara on T-shirts). The time of pop culture is so generous that it has some of everything; its habitat is, at the very least, infinite, and it shows devotion to that which it does not oppose being remembered and finds its home in an indisputable time that has ceased to conceal itself. It is cult-like time to which everyone pays favors, a time that has done nothing to continue being influential but which, nevertheless, is. It is a time of posters and posterity whose songs are the autobiography of specific moments and emotional sequences remembered in an ideal state.

Therefore, to give free rein to the suppositions and simulations of memory, on August 24, the night before the nation's Independence Day, Uruguayans celebrate the declaration of National Dependence on Memory, that great commemorative celebration of national nostalgia. On the eve of the nation's birthday, the eve of the past is celebrated. What redundancy: the preterite is turned into tradition, into a favorite artifact. It is a case of fatherland and flashbacks, a Proustian trophy with an overdose of blind optimism, because nostalgia comes freed from the negative facts and acts of past eras. Their evocation ignores the dark side of earlier times. Some things that were among the worst can go unnoticed for a few hours in a demographic situation with an abundant memory that is useful only for those things that it wants to remember. Decades are rescued as perpetual time with the most indelible part of their aura, one that arrives at the place where memory forgets as much as it wants and as much as it could desire. It acts selectively. It discards. In its coffers, memories are an exclusive brotherhood.

In December 1941, Franklin Delano Roosevelt told Churchill: "It is fun being in the same decade as you." In Uruguay, most people have fun being in the same decades as others, no matter which ones they are. Any earlier decade is valid. And if they do not go all the way back to the time of Jesse James and Sitting Bull, it is because back then there were no LP records. In the festivals of nostalgia (and there are many festivals, but there is only nostalgia), the most celebrated one is that of the 1970s. Why? It is hard to understand. Creatively, in terms of pop and rock music, it was a poor decade. Politically it was disastrous. Nevertheless, DJs grow weary with requests to play songs that were popular in 1973, 1974, 1975, and later in the decade, when Uruguay was experiencing the splendor of a military dictatorship, which turned the present a place in which to experiment with ideas from the past. Can anyone understand it? History rehearses its tragedy with a smile on its face. Alcohol is its Google: in the outrageous partying it even finds things it would rather not.

People waste money to hear and dance to songs that invoke experiences from a miserable period in this South American country's history. On top of that—and on top of the dance floor—everyone dances, though not very much on top of one's partner, since music back then was for dancing separated, as far apart as possible. There was no romantic physical contact. Disco, disco, and more disco. "YMCA!" sing frenziedly the youth of yesteryear, even though, before drinking the next whiskey, no one will have the nerve to say: "Do you remember that when this song by the Village People was popular we were enjoying the marvels of the "Medidas Prontas de Seguridad" (Prompt Security Measures), or that when the Steve Miller Band's 'Abracadabra' was at number one on the charts, the *tablita* currency table, with its anticipated peso-dollar exchange rates, left the country and its people with empty zeros? That era was a real touchstone, because it was as hard as a rock. What a great time! Do you remember, brother? Those were the days." Forgetfulness has been excluded *ex professo*.

On the interminable evening of August 24 (interminable because it can last as a social attitude until the next Nostalgia Night), Uruguayans make current the pain of the past through drinking and dancing. How many of them will get up and still have enough energy to celebrate the exploits of Independence? How can that be! Country comes before the Beatles and Gloria Gaynor! The proof of this mess is liquid, and excess liquidates. The next day they cannot put their souls into the matter, and even less so their bodies. Oh, youth, divine treasure, you have gone out to return no more. Few today remember the complete scene. Uruguayans make memories by losing them. The past grants too many extra moments to its continuation. With help, it learned not to recede. Kant believed that nostalgia is not an illness of exile but rather one of poverty, that is to say, it appears to imply the loss of the promise of riches. In order to remember that they cannot forget such a loss, Uruguayans drink. To remember a lot they drink a lot, to forget that the present has already arrived. Returning incompletely with fragments that ceased to be worse, the rules of the world demand a sacrifice from comprehension.

Uruguay is such a slow country that the present has still not arrived from the past. It left some time ago but still has not made it. If we do a good job of promoting this native torpor, people from elsewhere, tourists by the thousands, will come to see how it is that such a place exists. In the country that sets the official time ahead, reality lives behinds the world's time. It is time that does not change its soul. Furthermore, the epochal time lag (modernity with viceroyal spirit) comes accompanied by bad taste in music. Songs to which no one paid attention before get a second chance on the turntable of memories that spins around and around, and they serve to build the Jurassic Park of national memory, which is always unveiled during the early hours of the next day, August 25, when Uruguayans, as they have for a long time, celebrate the nation's Independence, a day in which many things recover their origins.

Appealing to the past causes today a greater number of confused people than before, because in Uruguay nostalgia is more and more precocious, an adolescent Babel, a whirlwind of prepubescence and yearning moving forward. It is yet another attribute of the collective absurdity that makes us guests of what we are. What reason can an 18-year-old boy who is only beginning to put his memory to work have for feeling nostalgia? The meaning of the word itself is suspicious: is it nostalgia for that which has not yet been lived? Or do young people give themselves the luxury of forgetting that which they have not yet finished remembering? It has been said that in Uruguay there are those who arrive at the future looking back, even if the past to come is the same old preterite as always. Nostalgia, then, is a utilitarian vehicle for everyone to return to the first night, not that of the day after tomorrow, but rather of the tomorrow of days past. The spectacle of circumstances lines up to enter where it already was (the flash forward goes in the opposite direction).

"What you come to remember becomes yourself", wrote W. S. Merwin in his poem "Learning a Dead Language". Uruguayans go forth in herds to recover an empty time, even if their glasses are full (or perhaps only half full), and they do so to the rhythm of the stammerings of disco music and between segments of background psychedelia (because the advantage that informs desire gathers disorganized memories). They celebrate that which surely happened a long time ago and another way, a very different way, or perhaps that which never completely was, or even almost completely, and which memory, stealing the faculties of imagination, reconstructs by force as the fiction of a mistranslated preterite. This is because the future today is not what it was; the past now begins a half hour earlier.

In the era of CDs and iPods, people remember music that was popular on vinyl, with a 33 format. If the past continues to prosper like this, the good discotheques will soon go back to the phonograph. For one day that could last another 364, Uruguay turns into the "world capital of nostalgia." In the country of jalopies and Beckhamesque banana kicks, a country that lives in the day before today, there are those who also celebrate nostalgia the rest of the year, living off the nearly hollow and lifelong postscript of Maracanã. They also live at the cost of the memories of when the country, in school books and travel guides, was considered to be like the Switzerland of the Americas, and not only because Uruguayans eat lots of cheese and wear watches.

They are memories that are not always marked by sanity. All of this, in a condition of nostalgia-induced consternation— not constipation—happened so, so long ago that today not even Switzerland is an infallible referent to have in mind. The country's essayist, José Enrique Rodó, wrote in *The Motives of Proteus* (1909): "The countries and people that really *live* (italics are his) are those that change their love, their thoughts, their tasks; they vary the rhythm of that devotion; they struggle against their past in an attempt to distance themselves from it." And elsewhere, the author of Ariel had stated that time is the "supreme innovator." Uruguayans have not paid much attention to Rodó, either.

Nevertheless, for better or for worse, man has memory and depends on his preterite moments of delight, idealizing in the least objective way situations that might demand greater care when it comes time to settle accounts and frown. Not all past time was better just for being in the past, though a large part of it would be better if it were really in the past, bygones allowed to truly be bygones. In any event, including that of setting out not to do it and running the risk of chance, man remembers: he inevitably ends up being the victim of his partialist memory, a magnet of yesterdays. He is weighed down by a mechanism. Pascal believed that human beings do not live for the present, but rather a little for the past and a lot for the future. In Uruguay, many live a lot for the past. They find it beautiful— even "healthy" perhaps—to recall anything that occurred before. And with the past, the answer is most likely affirmative.

This past is an exclusive figure of its performance in the midst of a concert of possibilities and enthusiasms that is in no way opportunistic. It is a past that through the will of collective memory has been able to remain for longer, a past that constitutes part of a result. It is, I want to believe, the shared pleasure of having reactivated the sensitivity of that moment of life when "once upon a time..." In the middle of the return to an idealization that has not been sent back home, the bonus effect of a specific time echoes, accustomed to living in the second-to-the-last version of its existence. There is a struggle to ensure that in the loss of content, life does not escape, with the copyright of the past thus being protected, because no one allows *déjà vu* to conclude. In the end, in its abbreviated periphery, time winds up being the relieved motivator (desire is gratified by memory), conditioned by knowing so little about it. The end of its origin is also not in debate, nor is it a topic of bards. The question about its meaning only lasts as long as a flash of lightning. Why waste time on a lysergic utopia like nostalgia, when we well know that it is not desirable to turn into anybody belonging to the past?

Due to a matter that is, above all, temporal, Uruguayans see the past with certain noble fascination, as if so far back in memory they might find healthier, happier images—that is to say, ones that are not as old—where they can remain awake. This seems to be the premise of Nostalgia Night: rewinding times— yearning is not enough—in which we were happy, in which we were young, when we did not go to the doctor as often (back then the prostate did not protest). Life was a sponge, and it fired at point-blank range. Man likes to recover the preterite so that he can suck the marrow out of something that is as dry as a stone. He is persistent. As he floats on his aspirations, forgetfulness prepares his cancelation. And yet, he is insistent. There is nothing there, just a few dust-covered experiences that have music as the ideal broom with which to erase them. On that night of thirsty multitudes, people go out to dust off memories intimately associated with certain songs that were popular for several weeks in a row, and then were not. It is music called upon to remain as one of the obligatory purposes of the heart.

"An optimist is one who enters a luxury restaurant without any money and orders oysters because he knows that inside one of them he is going to find a pearl" (Anonymous). The optimism Uruguayans feel about the past makes them seek pearls where there are only catfish, if they are lucky. Remy de Gourmont said that "all vices have an internal origin. Cards do not make the gambler, or the bottle the drunkard." Does so much idolatry of a past with spurious reputation turn Uruguayans into antique pieces with more than one reciprocal purpose? What to say? I am not an expert on Nostalgia Night. I was not an expert on it before (when I could have been), nor am I one today, when the future pushes the rewind button less and less. I never attended any party or dance held in honor of nostalgia, so I do not know what types of things go on at such a merrymaking whose consequences are its intentions. Furthermore, time and again circumstances have prevented me from joining in on the national history of celebration, festivities which, I suppose, due to having the past as their main guest, are surely always the same, an inevitable signal.

Once, long ago, I received as a gift a ticket to attend something having to do with nostalgia. It was a party or some similar gathering. The givers of this gift told me that I was going to feel like I had 30 years earlier. I was very excited about that, and especially about the fact that I had a free invitation. It is always nice to travel back to the days when one was three decades younger, without having to pay for the ticket. I wanted to go to the party, which promised to be brutal (surely they were going to play Village People and Gary Glitter songs!), and I made immediate plans to share that mutual sentiment. I even shaved and got ready in an appropriate fashion, but without putting anything artificial in my hair, because I had the intention of returning faithfully to my era. "Guys in those days didn't use hair gel," says the tango. I continued with my plans to attend, even splashing on some Old Spice, my favorite cologne that unforgettable night. I had my glad rags on, I was radically clean, and, within my aesthetic parameters, I was looking elegant and ready, very ready, to join the young guard. I put all my effort into the preparations of appearance, just in case, because when nostalgia is in the mix, any social or physical contact becomes possible, even if, in the end, one realizes that all of it will change nothing.

Since the celebration was slated to begin very late (another Uruguayan irony: the past begins the next day), I decided to take a nap, which ended up being the only thing I took in that day (alcohol included). I lay down for those hours, which were going to be a short rest, imagining myself as the healthy looking young man I had been, when I did not need to take a marathon nap just to be able to dance slow songs, ballads, for 30 minutes straight. However, because my Chinese-made alarm clock did not go off as intended, I did not wake up until around 11:30 the next morning. By then it was a little late to start remembering. I did not miss out on anything ("No one can lose either the past or the future—how could anyone be deprived of what he does not possess," Marcus Aurelius). As a result, since then I have had to continue living in the present after having missed the chance that night to leave it behind. Those who went told me the party was excellent and that the people there danced and remembered, with nostalgia, of course. Nostalgia is never calm or unperceived when it reveals itself.

In Uruguay, people prefer to remember at night—they have dark memories—when the moon is there, spying on them, maybe so that they will not feel so alone. Couples go to banquets with dancing, accompanied by other couples, and they all remember together, in groups of two, three, more. Uruguay is strange even in this regard: a completely intimate faculty like memory is exercised in public as if memories were a soccer ball around which the game is set up and played. Men—married, bald, gray-haired, with paunch bellies, and dressing and acting

like preppy teenagers for a few hours—remember in the company of their wives the times when they went out with other
women. The wives, meanwhile, at that same moment are surely recalling things similar to those being remembered by their
shameless husbands, although some of the things they remember are things they did with other men, some of whom were
gentlemen. Since not all nostalgias are clean, an open bar is
offered at parties so that those with good memories can perform
the necessary cleaning, washing—generally with whiskey, wine,
or champagne—the dirtiest parts of the mind, those where
memory is housed. Liquor is a catharsis.

Someone once said—not to me—that no one is immune to
nostalgia. Some, it would seem, have their defenses down. In an
attempt to raise them, they attempt to have fun. People seem to
remember better when they drink and dance. Perhaps it is for
this reason that at wedding receptions they do the same thing
that is done on Nostalgia Night: the bride and groom drink and
dance to remember the beautiful past before the present begins
to become so. Newlyweds, however, have a different destiny
from those suffering from nostalgia. The worst that can happen
to the merry nostalgics is having to run into at the party the
very person they were remembering. It is then and there that
the conflictive situation shows them how much time has passed
between now and the day before yesterday. Today the former
girlfriend is nothing at all like she was, and she only continues
to resemble her old self in the invocation of him who remembers her with a whiskey in his hand and a faulty illusion in his
memory, which is as impaired as a man who has lost his
whiskey-holding hand. At that hour of the night, which is life
before the last twilight, such former couples are now complete
strangers, and this is the only complete thing that remains
between them.

In the middle of the dance, between the Twist and the *Lam-
bada*, between the exchanges of the emotions and ghosts that

remain, after dancing four songs in a row, though none are Mexican *corridos* (aren't these slow songs great, girl!), just when the body begins to suffer cramps and diverse aches that years ago would have been impossible, those involved become victims of the songs, which for three minutes will be popular again, and which bring back more memories than expected. Secretiveness has its motives. Hearts and minds are softened and phrases replete with clichés begin to roll forth: "This song was popular when I was in high school"; "This song was all the rage when Pelé was scoring goals"; "This song was number one when I met . . . " (and the men saying such things stop talking to avoid infuriating their current partners, women with the good taste to remember in silence).

The wood shavings of the felled tree fall without turning. The sawing action included the defenseless parts of eras. Everything else is prologue, dilemma, trivia. Between gossip and messages created by the sense of touch, reconstruction takes charge of the rest. During the function without collateral damage, the morass of experiences that emerges to the order of songs which last three minutes—a backward-moving rhythmic woodland—knows how not to deviate from expectations, even though it does seem as if it were asking, "How does one kill time? With a shotgun blast? With a hammer blow? By stabbing it? How? With what?"

In the express taxi of oldies music there arrives a diaspora of memories that crowd onto the dance floor without requesting anything, except alcohol. And this alcohol, included in the cover charge, takes charge of making less excruciating the movement of the feet and the unanimous parade of memories. Nothing that happens will fall outside the playbook. The blame for the bittersweet experience caused by an excessively nostalgic night will have to go to the past that returned for so little (money and time), to life in general, and not to the songs of Elton John, Queen, or ABBA. Remembering hurts, and for those who do not believe it, just ask feet: they hate being thrust

by force into the dancing time machine. They, more than anyone or anything, hate the oldies. Knees, calves, thighs, and heels
come after them. Bodily aches and pains collide at this point
with incorrigible experiences. As a second-to-last shield against
so much perfumed and sonorous masochism there remains the
present, which arrives promptly the next morning, much more
tired than 20 or 30 years ago, when everything was able to make
sense, because carnivals truly were those from earlier times.

Charles Manson, the demented murderer of Sharon Tate,
said in a 1994 television interview: "You know, a long time ago
being crazy meant something. Nowadays everybody's crazy."
Today, everyone with memories, both the crazy and the sane,
feel expatriated from a chrysalis time that is nothing more than
what it is attempting to summarize: everyone—from the
demented to the mentally healthy—is part of a regiment that
has not been able to find the way back to the area where it
belongs and which multiplies in direct correlation to how hard
it is to find access to the desired territory, the future plan.
Everyone thinks the same way. In this commemorative context,
the perspective of a collective curiosity is imposed. Dates on the
calendar take advantage of the opportunity. They are, after all,
days of vinyl and paraffin. "Yesterday's grass drying in the sun,"
as the tango goes. It is an elegy reshaped by the chosen reality,
the corollary of a country where forgetfulness lives day to day.

In the world's present time, the past is a very subjective
point of view. Everyone has his or her own version of moments
lived and think that it is important to give things that have
occurred "more" time, to give them a postscript and a gratuity.
Inside the past there are lives with a look of hypothesis, of
something that in many regards is indecipherable and which for
some emotional reason continues to persist. There is an inability to escape the efforts of reminiscence, which does not cease
to be curious. Nostalgia coexists with amnesia without taking
charge of anything. In an era when in technology and medicine

the only thing that matters is innovation, pure novelty, thoughts and results aimed at the day after tomorrow, we live as concubines with the past, as if we were learning "new things" with the discoveries of memory. Reminiscence is a dominant force. In the present, the past still possesses days.

We travel to the past to live in the place where we once went. When MTV debuted in 1981, playing the video by the duo Buggles called "Video Killed the Radio Star," the dominant premise was that a new era had arrived in mass culture. But this was not exactly the case, as was later told by the name of a Robbie Williams album in 2009: "Reality Killed the Video Star." Reality killed lots of things that had intentions of erasing the presence of past times, a reality with a period at the end, with a today and much earlier. There is no shortage of examples of today's reality. In the 2014 Detroit Auto Show, two of the stars were "very new" cars, but with an aroma of paraffin: the Equus Bass 770 and the Volkswagen Beetle Dune Concept. The first is an eclectic version of the so-called "muscle cars" popular during the 1960s and 1970s. The second is an updated version of the VW "Bug," which has been in the world since way back in 1938. In the automotive industry, trapped between before yesterday and the day after tomorrow, models similar to these define a retro-revival tendency according to which glory is in the past, with its multitude of rolling existences that prevent the triumph of amnesia.

Something similar occurs in the recording industry. So that memory need not exert itself so much in its travels toward a time that belongs to it less and less, the present entered into a virtual contract with music allowing this latter entity to appear today as much as possible to the way it was in decades past. "Old is cool" is the slogan of the network VH1. Furthermore, for this tendency to gain permanency, the songs that most appear like earlier ones are rewarded with prizes and with top popularity rankings. At the 56th Annual Grammy Awards in

2014, the song "Get Lucky," by Daft Punk, won the Grammy in the Record of the Year category, while its authors, the techno-house music French duo, won the award for Best Pop Duo/Group Performance. The catchy song bears the evident influence of the music of the 1970s, when people went to Studio 54 to dance wearing colorful bell-bottom pants. People might be distracted the first time they hear the song, believing it is by a group like Chic, or perhaps Earth, Wind & Fire. Not surprisingly, it was co-written by Nile Rodgers, who can claim authorship of some of the most iconic songs of that era, such as "I Want Your Love," of which "Get Lucky" is a direct descendant. One of the lines in Daft Punk's song says: "The present has no rhythm." If we compare it to the present of 30 or 40 years ago, we can quickly agree with this declaration.[3]

Even though this does not mean that memory is a device that facilitates the facile, each time it is proposed the past enters into the present like an untimely tsunami, filling our reality with doubts, especially with the one that gives rise to such a paradoxical situation. In the experience of nostalgia, the recognition of an idealized past bumps up against the question: "Was I really the one who was present in that time that occurred so much earlier than today?" Nostalgia is the encore of certain moments from the past in which small, medium-sized, and large events that have been lived refuse to stay behind, even if with the passing of time it grows increasingly harder to recognize them.

I am inclined to think that Jonas Mekas, who spent his life imagining the future, was correct when he stated that as long as

---

[3]The new fad about nostalgia boom is necro-advertising: the use of a publicity spot featuring a deceased movie star. Steve McQueen appeared in Ford commercials, while Bruce Lee did the same in those for Johnnie Walker. Marlene Dietrich, Grace Kelly and Marilyn Monroe made a showing in the ad campaign for the perfume J'adore, by Christian Dior. Monroe was also seen in Chanel No. 5 commercials.

someone feels nostalgia he is not dead; he knows that there still exists something that he loves. It is through nostalgia that an unplugged past is recovered, a life-scale past of the imagination. It is this imagination that is used to remember that which the world appears obliged to recognize: intervals of emotional lucidity, pending matters that desire resolves in its own way. It should come as no surprise that the narrowing of present time is taking place in the least expected direction. We hit the pause button on the past, wanting to recognize it in the recovered instants, in the immediateness of what happened long ago. By way of this temporality, we evoke "the next thing" that happened way back when.

What strange times we live in: Alzheimer's and an overdose of memory define one of the era's visages. The past, like a merry-go-round horse, makes a complete (counterclockwise) loop, arriving at the same place where the next loop will begin again, and then again. The past is a repository of phantasmagoria where the cadavers of understanding rest. Reflected in this archaeology that has returned to the present are the ruins of a backward panorama where years change purposes. The accumulation of indispensable and reactivated furors includes sequences interrupted by the present to which we desire to return, as if upon rediscovering the preterite we would like to go on a journey with it somewhere. Perhaps past days want to be given more time, and they, like the Bryan Adams song would like to sing: "Oh, yeah . . . Back in the summer of '69, oh . . . "

Yogi Berra has said: "The future isn't what it used to be." But the past is not what it used to be, either. Today's past aspires to become the future, and right now. Bob Dylan stated that "the future is a thing of the past," and he was surely right, at least somewhat, with this sweeping generalization. Nevertheless, we remain anchored in the time that we call the present, and there, because it feels unsatisfied, memory creates retrospective desires ("Recollection's love is the only happy love," said Søren

Kierkegaard), and it comes accompanied by questions. "What abolished kingdom evokes nostalgia?" Mexican poet José Emilio Pacheco wonders in a poem.

Love for the past is the answer to the stubborn yearning for an emotionally erudite place, one that belongs to an earlier era of changing dates, not to an easily recognizable mainstream past. It is, rather, the abstract construction of the remains found in a backward march. It is for good reason that it has become easy to dream about the perpetuity of certain events and facts from other eras. If the increase in *retromania* continues, we will soon be writing emails by hand (and if this stubborn yearning keeps up, we will soon go back to using dirigibles to fly from one continent to the other).

Finally (even though neither time nor the past have finality), in an act of gratuitous exhibitionism, life bravely highlights that the past, which did not arrive all at once, is an inheritance. It contains accumulated days that wear on the outside something that has also remained inside. In these days we identify hunches, we suppose that from them will come that which one day, we will become. The past is a cult figure that makes its cameo appearance by unfolding without losing eloquence. It is a counterculture, countertime blockbuster made up of sequences of disuse, of impartial montages, of synthesis and pantomime, turned into a climax of catharsis. This is why the past, the most hardcore temporal state of all, can only be partially dominated by rationality. It rebels, resists, and does not want to be excluded from "the here and now." It does not want to cease being a symbol, a collection of moods. This is the reason that the past has become Volume II of the present. It is a past that was fortunate enough to have been part of the world in some era. The nostalgia that we feel for the past is defined by a verb phrase indicating the future: to be continued.

So then, in a seemingly impossible way, the past returns, having changed into the prognostication of an admired moment, into an exaggerated hypothesis.[4] It has been called upon as a kaleidoscopic feeling that can only sublimate moments already lived. It is a painful mirage (because time also grows older), part of a sea of dates diffused little by little, as with an eyedropper, all of which defies definition, because in the eras invoked there is *something* inexplicable, something powerful, which is emerging between rhythms that were born with a future included in yesterday. It is a *something* (a mixture of want and yearning) whose existence is intimately associated with certain experiences related to enthusiasm and to the desire to no longer be sad (a feeling very similar to happiness). The rest of this fabulous movie's sound track, which the world tries to rewind time and time again, either in vain or in a different fashion, contains several memorable songs which memory enjoys singing in a *la-la-la* fashion. This past, where decades and ages mix promiscuously, has had some of everything, like the Bible next to the hot water heater, like the notion of the ephemeral next to the dissolution of time, like the beginning and the end as they were before. The rest is nothing more than the same as always, and is a domestic flight to forgetfulness.

---

[4]On January 7, 2012, Madrid's *El País* newspaper published an article, entitled "The Year We Lived in Retrospect," which constitutes a sort of cultural assessment of the events of 2011. It begins by stating: "The cultural year has ended, there has been a proliferation of lists to recount its fruits, and among the discordant chorus there has emerged a clear winner: the past. There is no shortage of examples: while *The Artist*—a black-and-white silent film!—has received an Oscar nomination, the most novel (?) stylistic contribution to music turned out to be a hodgepodge of references called hypnagogic pop, which is based on the echoes of songs from the 1980s, processed with all the attention of a person operating between sleep and wakefulness. Jonathan Franzen's *Freedom*, which recalls Dostoyevsky, sold like 'the great 19th-century novel of the 21st century.' Meanwhile, gastronomy, the motor of modern democratization, turned heads with a surprising exercise of contrition as it glorified grandmother's food. At the same time, hipsters, the ultimate paradigm of youth in the know, decided that their beards—rescued from the memory trunk—should only be groomed by veteran straight razor craftsmen."

In light of these things, one might well wonder: is there such thing as an "unchanged perspective" of reality, a point of view of intransigent validity that returns, trained, to that which it has already seen and experienced before, and recognizes it *a posteriori* as something new? Today, the past—so well preserved, for example, in that infinite and non-linear piggy bank that is YouTube—triumphs, opening up access routes. It is the time-neutralizing (and at the same time paralyzing) dynamo of the progress of the present toward the same place as always, if such a place exists. The invoking of a deformed past is the great democratizer of contemporaneous experiences, or of that which happens to human beings when they realize that the days before yesterday must be preserved with care. These past days are taken into account as if there emanated directly from their paradigm—with a greater amount of things than memories inside—one of the main tendencies of this era after the latest modernity. The revival, which before was already old, is now even older. Like the main character in *Midnight in Paris*, who travels back in time with the same ease with which others travel to the corner market to buy a carton of cigarettes, no one wants to give up the security of what already happened, and which happened in a glorious way to boot. Or, perhaps it did not happen quite that way, but memory nonetheless perpetuates it, perceiving it gratuitously as having happened that way, as a new idealized authenticity.

The tendency is a retro-tendency. Everything now comes from before. The entire present is nothing more than a contribution from the past (a certified copy of the "yesterday" from different eras) to what is occurring today, even though in the preterite temporality the frenetic pace of change was not as dramatic as it was later perceived to be, since the social and technological transformations went nearly unperceived back then. They arrived only after having been there. Someone once said: "The past is a foreign country." I cannot remember who said that, but he should accept his mistake upon seeing that today the past is the country where the majority of Western humanity lives. (Now I remember who said that; it was L. P. Hartley, whose novel *The Go-Between* starts by saying that "the past is a foreign country; they do things differently there."). The past, that great mental configurator of tendencies and customs, lends comfort to the anxieties of expectations. Life has fewer disappointments if it is seen in the rear-view mirror, or at least that is what it wants to believe. The fear of losing the authenticity of the human experience, the true vintage of our condition, leads one to think (but without thinking about it too much) that by traveling back in time life will be better "again." Life goes back to being the same thing that ceased to be identical, but this very thing is an indication that at some point in time it was seen in a similar way. The translation of the sublime in the phenomenon of retrospection follows the same path.

PLEASE, MR. POST(MORTEM)

WHEN I WAS A CHILD, around age five, a sizeable neighbor woman, built in keeping with her brutal threat, told me up close: "I could just eat you up with kisses." I took off running. I imagined myself on a plate, surrounded by a knife and fork, with salt and pepper sprinkled over my tenderloin, the victim of a carnivorous tenderness. Like her there are myriad others. We take death and wrap it up like a gift, using a delicate romantic vocabulary (our times, despite their frenetic pace, continue to be romantic). And as if that were not enough, there are those who show their love for humankind by eating it. If there were thousands of such people, like Hannibal Lecter, our race would be on its way to complete extinction, just like koalas and white tigers. In any event (and all these events look the same), imagination celebrates modern cannibals. Granting them a saturated visuality renders them conducive to popularity. It gives them certain qualities; it finds glamour in their bloody verisimilitude, which is about to be confirmed and take shape. This token of exoticism is stronger than the gastronomic imperfections of the practice. Cannibalism, when it is practiced with good manners, as in the case of Lecter, entertains, even amuses, especially if one is not on the menu. The world is a more entertaining place with cannibals in it.

Cannibalism causes horror and humor; beyond representing a transgressive exercise, visceral dinners consisting of guests prolong an expansion of empiric reality that the spectator wants to abandon and yet ends up dragging out. Cult films with scenes depicting cannibalism, which were popular during the 1980s, such as *Eating Raoul* and *The Cook, the Thief, His Wife & Her Lover*, stimulated the complex sense of incomprehension that anthropophagy fosters. Most people recognize their own double Jekyll and Hyde personality in this not always exhaustive activity. They feel indebted to cultural circumstances that keep the population of the species in check. Death is not beyond anyone. In the face of these purposes with different needs, there remains no quicker way to deal with this than to laugh. In the mirror of shared barbarism we see a face all too much like to our own. How similar we are to those we thought we were! We are just like ourselves! In the end, then, it is the laugh of him who knows he could do it but does not dare and yet is not enough of a vegetarian to reject such a temptation outright.

Serial killers who kill to eat—the life of a man and that of a cow have the same value to them—are a literary genre apart. They are cut from a cloth that dresses with abomination the deviations in human behavior that give rise to the unforeseeable. With a pathology verified in the existence of their fellow men, in others who cross their paths, they set in motion—moving back and forth—a decadence, in no way axiomatic, whose gratification produces works of nonconformity; they do not conform to the idea of normality. What is confirmed is an unnatural catharsis, or criminality understood as a similitude of beauties. The character of Mickey Knox in *Natural Born Killers* states: "Killing you, and what you represent, is a statement. I'm not one hundred percent sure exactly what it's saying, but, you know." With much seriousness and complete serialness, those who are killers by nature—and who thus go against nature—have long captured imaginations, even before Thomas De Quincey (1785-1859) wrote *On Murder Considered as One of the Fine Arts*, putting in order some ideas about the virtues of death. Though it is not completely beautiful, death also held an artistic quality for Raymond Chandler, the author of *The Simple Art of Murder*. Simple because it is easier to put in practice the verb "to murder" than the verb "to write." Both murderers and writers know this.

Although the term "serial killer" is of modern origin, the word used to refer to a person who commits homicide dates from the 12th century, according to Bernard Lewis in his splendid book *The Assassins:* "The word first appears in the chronicles of the Crusades, as the name of a strange group of Muslim sectaries in the Levant, led by a mysterious figure known as the Old Man of the Mountain, and abhorrent, by their beliefs and practices, to good Christians and Muslims alike." In 1175, an emissary to Roman Emperor Frederick I Barbarossa informed him thus: "On the confines of Damascus, Antioch, and Aleppo there is a certain race of Saracens in the mountains, who in their own vernacular are called *Heyssesseni,* and in Roman *segnors de montana.* This breed of men live without law; they eat swine's flesh against the law of the Saracens, and make use of all women without distinction, including their mothers and sisters."

Around the same time, the Archbishop William of Tyre (1130-1186) made reference to a sect with approximately 60,000, or more, members called *Assissini.* But while they had a master and a sectarian character, the first individual serial killer, who only arrived a century later, came to represent the antithesis of the method. Regardless of how much he repeated a procedure in his practice, he received orders from no one, only from his agitated instinct. He began killing for hire, but the pleasure of executing people with such frequency turned him into an amateur by choice, into a professional amateur. This practice, then, comes from earlier times. In 1332, a German priest by the name of Brocardus reported on the danger of the era: "I name the Assassins, who are to be cursed and from who people must flee. They sell themselves, are thirsty for human blood, kill the innocent for a price, and care nothing for either life or salvation." At that time, the term "assassin" began to be used in Europe as a synonym of "murderer," with no connection to above-mentioned sect. The word "assassin" referred to paid hitmen. Francesco da Buti wrote in the 14th century: "An assassin is one who kills others for money."

Since then, and up to the most recent and bloody present (life would not know what to do if there were not so much death around, which is why cannibalistic serial killers tend to conceal the current lack of good wars), the verb "to assassinate" has given rise to various metaphors regarding the suspicious relationship between ethics and aesthetics, even if at times one of them fails to show up for the date. Resorting to a tentative metaphoric solution, despite its questionable finality, represents a captivating approach when morals are incapable of abolishing the differences between good and evil within an act that has no beautifying purpose, but which despite its load of aberrations manages to achieve such a purpose. Music has given it dance steps ("Psycho Killer," by Talking Heads) and two best-selling writers, Thomas Harris (*The Silence of the Lambs*) and Patricia Cornwell (*Postmortem*)—the latter also being the author of one of the most ambitious investigations into Jack the Ripper— turned urban cannibals into an unsettling literary mouthful.[1]

---

[1]Serial killers have a ubiquitous presence in mass media entertainment. Until a very short time ago, they were a topic belonging nearly exclusively to the movie industry (where films abound in all languages), but recently, as if they had become the in-style entertainment trend, they have also made it to television. And this no longer occurs only in individual episodes of police dramas, but as a central theme in shows dedicated entirely to the exploits of killers with multiple victims. In January of 2014, the television series *True Detective* debuted on HBO. Woody Harrelson and Matthew McConaughey play Marty Hart and Rust Cohle, respectively, two homicide detectives hunting a serial killer in Texas and Louisiana. In February of the same year, the series Hannibal premiered on NBC. It is based on the novel *Red Dragon*, by Thomas Harris, whose main character is the well-known Dr. Hannibal Lecter, who is also capable of terrorizing on the small screen. Another three novels published subsequently by the same author, *The Silence of the Lambs*, *Hannibal*, and *Hannibal Rising*, established worldwide one of the best-known sagas regarding serial killers. For its part, the Spanish movie *Caníbal* tells the story of a tailor in the city of Granada who enjoys eating women. Therefore, to ensure the success of his anthropoghagic banquets, he must first seek out victims. The attractive women who cross his path run the risk of ending up on a plate, diced, covered in sauce, and all in succulent portions. For this monstrous cannibal, evil has the same transcendence as eating a hamburger, in this case a female one.

Besides being cannibals, some serial killers are also necrophiliacs. During the trial, which took place in Wisconsin in 1992, the lawyer of depraved predator Jeffrey Dahmer said that his client was a sick man, a necrophiliac who loved to have sexual relations with non-loving objects. Dahmer is a nominee in the category of "Most popular serial killer in the history of pop culture." In 2012, John "Derf" Backderf published *My Friend Dahmer*, a graphic, 200-page novel in which he recounts his relationship with "The Butcher of Milwaukee," with this man-eating misanthrope, when the two of them were teenagers and spent time together in their high school band's practice room.

History insistently tells us that there was a time during its respective pasts when several historic serial killers were, and acted like, normal beings, and their anomalies (which they must have had by then) went unnoticed. Their lives were the legacy of crime, including before killing someone. Nevertheless, according to Backderf, Dahmer came with defects from the start (he used to sacrifice animals on an altar in the woods), something that his classmates detected, but not his teachers. Operating on this hazy edge of humanity (with his coming to an end in 1994 when he was murdered in prison as he was serving his life sentence), Dahmer moved with phenomenal speed as soon as he reached his adult years, killing 17 people in short order and leaving a wake of grotesque brutality that, to the present day, no one else can claim.

From the figure of the serial killer, in his various types, there arises an extrageographic fascination due to the detail and position of the stimuli involved (a somatic relief among the details of the avatar). Like a feline soul exempt from redemption, these predators of the street and bedroom kill and devour anything and at any time. They are serial killers but also cereal killers, since they are capable of eating their prey during dinner or breakfast (in this regard Dahmer was very democratic, since he would eat his victims at any hour of the day). Readers feel a forensic curiosity about these unsettling, dark characters because they want to determine what triggered such behavior, even if the effect is always superior to said causes (superior at least in visuality).

The expression "serial" highlights the habitual: the sinister labor leaves behind it plural aftereffects. The paradox of serial killers' dilemma is something akin to this: they hate people but cannot be alone. Charming and normal beings on the surface, they find their destiny at the margins of society, turning the post- of mortem into pre-. They anticipate the unexpected and, with the spontaneity of a chameleon that has learned to read and write, they move with extraordinary ease from one behavior to another, from one identity to the next, which might also be their own, and if not, they assume it anyway. For this reason they have been provided with a chameleon-like mind. Furthermore, they have as a compass a mutation of aspirations. By day they water the garden, they are nice to the neighbors (they say like no one else, "Hello, my friend"), and occasionally they work. By night they change topography to fulfill a specific design: they invent the dissolution of a foreign body, raw material with which to find, beginning now, that which lies beyond.

As a cruelty that tempts their exclusive intentions, serial killers sign a pact with an abjection by way of antonomasia. They are the Titus Andronicus from Shakespeare, or from Dante's *Inferno*, who finds his resurrection in the death of another. In their second, disproportionate identity, those who love such things end their oblique experience in calamity. They are spurred on by a lesson without teaching and a multitude of physical options for the same purpose. Without euphemisms, non-negotiable, and having as their point of departure the unbreakable solidarity that they share with horror (that great ingredient of the human condition), serial killers handle all that occurs as part of their actions and movements without feigning, even controlling the times in which they act. They manipulate the lives of others according to their will and pleasure, demonstrating (until one day they grow tired of desiring it) parameters of Cartesian precision in the moment of taking action. Linked to the mechanisms of their macabre seduction, they feel like natives of a different type of realism.

As an incurability difficult to recognize and adverse to the social scene—they are their only spectators—serial killers bring with their surrender a funereal scent, characteristic of a deidealized romantic being, that belonged to those who in the 19th century went out at night, like bats, so that no one would see them walking the streets of London or Paris. Their surrender into the ruins of behavior represents the portent of a life lived in reverse. Their motives represent that which is sinister, even if they invoke other topics favorable to sordidness. It is a one-way narcissism. The funerary delight with certain aspects of extermination (before being completely fulfilled, since what they enjoy is the step before the conclusion of the bloody act) establishes a hyperreality more certain even than reality, as it allows such people to assume literal senses of identity.

Due to the fact that Communism and its spies ceased to be a threat to humanity some time ago, now it is the excessive individualism of serial killers (Draculas with Anglo-Saxon names, all of them white, misogynistic, and well-educated) that has become the last intermediary capable of making readers' adrenaline race every time they turn a page, and another. The end is postponed and the murderer has no end. His activity eternalized him. The same as with Lecter (Hannibal, not the town in Missouri where Mark Twain was born, but rather the doctor), his voracious appetite fosters continuations, sequels to a work of synthesis. He adds up his victims with the numbers of a bankrupt mind.

The horror represented in the person of an honorable psychopath—a ripper or not—alludes to an anxiety that finds no satisfaction, explanation, or antidote. He is the new bogeyman.

It should perhaps come as no surprise, then, that after the fall of the Berlin Wall, serial killers have replaced ideology as the new arbiter of danger. They are the operatic re-creation of Satan, and he, as we all know, is by no means a vegetarian (unless things in Hell are going to be different from how we have imagined them until now). Evil reincarnate prefers meat, and when we feel that he lies in wait for us, we confirm our everyday vulnerability, our absolutely edible character. The soul can also be seasoned.

There have always been serial killers, ever since man has been a serial animal with aspirations of being taken seriously. There have been Cain (and since at that time there were only four people on the earth, one of them being murdered was a lot), Caligula, Tiberius, Tamerlane, influenza, the bubonic plague, other illnesses before AIDS, then AIDS itself, Saddam Hussein, Osama bin Laden, and drug traffickers (serial killers working for a criminal enterprise). However, the specific examples of the term (incorporated into universal vocabulary in 1980), only began to draw attention and lead to comparisons in the 19th century, with the appearance of Jack the Ripper. He was a pioneer. People sometimes forget this.

He was something like the Christopher Columbus of murderers: he discovered a new territory in the human condition, which was soon inhabited by others of his ilk without salvation. Cinema modernized him, idealizing a scene of abominable behavior and meticulous transgressions. After him everything was a lot easier. Movies featuring maniac murderers consolidated the transition to celluloid of the degradation of the modern person attracted by the image of the executioner: *M, Psycho, A Clockwork Orange, The Hitcher, The Texas Chainsaw Massacre, The Hills Have Eyes, Henry: Portrait of a Serial Killer, The Silence of the Lambs, Seven*. In these Hollywood Auschwitzes, the remnants of a domestic apocalypse permeate the actions, bearing witness of the triviality of life (its condition as detritus) and accepting the period between birth and death as a transitoriness that is anything but fraudulent.

Though it is true that M, by Fritz Lang, had the first serial killer as its lead character (something viewed at the time as a peculiarity without privileges, and Peter Lorre's face was peculiar, very peculiar), it was only with the arrival of Norman Bates (Psycho), drawing back the curtains of prejudice and stabbing one of his victims in the shower in that extraordinary scene (interpretation: violent death is not so dirty; Hitchcock was brilliant for a reason), that cinema opened up to physical barbarism, by this time charged with neurosis, perverse euphorias, and well-conceived chills. There appeared new scenery for an act as old as the illness. But this is the civilized world which is our lot to share, the universe of fast food and of fast reading with little verse. It is, as Denis Johnson describes in his novel Angels, a small world that is half machine, half meat.

As had already been sensed by Jack the Ripper (who they say once saved a young girl who was drowning), a murderer becomes his victim's least favorite accident—an intentional accident. Jack made it clear that the serial killer is never a "one-hit wonder." A late product of the British Empire, when he arrived on the scene he was lagging behind the neurosis of the world's new time (Jack carried out his work as an invisible butcher between August and November of 1888), a time when soccer had already grown popular among the English. Could this enigmatic character have been, as has been suggested, a physician to Queen Victoria who killed women because one of his family members had contracted syphilis from a prostitute? Could it be that there are doctors who "save" people by killing them?

What irony! The first great serial killer of the modern era had perhaps been trained to save lives. Incidentally, his presence marked the narrative break of a period in which multiple historic novelties piled up rather indiscriminately. A character with his own *zeitgeist*, the Victorian murderer who is suspected to have had impeccable manners and who could save people who were not his victims (like the above-mentioned case of the young girl) was someone willing to ignore verisimilitude. This disrespect for contemporary solitude, this great chameleon-like profaneness (police were never able to capture him), made its appearance two years after Robert Louis Stevenson published *The Strange Case of Dr. Jekyll and Mr. Hyde*, coinciding with the worldwide expansion in the positivism of science and with the passion of the nascent sport of the masses, soccer. The British Empire did not know which path to take, that of the murderer as spectacle, or that of the ball game as entertainment for the masses. These were two different monstrosities.

Two years later, in 1890, Emile Zola wrote in *The Human Beast*: "She loved accidents: any mention of an animal run over, a man cut to pieces by a train, was bound to make her rush to the spot." Also, the novel *Crash*, by J. G. Ballard (which inspired the David Cronenberg movie of the same name, and the song "Cars," by Gary Numan), is an inescapable example of symphorophilia, one that re-creates that highly impenetrable and viscous region of the human mind, so laden with non-reciprocal actions, where physical disaster finds a way to draw attention to itself and become literature and cinema. Messy wounds seduce people into morbidity. We live in a culture were such wounds attract curiosity, just as sharks are drawn to a ship-wreck. The scene can take place in the privacy of a bedroom or outside, between two destinations.

In a hotel room, the police pick up pieces of a chopped up body. A few hours earlier it was alive and walking around. The hand, which until a while ago was able to ring the doorbell, has been sliced as if it were a piece of salami. There is blood every-where. The television cameras have already arrived. No one knows how they got there so fast, but they did. It appears that destiny notified them. Exhibitionism of violent death cannot be complete without the widening of the public eye, the "Big Brother" that we all carry inside. Flesh by itself feeds the ratings. The public tunes into the nightly newscast that shows the butchery most explicitly. Outside, the activity continues. The police pages publish the results of the death: their games are played in different places. Along a roadway several drivers stop to look at an accident with fatalities. A pair of bodies, still alive, lie breathing on the ground. The scene is completed by bloodstained clothes and maroon spots of newly coagulated blood. Everyone looks intently at what has happened, and yet they are able to escape the scene open to view. The mind goes in another direction because life is in another place, and in yet others. The liquid landscape of the *trauma* ("wound" in Greek) transports them at once to a different injured reality: they find themselves in front of the stage and the action is suspended. Death is a spectacle before the living.

Spectators of wounds are invited not to make up their minds as they stand at the abject mirror where they discover a face that was not planned. Those who find themselves face to face with themselves foresee the beginning of a state of calamity moving asymmetrically and allowing spasms to bring order to the chaos of the senses in their own way, in any fashion they happen to fancy. It is the pantheon of the Identi-Kit, the genealogical death of affiliation. From Norman Bates to Patrick Bateman (*American Psycho*), and passing through Alex (*A Clockwork Orange*), the scenes prone to the public destruction of privacy through the presence of a serial killer have possessed, throughout time, an inexplicable magnetism, causing the repugnance of the abnormal and the seduction of the promise of unreality to coincide. In this there is a shift to something even more repugnant and less preferable from which, nevertheless, it is impossible to look away. The nadir of an ignoble activity reverses the intrinsic nature of curiosity (senseless death exacerbates the senses) and thus calms expectations when there is a shortage of solutions.

With the good health of their irresponsibility, serial killers practice their solitary ritual in diverse ways, establishing specialties that are far from ideal: stranglers, suffocators, poisoners, mutilators, throat slitters; in short, annihilators of all parts of the human body. For them, none of these parts is more important than the rest. The hedonism of this whole and predatory entirety can only be stopped by a noose around the neck, a lethal injection, an electric chair, or a good firing squad (which is what Gary Gilmore requested in Utah in 1977: a decent execution by an effective firing squad, and not like the one faced by the character in the joke told in Spain, who was walking down the street completely covered in blood and, when asked what had happened to him, responded, "They put me in front of a firing squad but they botched the job!"). But they run the risk anyway. Engaging in vampirism once and then again, these predators feel original. They emerge victorious from anomie. Their psycho lifestyle, grotesque and dissolute, becomes a life vest for their very unconventional appetites, and as a result it allows the cheers of these appetites to be heard. This explains why the adjective factory lives at the expense of such acts.

In their disrespectful gluttony, serial killers, even the most inconsistent in their precocious ferocity, are killer angels who make house calls. Before anyone opens the door they are already inside the house. They knock, knock, knock on the door, and then they move quickly to the knockout. They are ghosts of premeditation who find their reward in a progressive but irregular way: they attack, they escape, and they attack once again. The reasons for their actions resist being captured. They are eaten up by worry and at times defend themselves by doing the same thing, eating. In this way they gratify their sumptuous instincts through a modus operandi that is by no means axiomatic and which is characteristic of an intuition not in conformity with their mental health. "Great crimes are never single, they are link'd to former faults" (Racine).

Acting behind the back of conscience, and subject only to the perplexity that they generate, serial killers define their depraved self-portrait. At the same time that they lie in wait in a sublimated identity, in a dead family tree (they erase their tracks because they do not know where they come from), they change the name of horror with the stroke of a pen. They give it a different name, and it is easier for them to re-christen with blood than with water. For them there is no redemption or quick forgetfulness that can conceal them, only the interruption of a visceral allegory. With their thriving fame, they allow themselves to be free of fear, since they know that their victims will not be compensated. They come from that which is unforgiveable and create curiosity regarding the game of discovery, committing the public to an aberrant plan: any fellow human could be next, and next is very close, perhaps next door. They are there, awake to what they plan to achieve and to all that which they are not thinking or planning. They live in the word "wakefulness," placing reality at the disposal of nightmares, because "dreams take no account of the world's dimensions" (Graham Greene).

In their distraction of brutality, serial killers set in motion a shared strategy: their victims (most of them women) emerge at random, because luck moves in bodies and changes both destinies and consequences. It is precisely their condition as elusive beings that sets the stage to make them nonconformists in one single way, the only way they know how to be so. Being as they are, a condition without penance, they cause lucid and talented shivers from the moment that they turn panic into reverse comfort. We are there, watching and reading attentively, and we feel a certain nervousness as we recognize as sublimated some of our least visible phobias. We are afraid to feel alike. Fear, it would appear, is a telescope that takes us closer to the place where we do not want to be.

THE FALL AS SOMETHING INDIGENOUS: ICARUS, MUSEUMS, THE WORLD TRADE CENTER

MAN HAS ALWAYS HAD A HYPNOTIC FASCINATION with beings and objects that crash to earth. Hypnotic, hymnic, optic. Anything or any mass that slams against the surface of the planet achieves an aura of venerability and transcendence. In the beginning was the Word, but before then was the Fall. We believe that the impact of something large, such as a meteorite or a comet, changed the history of Earth, annihilating an entire period of lives and possibilities. This is how we explain the disappearance of millennia of flora and fauna. And even though there is still no proof, imagination is sufficient to conceive of it. It knows how hard it is to change the trajectory of a verticality in decline. That remote, preterite past—which is so distant from the present that it makes us feel as if we did not belong to any era, which is unreconstructable except in terms of certain relics and dinosaur skeletons discovered from time to time— interests people as much as the future, whose predictability depends less and less on one's desires.

We look at our great oracle, the past, through a big crystal ball (which can also fall to earth), and we see more realities crashing against the planet. Ships, living beings, asteroids. We see rocks of all sizes. As a result of all the things that have come from space and fallen here, the planet could very well be flat instead of round, the latter condition being proven not so long ago when man set out in search of gold and spices only to find a new map, with Indians, Amazon women, and pearls from the ocean's depths (which so fascinated Gonzalo Fernández de Oviedo, 1478-1557, the great chronicler of the Indies). We

89

look and we see. But what? How many valleys, canyons (brown
and red), and hollows give us the impression of a surface perfo-
rated by something large that fell from above in an era different
from ours, when things fell just as much as they do today? Better yet, fearing a fatal encore, we envision some huge ending
repeated for our species and all others, with an object the size of
another planet crashing to the Earth and leaving it as flat as a
penny, with us underneath. After gazing so much at heavenly
bodies, we will die crushed by one.

That daunting and as-of-yet unrealized thought has a mythical genealogy. Soon after its birth it turned apocalyptic. Perhaps knowing that the best things are those that fall—leaves,
hair, teeth, kingdoms, and the stock market know this well—
man has speculated about a plan of marvelous descents that in
his visible future (a future of imagination) includes other men,
ships from other planets, objects, and beings comparable only
to themselves. Water also falls, and if we observe things correctly, the first great disaster in history began with a successful
case of falling: the rain of the universal flood could not be
impeded. Could that have been the rain of which Bob Dylan
was singing? "And it's a hard, it's a hard, it's a hard, it's a hard /
It's a hard rain's a-gonna fall." There was another extremely
great fall before that one, and this one *was* the first: the Fall of
Man into sin. No parachute could match the temptation of that
woman. Eve did not fall by slipping on a banana peel. Her fall,
rather—and that of her companion—was precipitated by an
apple, not one that fell from an ordinary apple tree, such as the
one that helped Newton discover the law of gravity, but rather
from the tree of temptation, something of greater gravity. This
is a leafless tree whose shade we all seek in order to fall into it.

The Bible alludes to different falls, especially notable
among them the one where the demons, by divine decision,
enter into a herd of swine, which then rush over a cliff to their
death. Mark 5:11-13: "Now there was there nigh unto the

mountains a great herd of swine feeding. And all the devils besought him, saying, Send us into the swine, that we may enter into them. And forthwith Jesus gave them leave. And the unclean spirits went out, and entered into the swine: and the herd ran violently down a steep place into the sea, (they were about two thousand;) and were choked in the sea." The moral would be, "With the swine dead the evil is gone," but man, perhaps out of respect for the meat from which ham is taken, chose the syllogism popular in Spanish: "Muerto el perro se acabó la rabia" ("With the dog dead the rabies is gone"). Dogs also fall— or they make a flock of sheep fall, something that occurs in Thomas Hardy's 1874 novel *Far from the Madding Crowd*—and one of the canines best at falling is the one in Goya's seminal painting, "Half-submerged Dog," from the artist's black period.

The constructed tradition has it that every fall is the metaphor of something fatal that has not yet come down but which could fall at any moment. Reality starts with a warning: "Avoid falling into sin" (but Eve, as a forerunner to Icarus, fell anyway). The expression "fall into sin" would indicate that sin is not up above, but in some lower part of the body, a place that has generated other dubious expressions: "What you did is very low." And it is not like we are all dwarves! Since his origins, man has been tempted to fall but also not to do so. In some aspects of reality, life can still choose. Between *yes* and *maybe not*, man is still able to find the delicate balance that allows him to think and to see his world from a point of view of immovability, from the vantage point of that which does not move (since the main source of security lies in existing in a perfectible place), from a perspective of immobility that can end at any moment, because not doing anything is also falling, into passivity.

Beginning with Plato, thought has been concerned about drawing parallels with falling, an ideal that goes against the grain. And the matter does not end there. In the *Phaedrus*, the failure of elevation arises. Due to his subplanetary, sublunar descent, man enters into a disharmony with his own being, a situation reflected in the waters of the Lethe, where the worst of all condemnations is experienced: the forgetting of one's origin. This incestuous relationship (in which metonymy is superimposed on metaphor) is insinuated in the lifestyle and thought of the Greeks of that time, both before and after Plato. One who preceded Plato, Empedocles, died when he leapt into the depths of the Mount Etna volcano (due to the high esteem in which he held himself, he did not want to die the same way as other mortals). And regarding the death of Aeschylus there are several versions. One of them holds that he *received* a fall: that an eagle carrying a tortoise dropped it and it fell on his head, killing him. Another version indicates that he died falling from a horse, though most believe that he died of old age, or rather that advanced age fell fatally upon him. There have also been historic falls in fiction, such as that of Sherlock Holmes and Professor James Isaac Moriarty, who die when, locked in each other's arms from their struggle, they plunge together over Reichenbach Falls, a wet Swiss abyss.

Falling and its postfaces have been the direct representation of a purpose without objective, a purpose which, as an elliptical figure, has been stimulated by the lack of specific time. In this way—and this is not the only one—falling is depicted in Milton's *Paradise Lost*, where man can barely find remorse among so much inexistent territory, and falling is exactly that: an inexistence that takes form and that informs on its ethereal omnipotence. There are few things more timeless and more recyclable (the place changes, the fall does not) than the irreversible idea of descent. In Neoplatonic philosophers such as the Italian Marsilio Ficino (1433-1499), a man ahead of his time (he was both a vegetarian and a closet gay), the impossibility of reconstructing preexistence is added to forgetfulness and disharmony as corollaries of falling. Thus, falling is not a final sign, but rather the absence of the first sign, the loss of any trace, existence emptied out by that which began without being finished.

Man, the victim of a fall that came before his own, was condemned to perpetuate it, as the Fall is nothing more than an
event without origin, the stigma that we have through ancestry.
A radical sign of that same mythological context is the sinking
of Atlantis, a monument of falling to itself, as it includes what
was before and that which did not come after. So large was that
fall from which no one swam away that it did not even leave a
trace. Therefore, the first ideal world conceived by man ended
in the depths, and it sank so far that it became invisible.
Atlantis represents a fall without existence, since it was never
able to be seen. Sunken civilization is one of the great conjec-
tures there is to make sense out of that which once existed
without being able to be verified.

In the *Bible*, the word—whatever it is—interposes between
acts and results. When the disciples inform him that the Phar-
isees are taken aback by his teachings, Christ responds: "Let
them alone: they be blind leaders of the blind. And if the blind
lead the blind, both shall fall into the ditch" (Matthew 15:14).
Toward this same place meekly march the characters depicted
in the 1568 painting *De parable der blinden* (*Parable of the Blind*
or *The Blind Leading the Blind*), by Pieter Brueghel the Elder
(1525-1569). Life placed these individuals on a one-way path
with no return. Man pays the price of his descents. All his falls
together synthesize into the absence of sight, the lack of a convincing visual instinct. As a corollary of the examples seen
above, as well as those to be seen hereafter, we might think of
it this way: that when Daniel was thrown into the lions' den,
the Tower of Babel and the walls of Jericho fell in with him,
with all of them coming together in the last book, Revelation,
where the world in the last days falls into a great pit of fire.

For Empedocles, carbonized by a volcano, there was fire in
the beginning and also in the end. We are here because the
valiant archangel pushed Satan into the eternal flames, a
metaphoric fall to justify the postponing of the one experienced

by us, beings half Icarus, half phoenix. Sooner or later, the ashes—the postscript of the fire—will also fall. In the end, the synapse is always interrupted. Ovid, in *Metamorphoses*, and in the poem "Daedalus, Icarus, Perdix" refers to the myth of Icarus, to that fall which occurred between premature visibility and physical water, an ironic comfort for the failed human bird: since he could not keep company with the stars in the sky, he will end up in the deep, along with the starfish, even though a wet sky was not what he wanted to touch.

The subject of the physical fall of man has been taken up again countless times in art, poetry, cinema, and even pop music. Jovanotti's song "Mi fido di te" says: "vertigo is not / fear of falling / but rather a desire to fly." Different eras bring varied pictorial examples of Icarusologies. In *Peacocks*, a 1683 painting by Dutchman Melchior d'Hondecoeter (1636-1695), Icarus is a decorative bird of limited flight. Just as with d'Hondecoeter's peacock, the mythical character specializes in appearing as his mutant image, because in this state (and it is unique indeed) he reassumes the angelic appearance that Ovid never sought—or knew how—to give him, even though angels tend to be young, as was the boy with wax wings, who paid dearly for his disobedience. In several paintings by Tiepolo (1696-1770) there are anthropomorphic angels who are either falling or who are at the same height as their fall, since they found in its visibility, that still unharmed beauty, their greatest virtue. It is for this reason that they never fall downward, but rather from one side of the broad heavens to the other, as if descending from east to west. Nothing stops them from navigating this space however they might and with their sight.

From the entire gamut of examples, the best known pictorial interpretation of the fall in question appears in Brueghel's painting *Landscape with the Fall of Icarus*, from 1558, where the activity of a seemingly normal day presents some inconsistencies which are forgiven. After all, Brueghel was a painter and not a photographer. In essence, the image of the fall is the following:

a farmer is plowing with his horse, a ship is sailing nearby, and in the water can be seen the legs of a man drowning amid the generalized distraction. It would appear that the problem was not the failed ascent but rather the mortal plunge. Meanwhile, the farmer continues working as if nothing has happened. We can suppose that the person who has fallen never asked for help. Silence fell upon him, and then he fell in silence (words fall, and fail). It is also possible that no one was able to pay attention to him since on that day reality invited solipsism. It is another possible theory. Brueghel's theory is a synoptic view that makes a map of its itinerary, though not its conclusions. The scenes at the bottom of the ellipse precede the beginning that comes after the fall and allude to an inconclusive exactness.

According to the information coming from the ship's sails (they never lie), it is a windy day. The wind has driven a man into the water. Nevertheless, the only evidence of wind is in the sails themselves, since not even the horse's tail or the trees show activity. Or did Brueghel's horse and trees know how to evade the wind? The water also shows no signs of turbulence. There are no waves, meaning there are also no surfers. Nothing or no one seems to feel uneasy due to the day's primordial activity, except for the sails of the ship. How strange! They are restless. If not for the title of the painting (without which nearly everything would be different), we also would not be able to know if the man fell from the sky or simply dove into the water to take a swim (as swimming existed by then). In any case, he is flying in the water (the liquid will liquidate him). We see his legs, but a pair of them is not enough to reconstruct a complete scene. The light is still there, resisting; the man has done a nose dive and brought part of the sun with him.

With its omniscient presence, the sun remains more than sight, and nearly as much as the fall that has just left a man abandoned in the sea. Between the premature and the premeditated, Icarus reveals a fitting message. The behavior of the topography and its inhabitants is subordinated to one single aspect: the important thing is the fall, the small detail among the complete peace of the bright day. Such impassivity highlights an imperfection, not of the painting but of life itself: nothing is tragic, not even the end with all its complete parts. *Landscape with the Fall of Icarus* organizes reality established in accordance with another, earlier reality but seen in a different way. The vision that is constructed takes it upon itself to grant the character the authorship of his actions. The fall is responsible for him and vice versa.

In another work by Brueghel, *The Fall of Icarus*, the situation is even more evident, because the boy is about to fall, although his descending action lacks the dramatics of the earlier work, in which the semi-submerged body highlights the drama in process, the exclusivity of the moment when life abandons its standard destination. The wisdom of the meeting between something (the fall) and someone (the "faller") is fulfilled in a place that is instituted, instructed: reality maintains its good manners despite what is happening. Inspired by the Icarusology of Brueghel, in 1553 Georg Hoefnagel etched *Landscape with Winding River and Fall of Icarus*, a piece in which a boy is falling (a younger Icarus?) among the thick clouds toward a river full of boats, hinting at the beginning of a theme in its museological uneasiness. The planet's important days are always windy. Close to him, a winged man—Daedalus?—looks distractedly in that direction. It is a windy day and the caption says: "INTER UTRUMQUE VOLA, MEDIO TUTISSIMUS IBIS" ("Fly between the extremes, the way is safest in the middle"). The words seem copied from Ovid. Daedalus, or whoever it is up there, must be thinking: "Icarus did not realize that what he was seeing / Meant danger for him." But in Hoefnagel's work, Icarus falls into the water on his back, looking up at the sky, a sea that is not at all liquid and which that day is nearly overcast.

The topic of transition between one height and another, of an unwanted fall, is the theme of the already cited work by

Brueghel (*Parable of the Blind* or *The Blind Leading the Blind*), from 1568, which encapsulates in the form of a precipice the destina-tion of a premature return to nothingness, the useless fall into randomness. (On this matter see the scholarly book *Museum of Words. The Poetics of Ekphrasis from Homer to Ashbery*, by James A.W. Heffernan.) In Brueghel's master painting, a group of peo-ple is being guided by a blind man who—everything indicates—will be the first one to fall into a ditch. None of them knows that they are being led by someone who cannot see or that he has already fallen; only we know it, although we see the fall from out-side, as an allegoric signal falling into interpretation.

In this way, the painting reveals themes ignored or not nar-rated by the image but which are present nevertheless. This Icarus without eyes or sight is the final stumble of an illusion, but it is also falling evidence of a landscape determined by calamity. The image of the passage from Matthew cited above is sum-moned. We see Brueghel's painting and cannot help but ask: what will happen when they all fall? The void responds only after everything has transpired, and the last one to fall will be the demonstration of an ontological fulfillment: there will be a defin-itive absence of man. It is the transition from *yes* to *no*, from the paradigm to the margin, from the ideal to the loss of privileges.

The different versions of Icarus' destination created by Brueghel gave birth to three notable poems with different aspi-rations. In these poems, the information about the mythical character manages to acquit itself well in dealing with the com-monplace. They are examples of reciprocal poetic speeches, where everything has something specific to be expressed. The situation represents a strange movement on the part of the myth, traveling from here to there and back again: it began in literary fashion with Ovid, it moved on to painting, and it then returned to language. They are prodigal words: after seeing what was out there, they feel comforted and, as a result, they return. They enter and exit ekphrasis, the same as with their epistemology of the ages. In the 1938 poem by W.H. Auden, "Musée de Beaux Arts," inspired by *Landscape with the Fall of Icarus*, the winged man in the fullness of his idiosyncrasy turns out to be, in appearance, just one more detail of iconographic wisdom.

> In Breughel's Icarus, for instance: how everything turns away
> Quite leisurely from the disaster; the ploughman may
> Have heard the splash, the forsaken cry,
> But for him it was not an important failure; the sun shone
> As it had to on the white legs disappearing into the green
> Water, and the expensive delicate ship that must have seen
> Something amazing, a boy falling out of the sky,
> Had somewhere to get to and sailed calmly on.

The poet creates a self-portrait of others' lives and reconstructs the undetermined indeterminations of the pictorial work. In this way, he allows for a distinction between the particular and the general, something that can lead to the detection of another reality within that which is "real": the moment in which agony and disinterest cross, leaving unexplained what was there before and that which will come later. In "Musée de Beaux Arts" (the title alludes to the Museum of Fine Arts in Brussels where the poem is located), the important thing is the fall, the worry that the boat is sinking without anyone in it being capable of realizing it. Marked by indifference, that moment signals the face-to-face encounter between the marvelous and the routine, with an unexpected result: the boat will continue on its path and the winged boy will end up fighting against sinking. He swims toward nothingness with wings of melted wax. There is a man working, and in the other it is marvel that is at work, but among those present no one sees it. The world of that day falls into the lack of wonder. It had all, and yet none, of the makings for a symbolic act.

Daedalus' disobedient son has been falling from one decade to the next, having come before the rebelliousness of the hippies, who today have fallen into disgrace. A great explorer of the fall, he detracted from the dramatic nature of the surface that was about to be impacted. It its different lyric and pectoral iterations, fundamentalist of the fall drags along with him metaphor and metonymy. It serves as a pretext for art and poetry and describes a visual idea whose motivation contrasts with its objective. The poem by William Carlos Williams, "Landscape with the Fall of Icarus" (published in the magazine Hudson Review in 1960 and two years later in the book *Pictures from Brueghel*), a direct heir of that aesthetics which resists tradition, begins with three verses of marvelous innocence (that era was innocent in many things): "According to Brueghel / when Icarus fell / it was spring" (he did not fall in autumn like the leaves). And it finishes by saying that the splash that no one noticed was that of Icarus, drowning. No one had the slightest doubt about what was happening. At that point he was flying very low, as if to show he was important.

While in Auden's works the writing seeks to understand the event through the empathy that the author feels for said event (at least regarding the poetic wisdom emitted by its images), Williams' poem exalts a naïve wonder (a naivety reminiscent of the painting by the customs official Henri Rousseau) customary in a person seeing things simultaneously and for the first time (Icarus was but a boy), even if the fall here is not live and in person. No, this fall, rather, is seen through an earlier painting, one capable of capturing the wonder caused by a domestic scene that has not been taken into account by compassion. None of all this open to view is completely possible.

The poem by Jack Gilbert, "Failing and Flying," contributes one of the most accurate looks at the inescapable character of Icarus, who not only fell from the sky, but who at some point in the adventure managed to rise and to believe, optimistically, that he could continue moving upward, and then a little more, until reaching his goal, even if he was still far from that extreme place that he could only reach with closed eyes. The poem, belonging to the book *Refusing Heaven* (2005), contains a masterful beginning that helps one to better understand the dysfunctional purpose of Icarus and of all the amorous Icarusologies and the many failed utopias that have used him as a referent:

Everyone forgets that Icarus also flew.
It's the same when love comes to an end,
or the marriage fails and people say
they knew it was a mistake, that everybody
said it would never work. That she was
old enough to know better. But anything
worth doing is worth doing badly.

In the century of the airplane, and thus the century of plane crashes (collective Icaruses), several poems have been written about the myth turned mediator of a modern sense of frustration, above all with regard to the impossibility of achieving the goal, whatever it may be. Nature and the character with melted wings did not have mutual feelings, a disagreement has inspired literary imagination. Besides the three poems cited, the following also deserve to be mentioned: Steven Spender's "Icarus," 1933 ("Til now, like Icarus mid-ocean-drowned, / Hands, wings, are found"); Anne Sexton's "To a Friend Whose Work Has Come to Triumph," 1962 ("Consider Icarus, pasting those sticky wings on, / testing this strange little tug at this shoulder blade"); and Muriel Rukeyser's "Waiting for Icarus," 1973 ("He said all the buckles were very firm / He said the wax was the best wax / He said Wait for me here on the beach / He said Just don't cry").

Visual poetry like that of every fall, the poems of Auden, Williams, Gilbert, Spender, Sexton, and Rukeyser invite the use of words (and the images that accompany them) with another perspective, one capable of seeing even that which is not in sight or named explicitly. It is perhaps because of this that the final stanza of Auden's poem is cited at the beginning of the movie *The*

Man Who Fell to Earth, by Nicholas Roeg, in which David Bowie plays an alien Icarus, but one with more metaphysics than Steven Spielberg's *E.T.* (Coincidentally, Roeg's prior film was called *Don't Look Now*, an appropriate title for summarizing the boy's fall: Icarus—like in Hoefnagel's painting—cannot look now, and as a result he is falling, sinking definitively into a timeless present. And the movie was filmed in Venice, which is also sinking.)

Icarus sinks in the painting of Henri Matisse, *The Fall of Icarus* (1943), a high tide of bright colors under control. The stars that surround him and testify of his vertical descent, or ascent (the greatness of the painting lies in the lack of definition in its perspective), six in all, so peculiar and yellow like individual suns, are located on high, or down below and off to the side. Is Icarus going up or down? Is it him, the disobedient boy, who is falling, or is it actually universal matter plummeting to earth with no one expecting it? Or are both falling at the same time in order to feel the closeness of mutually frightening company? If Hollywood were to make a film version of Icarus and his heavily reported fall, the sequel, or Part II, would be called, "Icarus Accompanied in his Fall," or "Icarus and Company." If Batman has Robin, and the Lone Ranger has Tonto, why not find a similar human sidekick for Icarus? Would anyone dare to fall with him? Who? Perhaps some animal? Pelicans, those Icaruses of the high seas, kamikazes of their own solitude, fall down into the water seeking food in the form of fish, shrimp, and distracted crabs. Many go blind from repeatedly hitting the ocean surface and they die, lost on the horizon. As a result of falling from so far, did Icarus die, or simply go blind?

The storyline represents an action without precedent: the recipient of an excess of imagination, the envoy falls from a lack of priorities. It is the fall into the void of knowledge, the dilemma of not being able to understand beyond that which is taught by randomness. The stranger falls to earth, as well as from side to side, and in the open air he feels emotional claustrophobia. Icarus was something like the ugly duckling that ran out of strength in mid-flight. In the same way as with the one who fell but who continues to see things from before the fall, he observes the failure of themes and appearances, that new place of understanding. He has found the place through which to pass and where he as yet cannot be. What is more important and dangerous than that?

Due to its feathered character, the myth of Icarus has been compared to other winged beings flying around out there and which can be seen in movies and also at times in reality: angels. They are not all brethren of Lucifer, and their hagiology has occupied various recent beliefs—actually old but updated— which state that the number of angels visiting us is on the rise. This topic is so relevant that some time back *Time* magazine dedicated one of its covers and main articles to the topic: "The New Age of Angels: 69% of Americans believe they exist. What in heaven is going on?" (December 27, 1993). It is pure speculation, so that a few readers might think themselves more pure, redeemed from their second-to-the-last fall by the temptation of feeling as if they were everything, except angels.

A fictitious being, or one belonging to others, the angel who appears in the movies of Wim Wenders, *Wings of Desire* (1987) and *Faraway, So Close!* (1993), exchanges his wings for feet in order to plant them firmly in reality. Just as the New Testament points out, it is more difficult to walk on water—only one man in the whole book can do it—than to fly from one world to another, as angels and archangels did in the Old Testament. His fall due to this intransitive exchange means he cannot fly except for in some thoughts that function as an antidote. Perhaps the greatest emotional impact that he obtains as a result is allowing himself to feel close and immediate in the midst of a world that still has not managed to recover from the fall but which nonetheless celebrates any new fall that might occur.

Wenders' unredeeming fable is not new in the German context. Reinhard Johannes Sorge's play *Der Bettler* (*The Beggar*) came out in 1912 (the same year that the Titanic fell into the depth of the sea). The play (an abstract, neo-expressionist production that debuted in 1917), whose theme is the clipped wings of desire, showcases an eagle-man who attempts to reach the heavens (he came before the later and more fortunate cinemagraphic angel of Wenders). The "beggar angel" grows wings (actually, not having any, he fashions some and puts them on) and begins to fly. Time after time, for the same reason, he fails. The bars of a cage come between him and the sky as intermediaries of the progressive and final fall. The eagle-man returns repeatedly to the point of departure, without knowing from where he has come or where he is going.

Like Brueghel's farmer who does not see the man's fall—because the import of what is occurring does not fall upon him—he does not know how to look. It is as if he has said to himself, "Don't look now." And as a result of having imposed this blindness on himself, it became his lot to fall (and his author, Sorge, fell into the forgotten). A year later, in 1913, Max Beckmann finished *The Sinking of the Titanic*, the first painting of this nautical disaster, and one that defies comparison. Among the images of aquatic desperation (falling can take place in water, fire, air, or on land) appearing on the faces of those present, allowing themselves to be seen without being able to be seen (much like a lightning bolt), a nervous truth can be verified: the life of man is nothing but a permanent training for a shipwreck, and it does no good to despair. Resignation takes the place of what cannot be continued. Nothingness is not worth very much, especially if it comes at the end of everything.

After the events of September 11, 2001, reality and imagination have become homonymous, being one of the first complete signs of the 21st century. It wants to be new in some regard. The move from fictitious to verisimilar has happened in reverse and now it is fiction that is impeded from copying reality with regard to the magnitude of its falls. Reality ceased to be an abstraction that we needed to keep explaining. Destiny arrived without any-one's permission, and for this reason the tale of verisimilitude, as with that of soccer games, was forced to resort to rhetorical inven-tions in order to understand, to the extent possible, the limits of reality and the magnitude of the falls that occur inside of it.

In the lapse—or interval—between one century and the next, man has lived depending on falls. In the poem by Vicente Huido-bro, Altazor was falling with a parachute and thus he was able to write. Descent is the position of man in his purposes. Since he is a being born of the fall—which proves the gravity of its law—man has reproduced the wonder caused by other falls that had no type of moral but which did have a distant absence of language.

These falls lack the words to accompany them. Robespierre liked to see fall the heads of innocent citizens—and heads fall when the guillotine falls—because he knew that terror changed the place of people's hearts (the spirits of someone condemned to death sink low to the ground). The fall, any fall, represents the impossibility of control and the definitive loss of willpower, the rejection of intelligence by unforeseen forces. In short, it represents everything that makes life more vulnerable and less peaceful. It is the being of every human being changing its con-dition. "Dust in the air suspended / Marks the place where his-tory ends" (T.S. Eliot).

"The era of falls" began with the fall of the Berlin Wall, and we continue living in those days. First there was the Concorde (it had been said that the safest airplane in history would end its history undefeated); then the Kursk submarine (since the sur-face of the earth is insufficient, there are other more liquid sur-faces where falling can continue); then came the Russian space station Mir (whose fall alerted the world, and yet it ended up without dramatics at the bottom of the sea with the fish and octopi); in the middle—history is full of intermediate points—there have been several falls in Wall Street stocks and politi-

cians who have fallen in disgrace; and finally four Boeing airplanes, two of them crashing horizontally into vertical buildings.
The day that this happened was also sunny, just as in
Brueghel's painting. It was not spring but rather still summer,
and among the Icaruses who had their seatbelts on the majority did not want to fall. In the illuminated surroundings there
were ships and people planting. It was reality being converted
into a museum of movement. It has long been thus. Hiroshima
and Nagasaki were the conclusion of a steep fall, that is to say,
toward itsel—first the movement of a trajectory toward its dissolution and then the stoppage in the twilight of the schism—
where we are still inert in mid-fall. And stillness does not accelerate: we hear its melancholy memory speaking of the budding
future as if a monologue were about to begin. Poet Olga Oroz-
co wondered: "Is it perhaps nothing more than an area of
abysses and volcanoes fully boiling, blindly predestined for the
ceremonies of the species in this inexplicable trip downward?"
("The Garden of Delights"). And history offers several answers.
On that downward morning, the glass of the two towers
seemed—and it was—the water were the Icarus of the painting
(that precious Icarus) was sinking, moving his legs. For a few
hours we were all him, Icaruses suspended between emptiness
and the end: "The truth: / to know that we are, / from the beginning, / suspended. / Brotherhood over the void" (Octavio Paz).
The same calm as always awaited the most unexpected fall. The
same thing happens all the time. Dennis Tito, the first space
tourist, confessed upon returning to Earth on May 1, 2001, that
although he had paid millions for the trip, the descent was the
most marvelous part. The terrorists who four months later came
down with the hijacked planes spent thousands of dollars on
their flight training, because, on the modern scene, falling is
nothing more than the conclusion of a freedom of movement
that leads to the lack of action. And it has a high price. While it
is the fulfillment of prediction that on occasion may be accom-

panied by reality, falling is the continuity of a preceding event for which randomness is not completely responsible. The action is barely perfect, as if it had just acquired its immortality.

On September 11, the television showed people jumping from the 105th floor, and even higher (the height is not always proportional to the fall). Between the fire of Lucifer and the dive of Empedocles into a volcano, they chose the latter, a way of restoring the inopportuneness of death right when life had become higher. In Abyssinia (modern Ethiopia) Italian soldiers threw their enemies from planes, and in Argentina the military government did the same thing several years later with political prisoners. The dead were called "the disappeared ones," a euphemism used to refer to the material lack of bodies, as if the invisibility of the air had swallowed them. Falling falls in different languages, and between the two towers of the World Trade Center it fell loudly into the void. They were skyscrapers that also scraped the earth. The lack of redemption always finds an opportunity for plagiarism in which to repeat itself, and its space comes with its own language, from the depths of history.

There is a photo by Gerard Malanga, from 1978, in which William Burroughs is pointing a shotgun at the twin towers of the World Trade Center. Might he have mistaken the towers for an enormous bird, divided in two parts, which he wanted to bring down with a blast of his gun? On that September morning in 2001—a beautiful day, precisely as the previous night's forecasts had predicted—mortality had to do with a crash so that it might fulfill the intimacy of an eidetic collapse, seen from outside, as if the images captured in the act wanted to seem like an incomplete thought. From the highest floors, some 1,300 feet up, there were people plunging downward; in an average of 11 seconds they were on the ground. Theirs were the screams (Icarus with a swan song) heard by the deaf sky when the first tower fell. A redundant death prepared the scene for each one, emitting a disconsolate noise, a noise willing to disavow reality. The image

was reminiscent of the beauty of kamikazes disguised as emptiness (an emptiness can, at times, disguise itself as beauty).

This history had begun at the only ending possible, no matter how hard it was to awaken the slumber of the emptiness, of
the change of expectations in the landscape. In that adventure
there was a structure, a story told by a sole and solitary figure. It
was like that moment in the morning when one awakens and
begins, little by little, to understand the world again. The high
and low points ended up at the same level. It was about time!
And to think that 27 years earlier, in August of 1974, Philippe
Petit, a tightrope walker capable of walking through the transparency of the air, had walked from the roof of one of the towers to the other, asking the emptiness if it wanted to accompany him during the chilling journey, and the emptiness truly was
chilling. Its docile nature is incomparable. At the highest point
of the two skyscrapers, those were the silent images that, when
hard pressed, found a way to express certain words.

It is not a cock-and-bull story to say that we are farther and
farther from the heights. And yet, in a beautiful cock-and-bull
story the impossible is achieved. This kind of thing happens. A
stranger arrives at a house asking for work and the owner tells
him: "There is a lot of work to do here, but we can only pay you
in one way, by teaching you how to fly." The wife is surprised by
her husband's words and protests: "Why did you tell him that
lie; we do not know how to teach someone to fly." The husband
responds: "He will work here for a long time, he will get old,
and when he no longer has the strength to work we will tell him
to climb the highest tree and fly. He will not be able to fly, he
will fall, and will die. That will be the end of the story." And
this is what they did. Time passed, a lot of time, and the man
did not stop asking: "When are you going to teach me to fly?"
One day, after many years had gone by, and when the visitor
was unusable and old, the couple told him: "The time has come.
All you have to do is climb that tree, and when we tell you to

jump, you will do it." The man climbed the tree, and when they gave him the order he jumped. But he did not fall. He flew away. Patience had given him wings. The corollary to the moral of this story has an immediate conclusion: having grown used to living in the Fall, man realizes that another fall is important. Living, then, is nothing more than accentuating the continuity of that which came to an end and which still has no end. And art has attempted to restore this paradox to that which is real, which can exist or not. It depends.

In the English language, the only unreal act in the life of man is a fall: *falling in love*. What a paradox: to fall is to fulfill an anagogical feeling, one of maximum ascent, or something that elevates us from reality but which at the same time strips us of the aerial aspect, approximating metaphysics to behavior. Seeing a man die in a painting is not as dramatic as burying him in reality, where things fall in a different manner. There is always, somewhere, a splendor that is superior to death. Icarus tried to reach the sun, but his wings ended up singed by the hot brightness, bringing him back down before his time. Man does not have to be an expert in falling to be capable of falling, and his age is also unimportant.

In the Empire of the Rising Sun there were Icaruses who exchanged their rising for falling; they called them, strangely enough, *kamikazes*, in reference to a sacred winged figure. Their brightness of fire while falling brought with it a dark heroism (generally, ending up below is always less glorious than achieving a permanent height). In the poems of W.H. Auden, W.C. Williams, and Jack Gilbert, falling brings the happiness befitting a beauty that is tragic and bereft of reward. Since the time that he began to be real and literary, man has dreamt of the heights, but also of the opposite, with an altered sequential order. When he falls, the prediction of the first day is fulfilled: from birth, descent is inevitable. And, in this new century of sun and wind, we continue in this fall without being here. That is why it is so hard to represent it.

INCLUSION IN VOGUE

WHEN WE SEE JUSTIN BIEBER, we do not see a person. We see a haircut. The same thing happens when we come across photographs of Cristiano Ronaldo and Gareth Bale, two of the best paid and most famous soccer players in the world. Or the unmistakable image of North Korea's supreme leader, Kim Jong-un, whose haircut completely characterizes the isolated nation and its ideology, at least regarding its male population.[1] These individuals show up on the scene and, instead of famous people, we see neatly groomed hairdos, as if the visual signs of our times were the first things to arrive at this part of human anatomy.

It might be the style, or it might be them, but there is something irreplaceable, something unique to an era about those heads where both personal decisions and a hairstylist's scissors have been. And not just any hairstylist: a *coiffeur* (why is it that to turn attempts at "good taste" into something elegant we resort, at least in language, to French?). There emerges in the mops of the above-mentioned singer, soccer players, and dictator—as in those of others with similar features, and perhaps owing to the year in which it became their lot to exist—a recognizable image, at least in its attempt to call attention to itself and emit a sense of currentness.

---

[1]Beginning in March 2014, young North Korean men desiring to go to college will need to cut their hair like Kim Jong-un. The women, meanwhile, must have a hairdo similar to that of the first lady, Ri Sol-Ju. Up until the official decree, men could choose between 10 different haircuts, and women had 18 such choices. North Korean barbers received the news with great satisfaction, since from now on no customer will dare to complain about their work.

The passage of time can be marked by haircuts, that which grows on top of the head and that which does not. In Elvis Presley's hair, with its immovable quiff, we see the decade of the 1960, whereas in the semi-Samson-like hairstyles of Aerosmith band members we see the 1970s. When we want to change from one time period to another within ourselves, we turn to a comb and a pair of scissors, believing that cutting off ringlets or tufts of hair (or neatly adding them), will place the beings that we are closer to the future, which is nothing more than the present with less nervousness.

We see a photograph of a person from the beginning of the 20th century and an initial comment crosses our mind, although this does not mean that the image which has flashed before our eyes has made us think. We see a face photographed in 1918 and we know that something more than an indefinable aspect distances us from it, something that amounts to everything that happened later and a long time afterwards. The face, framed by hair, with echoes of Charleston-style music, of dry laws, and of Carlos Gardel and Rudolph Valentino movies, seems removed from the vastly changed things of today, as different as a *Pithecanthropus erectus* (also known as *Homo erectus erectus* or Java Man), or an even earlier member of the Homo genus. The decades after the 1920s imposed an irremediably Jurassic premise on the hairdos of yesteryear.

In such photographs, the prehistory of the modern visage exposes the inequality of its different somatic parts. There is nothing strange about the eyes, mouth, or cheeks; the odd and alarming features begin a little higher up, precisely where ideas began to turn into hairstyles. We discover that combs and brushes were not always used the same way as today. In this image of the irreparable past there is an unwilling humor, almost involuntary, which, at first blush, tempts one to make a comment that would sound absolutely ridiculous if it were said in public: "People from the past were so different from us!" With their capacity to capture the moment of desire in an inconclusive fashion, photographs lie, or rather they tell the truth in another way, in an unknown way. With an ease that only photographs can manage, they demonstrate the fading power of fashions and styles (as tendencies in action that do not remain). And they leave behind something else: unfinished beauty.

With the cold beauty of battlefields, the first photographs of the past century take on an air of strangeness today, as if the preterite had happened much further back in the past than it truly did. The millimetric order of hairstyles belonging to the human race before it included us is surprising. Nowadays, seeing the future of these hairstyles in reverse, the reason that caused them to reach that point is anachronic. That rigor of hair and hairdos came to exist in the disfigured knowledge of something that is no longer completely nothing, because it no longer forms part of nothing, if in fact nothingness has form. The earlier elegance was corrupted by that which no longer is and by the reason—obsolete—which caused them to be what they were. Face to face with the dead past, we may even feel that we are superior, believing that now we are different and that current hairstyles symbolize a greater knowledge from that reconciled height where ideas depend on a comb.

The passage of time can be seen in the ways that people style and crop their hair. The lesser part of the outer qualities endowed the future with the present. In the traditional barbershops of Argentina and Uruguay, that geo-emotional existence called the River Plate, where the barber is a barber and not a *coiffeur*, the walls (covered with mirrors) are decorated with a photograph of Gardel. His hair, slicked down impeccably and implacably, forces one to conceptualize the head as the place where elegance is thought up, thought of, and combed. Is Gardel, nicknamed *El Mago* ("The Magician"), there to make us feel guilty about our current lack of elegance and to tell us that the boys of earlier eras used gel because they had a lot of free time to groom their hair? Hurriedness dispenses with combs. Rarely does a customer say to the barber: "Cut my hair just like Gardel's," or "Do it just like Errol Flynn's." Few barbers today know what Vitalis Hair Tonic is, let alone how to correctly combine comb and Brilliantine styling pomade. The overwhelming lack of ideas in our era regarding the beautification of male hair is enough to make one's hairs stand on end. And this is only if there are hairs, since shaving the head has enjoyed great popularity for quite some time. Men who are not bald want to be.

An entire, dramatic decade became symbolized by hair: that of the 1960s. When the Beatles became famous, everyone grew their hair out. No one wanted to be Samson but they did want to be John Lennon (and even Fidel Castro and Che Guevara, who also sported long hair in the form of bushy beards). Young people found in this mane one of the ways of expressing their modernity and their empathy with the accelerated times that made many feel like lions, even though the Metro-Goldwyn-Mayer lion had been there before and no one had paid any attention to it. These hairstyles of the king of the jungle did not reach down as low as the metro (there were no subways among the liana trees), but they did grow out nearly that far, beginning to measure more than 4 inches in length, and as much as 8 inches or even a foot. This long hair was an immediate hit and was much more attractive than Elvis Presley's tuft, which had a tinge of high school style from a much earlier decade. With the first invasion of British rock, society both East and West acted in uniformity and hundreds of good barbers went bankrupt, especially those who did not make any concession to the times when hair began to grow faster, or to the slight difference between now and not now.

For River Plate barbers, trading the photo of Gardel for one of the Beatles, or of Jim Morrison (always so well-uncombed), would have been an act of treason, and even more so would have been accepting the slavery of slovenliness. Just as dandruff and lice had their moment of fury in a century of passing furies, Beatlemania radicalized the ways of treating the head, making it less eternal than dandruff during the interim, because not even the best shampoo could vanquish the true snow of time. Having short hair in the 1960s was a symbol of unacceptable dissidence. The era did not call for such tidiness. The alleged freedom that the hippie movement tried to instill in behavior soon became a vehicle for the orthodoxy of attitudes, pushing the secret to the surface.

All those who behaved differently were immediately con-demned. All of this impropriety became the opposite, that is, the proper combination of behavior and adventures, both going back and moving forward. To be an authentic hippie, it was necessary to have long hair, dress in faded clothing, walk around barefoot, and replace the shower and soap with patchouli. The only thing radical was the smell. An aspect of childishness and unfinished puberty took over the surface, giv-ing a stereotypical look to the appearances of social breakdown characterized by the blackmail of dogma. The era took charge of its puberty. And at some point, the load became saturated with emptiness. It brought with it the weight of that which was too recognizable, excessively opportune to being convulsive.

In the 1970s, hair lost its symbolic value. Hollywood changed the perception of appearances. Tony Manero, the lead-ing character in *Saturday Night Fever*, made John Travolta famous, and with him arose a renewed sense of good grooming. As if the fortunes of the world were indirectly fulfilled in a hair-do, the other face of the hairstyling trade got its turn. The grooming arts reigned in the last masculine hours, when there was less to say. Having become a capitalist fetish, long hair came to represent the baldness of ideology. Unruly locks were held in place, aided by shampoos, conditioners, and any other unwholesome ointment that could keep curls headed in the right direction. It was no longer necessary to be the same as everyone else. This became clear at the end of the decade, when the advent of the punk movement revitalized heterodoxy. Hairstyles changed trajectory once again.

Everyone began to have their own hairstyle in a situation where opposites coexisted without knowing very well what they were but still feeling a sense of similarity. For the first time, the scalp and the brain came to cohabitate without mutual disrepute, with the freedom afforded by not having a purpose. The *memento mori* of beautiful hair was brought to light. Personal happiness from an extreme reduction, from hair cut down to nothing, included, nevertheless, a fullness of life. A triumph was gained by the capacity of caprice and the whim of liberating one part of the body more than others. Just as with neurosis and the illusory rite of television zapping, hair became an emblem of change and of shifts in moods, at least those of appearance. The message of alternative psychoanalysis guru R.D. Laing for people to do with their heads as they pleased was translated as, "Cut your hair however you want." There arose an abundance of dyed hair, shaved heads, and tattooed scalps. All this constituted a hairy rainbow.

Artists and musicians with radical tendencies, or at least viewed that way, opted for shaved heads, thus symbolizing a rejection of the beauty of the organized world and its codes of self-representation. Something similar was done by certain neo-Nazi groups with no interest whatsoever in music or art. The times, which include those of today, allow for anything to be said, heard, or uncombed. The variety of hairdos, of haircuts— or the lack of the latter—came to summarize the *fin-de-siècle* drift of a century agreeably crowned by a varied collection of mixtures. The exercise of saving and wasting, which has characterized capitalist civilization (accounting for half the world, with the other half trying to become so) from its earliest zenith, was transferred with enormous ease to the somatic zone, which by day needs a comb and by night a pillow. Hair, more than any other part of the body (inside or out), was always in line with the history which it shared, even if only by obligation.

In the mid-19th century, Charles Baudelaire was smoking hashish, writing, and combing his hair. One day he cropped his hair very short, and what little remained visible he dyed green. With his unexpected look (that of a punk *avant la lettre*) he went to visit a female newspaper reporter with whom he had agreed to meet. After an hour of conversation, and seeing that the woman continued to be indifferent regarding his change of hairstyle, the poet asked: "Don't you see anything out of the ordinary in me?" "No I don't," the woman responded. Angry, Baudelaire rebuked her, telling her not to be afraid to say what she saw. "But I have green hair and that's not very common," he stated. We live in different times now, although Baudelaire continues to be read, but less so. No one causes a reaction anymore with their hair, or the lack of it. The propriety of hairstyles has ceased to be a public issue. It is one of the greatest conquests of privacy achieved by life.

THE XEROX SYNDROME

CASES OF LITERARY PLAGIARISM ABOUND. Famous and unknown people alike have been tempted by the shortcut of replication. They believe one arrives faster that way. Long gone are the days when Richard Wagner made the following recommendation to Augusta Holmes: "The first rule, do not imitate anyone, above all, not me." Plagiarism has ceased to carry an insurmountable stigma. The pillaging of others' work is not considered a degrading practice. What is more, it is a topic that is almost no longer discussed. Or, the discussion is in favor of plagiarism. Even Jorge Luis Borges himself felt attracted by the idea of being him who he admired.

At the funeral of Macedonio Fernández, in February of 1952, he confessed: "During those years I admired him to the point of transcription, to the point of passionate and devoted plagiarism. I felt 'Macedonio is metaphysics, he is literature.' Not imitating that canon would have been an unforgivable act of negligence."[1] The Xerox syndrome is one of the characteristics of the era of Yahoo!, Facebook, YouTube, Twitter, Instagram, selfies (in person), Photoshop, and WhatsApp. It is literature turned into plagiarism of life. It is cloning inserted comfortably into language. It is facsimile writing.

In a century such as this one, with so much of cloning and clausular paraphrasing, of *pastiche* and collage, of the hyperproduction of words that circulate through the space that used to

---

[1] In *Otras inquisiciones*, a book published the same year as Macedonio Fernández's death, Borges wrote: "Those who meticulously copy a writer do so impersonally. They do so because they confuse the writer with literature. They do so because they suspect that varying from him at all is tantamount to varying from reason and from orthodoxy. For many years, I believed that the nearly infinite literature that exists was in one man. That man was Carlyle, was Johannes Becher, was Whitman, was Rafael Cansinos-Asséns, was De Quincey."

be occupied by the spoken Word (Twitter is a telephone where people write, not speak), *copyright* has turned into an entity with no established residence, a customs house with the door open. It is something to which increasingly no one pays attention any longer, just as no heed is paid to quotation marks, within which the phrases of the original author could remain, though such quotes would make everything seem like a transcription, when in truth plagiarism seeks to make the copy appear as an original creation. In the process, the inspirational phase disappears, being replaced by an ellipsis, in a shift from the reading to the copy of what was read.

Therefore, negotiating with imitation can be disguised. The plagiarizer is a type of "pickpocket"; he sticks his hand into the pockets of other writers' works without anyone noticing. The sound track of his action could be the unforgettable bolero that used to be performed by Cuban singer Olga Guillot: *Tú eres mi yo, yo mucho más que yo* ("You are my me, much more than I am me"). Two poets have their lyrical interpretation of the matter, applicable to a state of modern life, or whatever the highly mutant era that we are going through is called. The first is Charles Bernstein, an American: "Reality is usually a poor copy of the imitation. The original / is an echo of what is yet to be." The second is Carlos Germán Belli, a Peruvian: "In short it is the same / plagiarize yesterday or plagiarize today."

The number of plagiarized works that one can see—as the discovery begins with the eyes—shows that some things need to be rewritten in the same way so that they will continue to be different. There is much belated culpability in this increasingly popular practice, which was not so stigmatized before. To begin with, the expression referring to the accused is supremely ironic: "the author of a plagiarized work." Their practice of improper appropriation would come first, disqualifying them; authors of plagiarized material cannot be considered to be creators of something new. Nevertheless, such a person continues to be an "author."

That is to say, a text does not cease to have an owner despite the fact that its genealogy has undergone a counterfeiting. Plagiarism, then, is the last attempt at posterity of an imperfect ego, the paraphrasing of a mimicry which demonstrates that the signs of identity associated with language cannot change hands so easily (it is hard to cause words to have amnesia). Copied knowledge is rewritten knowledge, a visit to the same literary inspiration on which an owner and a derivative already rest. Therefore, beyond the absence of originality, authorship—illegitimate, defenseless— is retained by the plagiarizer, that is, the author (of plagiarism).

Humans are imitative from infancy. Before, children imitated what they read; now they imitate only what they see on television. They know this better than anyone, even if it continues to be unknown who this never-identified *anyone* is. Children imitate: language, attitudes, affection, rejection, and even gastronomic preferences. They want what others have. Psychologists call it the learning stage, which would be the fulfillment of the maxim "Suzie does as Suzie sees." Children grow up imitating, but no one sees them as plagiarists. What is more, when they plagiarize the manners of others their same age who are more polite, they are congratulated and rewarded. The same does not happen with writers who imitate; they are rewarded with lawsuits, sneers, and scorn. No one thinks that they acted like children, trying to improve by way of emulation. They are seen as vulgar thieves of intellect and of others' words.

Imitating good schoolmates, those who stand out for their good behavior and social comportment, is not easy. But it is not hard at all to plagiarize a nearby writer, even if he or she actually lives far off, or is from another era, or is a neighbor only in ideas and aesthetic commonalities that are impossible to avoid but not to disguise. In other words (which for the plagiarizer must be those of the person who has been plagiarized), copying a page of someone else's work is easier than transforming it so that it seems to belong to the plagiarizer and not to someone else. If style is the repetition of one's self, as T.S. Eliot believed, plagiarism is the repetition of one's self based on someone else. His most well-known poem, and surely also the most original one that he ever wrote, "The Waste Land," is a collage, patchwork, or collection of tales (a poetic form comprised completely of verses from other authors). Mexican poet Efraín Huerta recommended the following: "Thou shalt not covet thy neighbor's poetry." However, in literature, coveting often becomes possessing. Those who are plagiarized are so admired that they are stripped of their ownership. It is the most excellent way to praise them.

Plagiarism is the highest form of praise. It is a compliment that is not content with only complimenting. However, those who replicate must abide by their imitative decision. Someone who plagiarizes Shakespeare or Kafka can be called a thief, although such a person can also be considered a highly ambitious reader who merely committed the mistake of writing down a few extraordinary paragraphs that were already written, and published. It can also be that the plagiarism *per se* is not the crime, but rather the misdirected choice of the plagiarized text. Thus it is that no writer who steals ideas and words will be accused instantly of plagiarism. In any case, it will be said that the book is poorly written (a failed production), that its language and the plot require more work, but never that it is bad because it is the result of plagiarism. The talent of a writer is not measured by the number of borrowings used, but rather the way in which they are used. The task was to improve what was borrowed, but the writer failed. The debt, then, is not reckoned by what the writer borrowed, but rather by what he or she has, or does not have, to loan to the imagination of the next writer, who is the current reader.

A canon of copy, an elementary mimicry, a practice of vampirism, the changing of a man into a leech (not into an insect, like Gregor Samsa), plagiarism is an altruistic tribute according to which human beings testify that they have read, with an excess of admiration, a certain work of a certain author. The plagiarizer is somewhat like the character out of the work that is being plagiarized; he has enjoyed the experience so much that he wants to repeat it, with him inside. No sooner than they are written, words begin to be appropriated by those who read them. This appropriation is one of both praising and hocking. The victim of a sudden Alzheimer's disease with regard to the text that has been read, the plagiarizer forgets that the author of the beloved text is someone else and assumes the right to enjoy the accolades that were not meant for him.

Plagiarism is the exact opposite of envy. Is plagiarizing, therefore, an act of generosity? Why does the plagiarizer steal? To achieve a spurious and phony glory, or because his love for a certain text prevented him from leaving it once he finished reading it? Does he copy due to inertia, because he is bored with his own (allegedly) creative ego? Is it a gesture of courtesy? If his original idea—the plagiarizer's only original idea is the one that motivates him to plagiarize the work originated by another—was to gain notoriety, then he has achieved it; he is even spoken of in the police section of the paper. Plagiarism is the eighth deadly sin (even though lust is a lot more fun). Nevertheless, despite that fact that it is so condemned, plagiarism is not seen as a despicable crime, as the murder of an author might be, with bullet or blade, such as happened to Brazilian writer Wilson Bueno, who was stabbed to death in the back as he was writing. It ranges from the death of the author to the murder on paper of one author by another.

A plagiarizer is one who makes his literary tastes public by repeating in writing that which has been pleasing to him, copying it with very little variation. There is also something of an incomprehensible feat in his act—which is not accidental but voluntary—because he has taken his opportunism to the edge of absurdity.[2] This opportunism has now come to occupy a territory discovered by another, and he knows that in the long run, and actually in the short term, this will give him no advantage. It is a

strange way of praising himself. A personal note: each time I finish one of my poetry readings and a reader approaches me to tell

---

[2]The literature of "plagiarism," and of appropriation, one of the most successful
"absurdities" of the first two decades of this new century and millennium (an
entire illustrated dictionary could be dedicated to defining the most fitting
terms for this issue and for the proliferation of pertinent examples), is almost a
new literary genre. We find examples in several languages. In English, there are
"amanuenses" who have made a professional career from the reiteration of its
practice. The books *Day* (2003) and *The Weather* (2005), by Kenneth Goldsmith, are, respectively, the complete September 1, 2000 edition of the New
York Times and transcriptions of radio weather reports. On his Wikipedia page
(http://en.wikipedia.org/wiki/Kenneth_Goldsmith), it states that "Goldsmith's
practice embraces the performance of the writer as process and plagiarism as
content." It says that "As a teacher at the University of Pennsylvania Center
for Programs in Contemporary Writing, Goldsmith's courses include 'Uncre-
ative Writing,' 'Interventionist Writing,' and 'Writing Through Art and Culture.'" It notes that "Class tools are appropriation, theft, stealing, plundering,
and sampling. Cheating, fraud, and identity theft are all encouraged. For Goldsmith, the classroom is a free space in which ethical queries can be conducted
in a safe environment."
  Long before Goldsmith, Argentine poet and journalist Esteban Peicovich
began a book that, as the "author" himself said, aspires to be infinite: *Plagiarized Poems* (1970), which has been published in two different editions. They
are poems "made" on the basis of phrases found in reality: in newspapers,
walls, billboards, medical prescriptions, restaurant menus, public bathrooms
stalls, official documents, etc., etc. The book, like reality itself, can be infinite in the sense that the first version has been augmented with new poems
"found" randomly. The poem "La represión" ("Repression") say only:
Fish must always be white.
Blue fish are prohibited.
(From a diet prescribed by Spanish endocrinologist Basilio Moreno Esteban)
  In her book *Antígona González*, Mexican poet Sara Uribe (not to be confused with the Colombian actress of the same name; in the infinite high-
way that is Google, one thing can pass for another and appear to be the
same: identities are superimposed and are, at the same time, the copy of a
copy, etc.) uses strategies of appropriation and rewriting. Not only are the
works of other authors like Sophocles, María Zambrano, Harold Pinter and
Judith Butler juxtaposed, but so are the voices of other women speaking in
Uribe's voice. Which one, of all of them, is the voice of the author?
  In 2009 the Argentine writer Pablo Katchadjian published *El Aleph*, a
sort of new version or personalized remake of the short story by his compa-
triot Jorge Luis Borges. Katchadjian added 5,600 words to the original
story's 4,000. Although his book (self-published by the author) was released
in an edition of only 200 copies, María Kodama, Borges' widow and execu-
tor, sued him for plagiarism. The case is still pending.

me that listening to me has made him want to write, I feel compelled to invite him to plagiarize me. I thank him, I applaud him, and I give him advice, hoping that the possibility of the most brazen form imaginable of plagiarism will come to fruition, and that I be the injured party, or rather the one benefitted, the writer who has spawned the impersonation of a fellow human being.

A writer can consider himself a genius when he begins to be plagiarizable. Argentina writer Ema Wolf said the following in this regard: "The truth of the matter is that I do not know any authors who are worried about being plagiarized." She added that, "I think the fear, rather, is to assume, without realizing it, an idea that is not your own. How do you know what belongs to you if you have been reading constantly from the age of 8 or 9? I will not say that to write is to plagiarize, but I will say that it is to always be adapting." We absorb so much information that in the end no one knows what the original source was.

Plagiarizers recruit words that do not belong to them, motivated by the need to camouflage, though very superficially, a text with which they have discovered an unhealthy connection. When they reward what they read with exaggerated praise (which turns it into their own), they satisfy their desire to be in the text of another as a "replacement author." They take the identity of another (and if they are discovered they lose their own), since they want to reach posterity with a borrowed eternity. Like a smuggler who has altered where his product comes from, like a *bricoleur* who has made several attempts, plagiarizers find reward in saying, in an equal or similar fashion, that which someone else said before them. Feeling disappointed because someone beat them to the punch, plagiarizers let the world know with their risky acts that they could have said the same thing, and to prove it they say it. They reinvent what has already been discovered. Their nature, as the substitute for an individual example, is carried in the opposite direction, altered so that it can continue to belong to its specificity. The word is turned into a boomerang.

All writers incorporate discoveries—of whatever sort, be they words or strategies—that originated on other people's keyboards. Art is either plagiarized or revolutionary, warned Paul Gauguin. Modern art (and also written art) has achieved its revolution through the indiscriminate use of mixing. In the museum of *mestizo*-ness are tradition and its antithesis. Eliot warned in *The Sacred Wood*: "Immature poets imitate; mature poets steal" (*The Wasted Land*, his best book, is a systematic homage to several of his favorite authors, a well-executed "theft," because today no one cares about the sources but rather the result on the page). Ownership begins with theft, and this theft should be accepted as a valid strategy, since the intervention of the plagiarizer can help improve a work or make it less inconvenient. Knowledge and the restructuring of style expand, absorbing what was there before and what will come later.

However, it should be clarified that the authors Eliot is referring to, rather than beings thieves, are really scrappers, recyclers. They take apart an already finished text, resituating it *a posteriori* in a work and context that can be different or similar (new is not synonymous with novel). What occurs is the following: sometimes authors admire another's material so much that they reproduce it without camouflaging it. This material is so appropriate (for appropriation) that it prevents a separation between the person who reads it and the one who wants to write it anew, and these are actually the same person. In these plagiarizers' unscrupulous visits to the similar interests of others—an otherness on the verge of becoming one's own—they reproduce (reproduction, no rewriting) the admired text as if it were incomplete; it lacks an other, since the one it already has is not enough.

The plagiarizer is never accused of having copied an abysmal literary work, but rather one that, owing to its great literary value, invited excess of emulation. And if he did do such a thing, that is, steal from a poor source—one that no one pays any heed to, not even to read—would anyone even notice his appropriative action? Besides being a plagiarizer, he would be accused of being a poor reader. In order for the bad and most forgotten works to come out of anonymity, a call should be made for the public to plagiarize them indiscriminately. If translations can improve the original (there are those who believe that Moby Dick is better in its Spanish translation, and that the *Quijote* sounds better in English), why cannot the same happen with acts of plagiarism? It is not so much a matter of who wrote it the first time, rather who wrote it the last time. There are examples of this, examples that may be debatable, but examples nonetheless.

At one point in the movie *F for Fake* (1974), which was the last one directed by Orson Welles, famous Hungarian art forger Elmyr de Hory (1906-1976) looks at the camera and states with convincing naturalness that on his good days he painted Matisses that were, without a doubt, better than those painted by Matisse himself on his bad days. There are forgers who do better work than the original artists. They do not believe that their actions involve the verb "plagiarize," but rather "rewrite." In this regard, de Hory said he was confident that one day museums would only deem to be false works of questionable quality. Perhaps one day there could also be libraries dedicated exclusively to authors accused of plagiarism, but who, through rewriting, have improved works of dubious quality.

As a result of seeking to imitate Edgar Allan Poe in a disguised fashion, Baudelaire reshaped the work of the American writer; Poe went on to become the genesis of the modern Poet. The plagiarizer does something similar to what an imitator on television does; he parodies the original, doing all in his power to ensure that the parody in not noticed, and he achieves the exact opposite. And the imitator is applauded and paid very good money. "In order to plagiarize," remarked Josep Pla, a notable writer whose work invites plagiarism, "it is necessary to have read a lot, to have a good memory, and to know what is what. Because they had all the reading that was possible to have in their time, meaning the writings of ancient and medieval writers, Renaissance authors, those of the first modern era, plagiarized a great deal. Now everyone is original because people know nothing about anything."

James Atlas believes—and he may be right to do so—that "literature is theft." But calling someone a thief of words sounds like an exaggeration. With plagiarism, someone else's creation is hijacked for a time (until the action is discovered); the plagiarizer makes the language-oriented labor of another his own. Nevertheless, the plagiarizing act never becomes total; passages are stolen, but not the entire landscape. The extrapolation does not become an exact replica. Thousands of writers have pillaged phrases, ideas, and situations from Cervantes, Dante, Shakespeare, but no one has published *El Quijote*, *The Divine Comedy*, or *Richard III*, merely changing the name of the author, which would be a creative but non-transcendent act. The cloning of motives, plots, and meanings is never absolute. And if it were, the result would be something like the textual quotation of the entire text, a global reading that started at the head and ended at the foot, of the page. In the plagiarizing process, the literary identity of the admired figure is assumed in representative terms. This figure comes to occupy the invention in question as a new form of visibility. Time and time again a style is rewritten and retransmitted, and at other times the style is the material that is copied and admitted as one's own after having been the exclusive property of the first author.

The paradox is redundant, and contradictory. In a world where scientific and technological ideas, concepts, and discoveries move from place to place, from one company to its competition, and from an invention to its expiration date, in this exchangeable reality, there has suddenly emerged a stubborn interest in reaffirming certain attributes of originality, permeated at the same time by their previous origins. The birth of copyright, or the privatization of writing, caused the center of events to move from the text to the author. This shift is relatively new.

Before the Enlightenment, no one viewed plagiarism as a literary leprosy, and objective imitation could be practiced and enjoyed with the approval of society, which considered this practice as a way of channeling and cannibalizing contributions to a similar literary history in process. The plagiarizer was not denigrated, since his practice had a hereditary objective: to expand the canon through a disproportionately detailed focus on certain exceptions.

The borrowing of topics and characters was not considered dangerous, and the act of using other sources was part of the work of citation, inter-reference, and participation in a common property: language. Good writers plagiarize language, taking the best words from the dictionary (and the adjectives must be even better, as well as the adverbs, the least precise of all). Octavio Paz has made the comment that, "For the ancients, imitation was not only a legitimate practice, but also a duty." However, "Since Romanticism, works must be unique, and inimitable." The Mexican poet also gave the following counsel: "If contemporary artists aspire to be original, unique, and new, they should begin by putting in parentheses the ideas of originality, personality, and novelty: they are the commonplace of our time." Originality, then, would appear to begin with the weakening of imitation, in the lack of permanence that follows certain ideas or themes which at some point ceased to say or report anything about themselves.

Plagiarism, then, was inevitable in the past. It was the archetype of an accepted convention. That is to say, the information about procedures and origins—said information being nonexistent—did not perish with the specifics regarding the author. Upon changing masters, originality, adapted comfortably to replication, ended up being an involuntary accident, the conversion of private property to collective authorship. But the perception of this practice has changed. With modernity and the birth of the publishing industry, plagiarism became a disgraced strategy, since texts began to be seen as *ex nihilo* creations, as if author were not indebted to any tradition. In this way, appropriation with an aim of improvement began to be rejected. Times changed.

What before was considered homage is seen today as looting (and looting sounds like lifting something from a purse without permission). The outsider nature of the act filled the ancient privilege with stigma: a certain word order and grouping of topics and characters belonging to a work could no longer be transferred to another work without yielding to the force of its originality. Originality and intellectual property became homonyms (Lacan: "If there is at least one bias a psychoanalyst should have left behind thanks to psychoanalysis, it is that of intellectual property"), charging with subjective resonance the effects and affection of a text. Miscegenation with someone else's ink was not permitted. The commandment was reinterpreted: "Thou shalt not steal, but thou shalt be able to paraphrase citing the sources."

Despite the strict disparity between creation and production, modern art has, since its beginning, favored the predominant intermediation of mixing, with its fluctuating epistemological occurrences. In this tranvestism of texts and non-bellicose objects, that which is artistic has been produced through recombinative devices, by way of borrowing and the usufruct of fragments that usually end up belonging to the last of the users. A simple detail suffices to make a break from the prevalent synonymy, that is, to turn plagiarism into its opposite, into a device that is both inspiring and original. The Mona Lisa (with a mustache) ceased to belong to Leonardo da Vinci and is a legitimate tenant in the work of Marcel Duchamp, whose ready-mades are the mothers of an incessant plagiarism condemned to success from the start. There is nothing fatuousness about erasing authorship; rather it serves to verify presences inserted into other presences. The text, just as with Russian nesting dolls, contains in its interior an ordered diversity.

There are texts floating around the Internet which, in their repeated transitory nature, have lost their first origin and

gained others, bringing with them different intimacies and certainties that, as a result of having put their origins aside,
became predisposed to receiving external legitimizations. The
unifier of these anonymous origins is not a textual pirate but
rather someone who adds new mixtures to the changing recipient, which already contained many such mixtures, though not
all of them. This someone processes qualitative data, and in the
recombination of these data, authorship dissipates, while never-
definitive vacuums of intention emerge.

The work of synthesis and expansion cements the entrance
into a recent access point. Referents are interchanged to make
them function with privileges different from those of their initial
task, adding origins for themselves. Nowadays, originality is the
inability to process influences. The result is a "multiphonic" text,
where the originating voice and the last one become one and the
same, or at least almost. Originality is achieved through addition.
In this nomadic writing, which moves from one authorship to the
following ones, the prognostication of Roland Barthes regarding
the death of the author is partially fulfilled. There is a text to
which responsible persons and specific authors are added, even if
there are no such people; words prevent the definitive creator of
names from being named.

The proliferation of plagiarism coincides with the reign of
the culture of the masses, which designs and implements the cri-
teria of entertainment, as well as that which is associated with
words. At present, the individuality of the artist is feigned, and
in this environment of appearances triviality operates through
improbable evidence that treats the exception as unnecessary.
The contrast highlights the serial banalization, the
(im)media(te) reflex whose hierarchical order functions without
any clandestine plan. It is a reflex that summarizes an updating
of favoritism by way of the purely current: the yearning for
instantaneousness tore to shreds the exposure to different contents. It is for this reason that the lack of self-demand causes flat-

tery. It is worth pointing out that in such a context, the ruse of prestige has new tasks to fulfill. It is at the service of initial gains. Indifference triumphs over difference, which invites us to not go against "the mass that is within us," in the words of Peter Sloterdijk. Together with entertainment is the degradation of originality, which is predisposed to not having anyone take its side.

Creation has been reduced to anonymous facsimiles of certain repeated pretexts. There is a model to be replicated, a referent—industrial, not inventive—which, based on itself, decides the molds of "originality" that are to be reproduced. There has been a warning about the effect, which does not seek out risks, rather it avoids them even before taking them. (Suffice it to recall that the majority of the authors who sell the most books are from the United States, a country where the entertainment industry places artistic products on the same level as material results, without aspirations of transcendence, or even of individualization in some cases.)

These cultural commodities do not represent a proposal of meaning about the world. They are just one more piece of merchandise, like some products that are supposedly more utilitarian, such as a pair of socks, a television set, or a washing machine. Priority is given to the serial production of best-seller books. It is the hit parade in all its rigged splendor (the unreserved insurgence of frivolity). There are certain inviolable norms, and no one can be more original than anticipated. An exceptional validity of expectations is imposed to maintain first-rate attention. Beauty is not allowed to be exasperating or to promise a formal, superior arrangement. It must generate optimism, even though the only one who can be optimistic is "he to whom not all the information has been given" (Álvaro Mutis).

Cultural merchandise works in favor of homogeneous acceptance of a global state of sensitivity without innocence. It was behind the mass media mechanisms that formulism became universal, it being one of the most visible processes of the globalization, in this case, of taste. There prevails an exhaustive indifferentiation that places all its trust in routine expectations. Artificial products are created that are tied, through their origins, to a transnational idiosyncrasy, which responds to a historic moment where the world belongs to everyone and the *barrio* is delocalized. Even hypotaxis moves according to dependencies and not as the result of any eagerness for autonomy.

The Spanish sociologist Marcelino Bisbal has opined that "people, as social beings, are increasingly the product of mass culture, which therefore constitutes a distinctive way of living their existence." Perhaps that is true. This "distinctive" way of configuring the world view of reality, which can be interpreted as erasing the borders between high culture and popular culture, actually implies the disappearance of the former. This situation ceased to be seen with prejudice, simply because it is no longer taken into account by the globalizing project, in which everything is obliged to look alike. The *faux* socialization that means finding a million people tuned in to the same television program extended to all levels, including that of literature (I read what everyone else reads), where the identity of difference—that which makes a work original and not a replica of others—is diluted.

Elite culture (not in power but in the realm of thought), which historically has been the great producer of ideas and of aesthetic behavior unrecognizable until its appearance, was overwhelmed by the culture industry, whose restrictive plans make cases of infiltration scarce. The cultural facts of that which earlier could be discovered in another way became diluted in a by-no-means spontaneous vacuum that makes it impossible to evaluate these facts, simply because there is a lack of access to them. What is missing are alternative intermediations, other ways to create culture beyond those influenced by mass media and the big companies of the powerful entertainment industry. There is a need for a new economy of creation that makes meticulous room for heterogeneity and for desystematizing guidelines, inside or outside the system. The Internet and its proliferating rivers are not enough to move the surrounding areas to the center or to make them accessible to such a penned-in circumstance.

Horkheimer and Adorno said long ago that having fun means agreeing that it is not necessary to think. Under this not-so-recent agenda, culture must exclusively entail entertainment and have as its main objective pulling the subject out of his or her thoughts. Upon feeling entertained, the subject also feels taken into account by boredom, since said subject is designated by generalized passivity to be another one of the recruits in the series. The monopoly of aimless recreation defines the serialized processes of the culture industry (or commercialized culture). The use of the assembly line spread to artistic production. As the cradle of schematicism, this manner of taking part in leisure absorbs and erases both the independence of thought and the deprogrammed actions of creation. The background promotes the lack of demands and the idiosyncratic shortage of time. The idea that leisure time was not made for thinking has been well instilled.

The products of the culture industry, the global factory of plagiarism and recycling, are conceived to distract, to avoid reality, and to be consumed, rapidly and simply. Any example of a propensity toward difficulty and aesthetic risk is looked down on. The pasteurization of the contents displaces spontaneity, and standardization takes the place of originality. The industry of free time thus presents a simulation of supply, since the real supply became limited to patterns of unnecessariness and conformism that make the earnings more relentless. In life, presented live and in series, everything is planned in such a way as to favor the realm of the fun-loving heartless, which Max Weber spoke of at the turn of the last century.

In the era that popularized the words "cyberspace" and "cloning," subjectivities are diluted—writing involves a permanent erasing—and the idea of a text with a set author becomes irrelevant. The only marked origin is the last one, the one that has just been read. It is an origin without owners or definitive points of departure. In authorship there is a plural person, and all of them summarize the same thing: a becoming, *ad infinitum*, that in multiple ways characterizes the effort in which the only leading individuality is the textual one, a magnet and a sponge to attract people to its offerings. Creation comes through the accumulation of originalities without any previous control or trademark, alluding, in all the transformative stages, to the process that defines the simultaneity of confluences.

Currently, "original" ideas, which go against the *status quo*, are suspect and highlight the lack of referents, or rather the coincidence of several referents at the same time through simultaneity and superimposition. A union of similarities that is impossible to verify attacks the validity of copyright. What previously was plagiarism is today intertextuality, an emblem of inversely repeated origins, as if it were a non-reciprocal exchange of subjectivities. Intertextuality, it should be remembered—even though plagiarism appeals to the forgetfulness of the reader—is a literary resource. It is through this resource that one text irrigates another with fragments and phrases, transforming it and achieving with its presence the partial erasing of the initial authorship, at least for that reader who does not recognize the signs of said authorship or of the explicit homage that a completed whole pays to certain of its parts. Nevertheless, intertextuality, or literary collages, are in a different category, being neither superior nor inferior to plagiarism, since the parts appropriated by the new text undergo a process of legitimization and reprogramming.

Cases of plagiarism abound (this phrase plagiarizes the first phrase of this essay). The counterfeiting or copying of money, of plagiarized dollars, is not the only instance. Just as newspapers have political, economic, and sports sections, they should also have one dedicated to plagiarism, to its authors and victims, as there is no shortage of this type of news.[3] Being authentic means being original. The plagiarist, however, does not want to be original. What, then, does he want to be? It is certain that no current plagiarist believes that cutting and pasting and using information from Wikipedia without acknowledgment, lifting phrases from Twitter, Facebook, or WhatsApp, and mixing together in the blender any and all material that he has at his disposal, is a crime against intellectual property. He sees the practice as completely natural, an act of authorized renegotiation of someone else's writing. He sees inspiration as being within his reach, online and free, 24 hours a day (Google is the new Library of Congress). An example of this is the French writer Michel Houellebecq.

For his award-winning book *The Map and the Territory*, Houellebecq (his poetry, with which he endeavors to be original,

---

[3]In today's world there is an excess of both problems and news about plagiarism. Headlines, such as these from Britain's newspaper *The Guardian*, offer something for all tastes: "Shia LaBeouf escalates plagiarism row with Daniel Clowes via bizarre tweets"; "Poem pulled from Forward prize shortlist after plagiarism row"; "Plagiarism scandal has revealed an ugly side of Australian poetry"; "Katy Perry accused of plagiarism over new single, Roar"; "Rand Paul battles charges of plagiarism but blames 'hacks and haters'"; "Damien Hirst, Rihanna and Medusa: the latest plagiarism row"; "Rudyard Kipling 'admitted to plagiarism in Jungle Book'"; "New York Times columnist caught in plagiarism row"; "Maureen Dowd's column features paragraph virtually identical to passage written by Talking Points Memo blogger"; "Booker winner in plagiarism row"; "Author admits idea came from Brazilian novel"; "Booker winner in plagiarism row"; "Canadian columnist accused of plagiarism"; "Coldplay reject plagiarism claims over new single"; "Jane Goodall book held back after accusations of plagiarism"; "Seeds of Hope, the primatologist's new book, has publication delayed after newspaper finds uncredited sources"; "Quentin Rowan confesses to an addiction to plagiarism"; "Have Oasis plagiarised Cliff Richard?"; "Clone Wars: is plagiarism killing creativity in the games industry?"; "Harry Potter plagiarism claim struck out"; "Led Zeppelin sued for alleged plagiarism of Dazed and Confused"; "Romanian prime minister accused of plagiarism"; "Victor Ponta copied parts of his doctoral thesis from two law scholars, claims scientific journal"; "South African author accused of plagiarism"; "Nick Cave denies plagiarism allegation"; "Russian spy Anna Chapman embroiled in plagiarism row"; "Harry Potter plagiarism lawsuit could be billion-dollar case, says claimant"; "Quentin Tarantino faces plagiarism lawsuit over Kill Bill 1 and 2"; "Bob Dylan in plagiarism row over paintings"; "Singer's art noted for striking resemblance to photographs by Henri Cartier-Bresson, Dmitri Kessel and Léon Busy"; etc., etc.

is abominable; his essays, on the other hand, are very good) borrowed texts from the French Wikipedia without causing much of
a legal stir by his actions. This is because Houellebecq made it
clear that to write is to generate an operation of neutrality, even
one of depersonalization (of the text and the author), in which
words feed off other words, even if they have been used by others.
Writing is an act of phagocytation. Argentine writer Washington
Cucurto (Norberto Santiago Vega), without putting on airs of
originality, considers plagiarism "a progressive act," one that is
fundamental in his literary production. "I do not steal," he said in
La maquina de hacer paraguayitos, "I simply write 'after the manner
of'; besides, not even the most brilliant creator could plagiarize as
masterfully as I." He also stated: "Perón stole from Mussolini,
Menem from Reagan, Cortázar from Michaux, and so on . . . it
seems just fine to me that such people steal from each other. What
does it mean to be authentic? Do you know any original writer?
Yes, God!"

Because God wanted it thus, originality is the common heritage of humanity. Perhaps that is why modernity, such as Marcel
Duchamp took upon himself to demonstrate, is an operation of
reversion and undoing, of reappropriation and dismantling, of
piracy (including self-inflicted), and "extreme makeover." It is a
way of obfuscating origins. It is an act of helter-skelter cut and
paste; I take from here and place over there. It is the era of the
cocktail. If we combine orange juice and vodka, it is neither
orange juice nor vodka, but rather a screwdriver. Would the
orange juice complain that by joining with the vodka it has lost
its "individuality?" Why, then, despite the rotation of perspectives in reaction to the aesthetic act, the *sui generis* originality,
does the alleged moment of the radical split with tradition—the
appearance of something different—continue to be so important?
It may be said that in the fraud over "the new," with its corresponding anxiousness of influences, the chimera of a perfect simulation is being fulfilled.

The list of devout plagiarizers in different literary categories is long and is no respecter of language, prestige, or geography.[4] British writer Graham Swift was accused of plagiarizing the masterpiece of William Faulkner, As I Lay Dying (1930), in his novel Last Orders (1996), which won the Booker Prize. The accusations did not serve to prove a strategy of using quotes and tributes connecting one book to another; it was determined rather that the borrowed echoes were the appropriation of an unidentified voice. A fellow Briton of Swift's, novelist Linda Grant, winner of the prestigious Orange Prize, had to defend herself from charges of plagiarism. This stemmed from the fact that in her historic novel When I Lived in Modern Times (2000)—which has 80,000 words—on 17 occasions she turned into dialogue between her characters parts of the book Mandate Days: British

---

[4]A long list of acts of plagiarism, some more famous than others, can be found in Du plagiat, by Hélène Maurel-Indart (Paris: Presses Universitaires, col. Perspectives Critiques, 1999), and in her augmented and updated book of the same name (Paris: Gallimard, 2011). Two other books worthy of recommendation on the subject are Boleslaw Nawrocki's Le Plagiat et le droit d'auteur (Geneva: United International Bureaux for the Protection of Intellectual Property, 1964), and Robert Plaisant's Propriété littéraire et artistique (Paris: J. Delmas, 1985). In her nearly legalistic eagerness, Maurel-Indart presents a long inventory of cases, most of them having occurred in French literature, an area in which various authors and prizes were tainted by the scandal of plagiarism. The book reveals that some French writers who were fundamental in France's literary history, such as Montaigne, Pascal, Alexander Dumas, Emile Zola, Leon Bloy, resorted to the practice of appropriation. Montaigne, possibly the most original writer ever to put pen to paper in the French Language, cited, "without quotes," writers from the past. He was so original, that he could very well be considered the precursor of "cut and paste," (putting one's signature on someone else's work has its merit, as Duchamp suggested several centuries later). A copy, rewriting, trans-stylization, improper loan, or what? By the time Montaigne came along (in the 16th century), "pure" creation had entered a period of crisis. The idol worship of originality was working up the nerve to take an unexpected path. Literature was becoming the art of mixing, of the cocktail, in which different referents came together to "create" a new and shifting one in which an indistinction could be distinguished.

Lives in Palestine 1918-1948, by historian A.J. Sherman (1997).
In an effort to remedy the problem, she cited the historian's contributions in the Grant pocket edition.

Doris Kearns Goodwin, the prestigious US historian, winner
of the 1995 Pulitzer Prize, acknowledged that entire passages in
her book *The Fitzgeralds and the Kennedys* (1987) were acciden-
tally borrowed from three similarly themed biographies. Her only
defense was to say that in putting together a volume with 900
pages and 3,500 quotes, she made a few mistakes with some of the
index cards. In a novel, topics—and even dialogue—can be
repeated and no one calls someone who has retaken an idea or
anecdote used earlier by others a "plagiarist." In an essay, on the
other hand, this is not the case. Speaking to this matter, the
Spanish critic Darío Villanueva stated that "in content of a dis-
cursive, philosophic, or scientific nature, it is in general obligatory to mention the source whenever one uses an argument or
point raised by another author, and to employ a direct style when
the words with which said arguments and points have been
expressed strike us as the most adequate and superior." At times,
evidence of "non-originality," or a case of sporadic recycled text,
emerges and rescues the original influence from anonymity; only
that which reproduces earlier sources as a formal, perfect synonym can be considered authentic. In other words, for a coun-
terfeited bill to go unnoticed, it must be identical to the original.

The repeating and recycling of literary works has helped certain readers exhibit excellent qualities of imitation. This practice, however, can go too far. One can go from emulation to
copying without qualm. It is for this reason that examples
abound. There have been various such instances in Spain, where
the *Diccionario de la Real Academia Española* is published and
which defines plagiarism as "copying the substance of someone
else's works, putting them forth as one's own." The Madrid magazine *Interviú* sat Spanish writer Lucía Etxebarría on the bench
of dishonor, claiming that in her book of poems *Estación de*

infierno (2001) she copied verses from two books by Antonio Colinas, a minor and overrated poet. Etxebarría defended herself by arguing that a writer, especially a poet, "draws from literary referents and topics and pays homage to and quotes the masters who he or she admires." The writer was doubly accused, since the magazine concluded that literal phrases and scenes from *Amor, curiosidad, prozac y dudas* (1997), her first novel, came from the book *Prozac Nation* (1994), by Elizabeth Wurtzel. Etxebarría, who said her conscience was clear, will have difficulty clearing her name, which has been associated since then with excessive intertextualizing exercises, whose results could not hide the similarity between the latter author and the one who was already there demonstrating similar inspiration.

For Etxebarría, making amends for this unlimited enthusiasm for others' words has not been easy. Her defense: "The same thing happened to Clarín; in *La Regenta* they accused her of plagiarizing *Madame Bovary* on the theater stage. And, according to this standard, Joyce's *Ulysses*, the world's most important literary work, would be discredited, since two of its every three words come from Homer." There is some merit in this defense that she offered of her calligraphic karaoke. There are not very many topics in the world to develop. According to Eugenio D'Ors, in literature there are only some 150 such themes that are always repeated. And Jordi Ballo and Javier Pérez calculate that of basic movie plots there are only 21. Therefore, entering into a reality narrated earlier by others does not imply that such movement, many time unconscious, is a matter of intentional copying. Furthermore, in a day when originality is subjugated by the constant and limitless exchange of realities, no one can feel that they own the topics of the world. Due to matters of work, instinct, and the need to take shelter in a tradition that will receive them, all writers rewrite. Their task is to make new that which was already written, including their own work in progress.

In the boot, giving her a kick of prestige, Italian novelist Ippolita Avalli accused Susanna Tamaro of having used in the short story *Rispondimi* (2001) arguments, characters, natural and sociopolitical atmosphere, structure, and vocabulary from her novel *La dee dei baci* (1997). According to the accuser, in one story, whose title became that of a collection, there are 35 points of excessive similarity between the two works. Tamaro defended herself saying: "I must make an embarrassing confession. I've always copied. I've ransacked St. Augustine, Montaigne, Pascal. I've always thought this was called culture." It would seem, then, that the main problem is that not everyone defines culture the same way.

N.K. Stouffer, a U.S. writer, accused her Scottish colleague J.K. Rowling (a war of initials) of stealing ideas from a series of books written by Stouffer between 1984 and 1988 (*The Legend of Rah and the Muggles* is one of them) and using them in the *Harry Potter* saga. Even though there are certain parallels between both literary worlds (even the name of the main character, Potter, is the same: one is called Larry and the other Harry), it is an exaggeration to conclude categorically that the success of one work came from the inspiration of the other. Likenesses do not necessarily mean copying. Rather they suggest a coincidence of motives and characters. Literary history is full of ill-timed similarities. It is not a new occurrence by any means. Concrete cases had already appeared in the first half of the 20th century.

One fascinating instance of plagiarism is that documented by A.B. McKillop. This Canadian historian dedicated an entire book to investigating a case of plagiarism involving a fellow and unknown Canadian writer and a famous man of letters. In *The Spinster and the Prophet: A Tale of H.G. Wells, Plagiarism and the History of the World*, a detective-like and persuasive read about the case that held the attention of the literary world between 1930 and 1933, there reemerges the dispute between Florence Deeks and H.G. Wells. McKillop claims that Wells' book *The*

Outline of History (1919)—a history of the world—openly plagiarizes the unpublished manuscript of *The Web* (1918), which
Deeks had unsuccessfully tried to get printed. In this case, as
McKillop demonstrates, parallel universes cross, since the dis-
tinct similarity is verified in the structure, in the syntactic con-
structions, and even in words used. The evidence put forth is
too explicit to be viewed as mere suppositions. Deeks fought for
her rights, but she failed. She achieved nothing with the litiga-
tion that cost her $500,000 (her family's money), a large for-
tune at that time. Furthermore, the doors of the printing world
were closed to her. She spent her entire life unpublished. She is
barely remembered as the unknown Canadian writer who
accused a successful writer of plagiarism and lost.

    In times of recycling, of samplers, and of cut and paste, any-
one can write and be read to the point of exaggeration, that is to
say, imitated right down to the periods and commas. Only the
name on the book cover is saved from replication. Added to the
recognition of others are keys emerging from anonymity. Literature consists of a scattered heritage that Alberto Girri called
"one's own, and that of all." Idiocy written in one languages fits
nicely into another. A case in point is the 2000 best-selling novel
Sabor a hiel (*A Taste of Bile*), by Spanish author Ana Rosa Quintana, which reproduces entire paragraphs from the novel *Family
Album* (1985), by U.S. writer Danielle Steele; from the presentation poem in *The Thorn Birds* (1977), by Australian Colleen
McCullough; and from the 2009 novel *Mujeres de ojos grandes*
(Women with Big Eyes), by Mexican author Ángeles Mastreta.
In all of these passages, there is scarce variation in the name and
gender of the characters and in the context. Mastretta, who herself is not very original, stated: "I would prefer not to make a
complaint, but one must do something so that this type of thing
does not happen again." In the specific case of Quintana, the
great deception—in legal terms one would speak of fraud—is not
in having emulated with hardly any variation the writings of oth-

ers, or in having made too much her own something that did not yet belong to everyone, but rather in plagiarizing mediocre works that leave little space for improvement with their restructuring.

Plagiarists generally have good taste in selecting the object of their phagocytic practice. But some lack talent even in this. Even to plagiarize one must have certain qualities; not everyone knows how to choose a good book, go through the words, and loot them from beginning to end. He who copies Shakespeare is ambitious; he who does the same with Mastretta and Steele is an idiot. And there are many such idiots in literature. The lack of common sense does not teach immediate lessons, but it does make everything more common. At least in paintings the counterfeits are always of highly valued artists (for this reason Dalí used to sign fakes that were based on his own paintings).

In Latin America, cases of plagiarism in which famous writers have been involved in are not exceptions at the margin. The Guadalajara International Book Fair awarded its 2012 prize, worth $150,000, to Peruvian writer Alfredo Bryce Echenique, who three years before had been found guilty of plagiarizing 16 newspaper articles from 15 different authors. It would seem that the logic used is this: if we write on recycled paper, if some words in English and Spanish come from other languages, such as Greek and Latin, why can what we write not have come from "somewhere else" also? These are paradoxical times. At the same time that serial plagiarizers are rewarded (perhaps to put an end once and for all to the very 19th century sermon imposed by romantic writers, a homily that places originality above all), and while there are thousands of petitions making the rounds on the Internet demanding the end of copyright (these promoters of Copyleft, of Common Rights, and of the death of the author, are somewhat akin to amateur theorists of a world where no one owns anything and in which there is a proliferation of literary Julian Assanges, hackers, and wikileakers who seek to exhume that which in truth they are hiding), at the same time as all of this, there is also a deification of the author figure, of those who write to produce novelties, of those who project an aura of originality, whether in the arts or in the world of technology and medicine, where the production of novelty is everything.

But we must not be so harsh with our contemporaries. Back in 1787, Mozart was hunting fragments of operas to compose his melodies. And this behavior continued as history marched on. In 1976, it was proven that George Harrison's great international hit "My Sweet Lord" was a direct copy of the Chiffons' song "He's so fine." We live in an era of familiarities and coincidences, in which everything sounds too alike. Coldplay's songs sound as if the catchiest parts came from another song that we have already heard. And there is an infinity of bands just like them. And the same goes for movies and television. The television series *The Blacklist* and *Crisis* surely owes their popularity to the fact that they have a storyline with premises similar to those of *24*.

The expressions in vogue today—*sample, inspiration, rewriting, verbatim, modified copy* (like the cars to which turbo engines are added), *reappropriation, unauthorized reproduction*—are nothing more than euphemisms to refer to an act of plagiarism, or to "self-plagiarism" of the falsified copy of a work. They once brought Picasso a painting that seemed to be by him. The owner, concerned, asked him: "Is this your work?" Picasso looked at it, smiled, and then wrote his unmistakable signature across the bottom right-hand corner of the painting, responding, "Now it's mine." Today this painting could pass for "authentic" due to Picasso's signature on it, a signature that passes for "authentic" because it is always the same (Picasso plagiarized his own signature all the time in this same way).

Plagiarism is as old and universal as dandruff. The statement by King Solomon found in Ecclesiastes 1:9—"The thing that hath been, it *is that* which shall be; and that which is done *is* that which shall be done: and *there is* no new *thing* under the sun"—which was later plagiarized, excuse me, repeated throughout history, marks the beginning of a common practice. It is true that there is nothing new (even if Pound insisted later: "Make it New"). Perhaps Socrates, whom we view as an original genius, was a great plagiarizer, but because he left nothing written no one can say anything negative about him, except that he did not like to write. Did he know how? The Mexican nun Sor Juana Inés de la Cruz (1651-1695), the first great female poet of the New World, America, was accused several centuries later by Alfonso Méndez Plancarte (1909-1955), of, among other things, having imitated Góngora. He also claimed she borrowed (without returning) from Pindar. She once wrote before affixing her name to a document, Yo, la peor de todas ("I, the worst of all"), but might she not have written "I, the most plagiarizing of all"?

Borges, a great original recycler, has reminded us that inventing is the hardest thing. But invention also gets confused in its activity: "We dream we are reading a book, and the truth is we have invented every word in the book. But we don't realize it, and we take it as strange." Would this be the complete opposite of plagiarism? What etymology can we assign to that moment which came before, without being verified, and which modifies opinions to establish an itinerant origin? Not necessarily as a novelty, the new paradigms arrive by analogy and are completed by it. This is why it grows increasingly difficult to relate a written idea to a specific person. Plagiarism represents a creative reading that allows one to exercise in public the anxiety of influences mentioned some time ago by Harold Bloom. The plagiarizing act recreates a mirror of identities that turns literary works into a sort of twins with different mothers. Rewriting the works of predecessors and trying to improve on their efforts is an endeavor as old as the use of words themselves. A miscellaneous example of this documentary evidence of coherence are the Gospels, a replica in four different but very similar versions of the same book written by four different authors.

In other words, because the words belong to someone else, plagiarism is a way of imagining the same thing with the same words. Its novelty is novel for not bringing about anything novel. There is originality and post-originality; there is someone who said something for the first time, and someone else, an admirer who wants to step out of anonymity by repeating it in identical fashion, also for the first time. The Gospel writers Matthew, Mark, Luke, and John plagiarized among each other, with scarce variation, the oral words of Christ, and yet nobody considered them to be repetitive or lacking in originality. To the contrary, their written words are the foundation of Christianity.

The act of copying is condemned, though originality does not have everything going for it either. Adam and Eve were expelled from the Garden of Eden for having been original in their manner of sinning. Due to their original sin, they were left without the power to continue copying the marvelous days in that extremely original place where only God could see them. When poets want to be "extremely original" and write poems using only neologisms, words that for other readers are incomprehensible, they are accused of being inscrutable, of being difficult, of having created a useless linguistic Babel. They are not considered great poets for having written poetry that, due to being completely invented, has moved outside the bounds of language.

No one is beyond this influence of others. All good writers are also voracious readers.[5] Their spongy labor is to absorb realities and writings which are later turned (most of the time unconsciously) to one's own purposes. Furthermore, people forget about what they have read, and about the name of the first author: "Everything has already been said. But since no one listens, it has to constantly be said anew!" (Flaubert, in a letter to

---

[5] When the Cuban writer Guillermo Cabrera Infante accused Carlos Fuentes of writing the novel *Cumpleaños* (1970) based on one of his scripts, the Mexican writer responded with a question: "Is it possible that one single orphan book exists, a book that is not the descendant of some other book?"

his friend, Louis Bouilhet, circa 1850). This act of beginning over again—a type of recycling against nature, and at the same time in favor of nature so that everything is as natural as possible—entails derivatives and versions that are not always symmetrical. When unknown writers copy famous ones, they seek immediate recognition. When famous writers plagiarize certain ideas and phrases from other unknown ones, their act will likely go unnoticed, and no one, save the affected party, will dare to question it. Prestige protects the deserving volunteer.

These days, which in many ways seem like the last days (at least for originality), both types of examples can be seen. Inspiration has taken on a different role, seeping into the terrain of dangerous coincidences. Just as Eliot, Pound, and Apollinaire used mixing and the benefits of spurious material, incorporating phrases, ideas, and references taken from other writings to put an early end to modernity, the non-neutral practice of appropriation, which copies from head to toe (or to the hand, since it is what does the writing), came to sublimate the dying space of postmodernism, a space disposed to everything and everyone. In place of borrowings and transfers, what takes places instead is the synchronic occupation of certain simultaneous originalities (provided that the word "originalities" is the correct one for this case). In the literature there is inscription and erasing.

Almost at the same time that several separate accusations of plagiarism were coinciding, a literary discovery came along to put the degrading practice at the height of its justification. It was learned, according to a letter written in 1875 and not discovered until 115 years later, that the wife of Robert Louis Stevenson burned the manuscript of her husband's most famous work, *The Strange Case of Dr. Jekyll and Mr. Hyde*, because she thought it was "utter nonsense." Fanny's letter states: "He wrote nearly a quire of utter nonsense. Fortunately he has forgotten all about it now, and I shall burn it after I show it to you. He said it was his greatest work." Stevenson recovered from the consequences of the fire and wrote the second manuscript in just three days, achieving one of the best known cases of self-plagiarism. He so admired the first version that he wrote the second at the speed of a photocopy. Almost all of history's great literature has been written under the same conditions, with writers who so admired their words that they were incapable of copying those of others. In any case, the only thing they plagiarized was language itself.

In a legal document that I must sign I read the following: "Your signature is authentic only if it is a reproduction of its previous versions." I arrive at the conclusion that to continue "officially" being who I am, I must plagiarize myself, at least on official documents. Nevertheless, in other aspects of modern life we see a nearly fascist pressure regarding "copyright infringement." It is strange that so much importance is attributed to plagiarism. Strange because we live in an era in which everything is forgotten and deleted with extraordinary speed. There is not even time to know who the true author is. Ours is an odd sociocultural landscape: there is a proliferation of reproduction, and at the same time there is a solipsistic cult of the "original" that seems boundless. Everywhere we look we see the nearly fascist pressure of "copyright infringement." Where will it all end? Spanish uses the English words "whisky," "ketchup," "sandwich," "hobby," "hippie," and "offside." Shall we accuse the Spanish language of plagiarism? Shall we accuse the dictionary of wanting to plagiarize the meaning of words? We plagiarize common sayings and jokes by repeating them so often that in this process of perpetuation the names of the authors have disappeared. And what about fables? Are they the original works of Aesop, of La Fontaine, of Yriarte (who imitated La Fontaine), of Samaniego, or did they merely "write" them? Nothing comes from nothing, and everything ends up being something else.[6]

---

[6]No one signs a newspaper's editorial; the newspaper is the author, a commercial and opining entity. Therefore, the various authors of an editorial must copy the "institutional" style, the one that distinguishes the newspaper.

Plagiarists brazenly steal others' glory; they are a type of pickpocket of third party written treasures. Furor in the face of the glaring brilliance produced by the writing of someone else prevents them from enjoying it in private. They make public the pleasure of their reading by taking possession of the text they have read, changing only the very name of the author. More than a lesser way of imagining, it is a greater way of appropriating a text and rewriting it exactly, leaving it exactly as it was found. Inspiration has been dictated to the letter by the voice of "another." In this aspect, are not biography and autobiography ambitious attempts to copy someone's past, discourses stolen in one's own garden or that of someone else? Both literary genres highlight the fact that copies of reality and of real people can be unlimited.

Plagiarism in painting, the "exact copy" of the reality of a work, is called "counterfeiting" (exactly as it is with the creation of fake money). That is to say, this is the case when a work lacks a semantic and syntactic difference with regard to another work that served as its referent. But "counterfeiting" empiric reality is not the same as counterfeiting the work of another artist. The documentary *Tim's Vermeer* (2013), directed by Teller, shows that Vermeer attempted to "copy" reality down to its most minimal details, including the brightness and luminosity content of light. Vermeer did not want to create "his world," but rather to make "his creation" from a copy of the world. He wanted to copy reality beyond a copy, that world which was there and which he saw every day from the window of his studio (facing the town square in his native Delft, Netherlands). That world, which was so accessible and in plain view for all to see, was something that Vermeer claimed as his own, in order to feel like the possessor of something dispossessed. So then, is Vermeer the best example to illustrate the definition of "counterfeiting" or "forgery" given by Umberto Eco in *The Limits of Interpretation*? In this book of essays, Eco wrote the following: "Forgery could be expressed so: any object which is produced—or, once produced, used or displayed—with the intention of making someone believe that it is indiscernibly identical to another unique object." The counterfeiting of reality can be an extraordinary task, one of extreme complexity.

Today, there are very few writers who want to be "original"; nearly all seek to be "different." In the era of "cut and paste," different cases of plagiarism and the concealment of sources seem to be saying, each in its own way, that monopolistic originality has reached its end. Perhaps Jorge Luis Borges' dream is about to come true, that someday literature will be contained in one single, universal book in which everyone will be authors and, therefore, no one's name will appear as the author. It will be the epitome of the "death of the author" (predicted by Barthes and Foucault), of collective authorial exclusivity, and the definitive imposition of the "mimotext," (a term coined by Gérard Genette regarding the character of certain imitative or mimetic texts that desire to be this way). It will be the end of an extremely long collective act, one that at some point had a beginning and an initiator. The paternity of the work will cease to be a topic of discussion.

What would the perfect plagiarism look like? It perhaps would not be a bad idea to create a universal award recognizing the "best plagiarism of the year," and have the plagiarizer and the plagiarized share the prize money equally. Why not initiate a Nobel Prize for those who have usurped someone else's "nobelty." It would be a way to professionalize the practice of literary bloodsucker and eliminate the amateurs, because plagiarism is a serious affair. One must know how to do it, with impunity and without reserve. If someone makes up his mind to do this, he should not employ half measures but should do it compulsively, even knowing beforehand that he will not be able to leave everything inside, since something of the original text is always left out. And yet this is the way that plagiarism should be done; to the contrary it would be a facsimile version of the work in question.

Each time that a writer sits in front of a blank page, he commits plagiarism. There is nothing more enjoyable that being able to imitate one's self. Seeing his face reflected in the waters of the fountain, Narcissus was not looking for anything else. He was copying his beauty by looking at himself, feeling original due to the reflected copy of himself. That was why he went to stand in front of the same fountain every day, to look at himself differently, to feel always the same. The final version of this essay, which concludes here, is the supposedly improved copy of several earlier versions, which were the same essay and yet a different one at the same time. Are we, therefore, witnessing a reproduction? A case of self-plagiarism, perhaps? A copy? Right.

EPICALLY OLYMPIC

WHEN THE OLYMPIC GAMES WERE BORN, the world was young. It is no longer so today, but the games continue to be for the young, nearly all of them Apollo-like, except for the African marathon runners, who are scrawny. Apollo, the first winner in the Olympics, played the lyre. Nowadays the lyre is of no interest to anyone. The name of this instrument in Italian is *lira*, the same name given to the former Italian currency. There is no interest in this or any other pre-*euro* monies, including the *franc* (though few people are frank about this). The same goes for the *peso*, a Spanish word indicating an object's heft, though for the currencies of this name found in more than one Latin American country no one seems willing to lift a finger, let alone heavy weights like a bodybuilder. What matters is the almighty *dollar*. The only *mark* with value is the frame that marks the portrait capturing the victor's smile. It is a photograph stolen from time, so that its vanity will not grow old.

Greek athletes came from the Peloponnesus; those of today run with closely cropped hair. For this reason, hair carries more weight than conscience. It is like the hair of gazelles with bald calvarias designed to conceal Calvary. But rather than hairstyling in Cinemascope, it is a giant circus. Curiosity takes them under the canopy of appearances: swimmers whose hands and feet grow due to stimulation from potions made in secret labs; runners with vigorous muscles developed through the use of some prohibited concoction (the law does not want us all to be able to look like Tarzan), javelin throwers who shave their mustaches in order to not look too much like Stalin; rowers with wings of wood who row like a row of supermen, and Cuban champions like the one who was fond of coke—not the sponsor (Coke), which is also addictive, but the other kind. Addiction to victory generates additions, and diction is expressed with figures.

Added to the athletes and their invisible syringes are scenes of a Caligulesque parade: Olympic executives receiving bribes so that they will choose one city over another, multinational companies paying million-dollar sums to secure exclusive sponsorship rights. These are doses of exclusivity. The athletes, besides wanting to beat their rivals to win the gold, sign contracts with anyone and anything. Well, not anything, but yes with anything that pays, from a refreshing beverage to a deodorant to a brand of underwear named Jockey (and, since this is not horse racing, they are their own jockeys). Neither steroids nor other anabolic drugs are amateurs anymore. Victory sells, and it serves as an antidote against forgetfulness. Memory (a swift Mnemosyne) builds its podium in tenths of seconds, pushing the fastest times forward (a timely onslaught), because the name of the game is beating records.

Even before the motorcycle, the automobile, and the airplane existed, man already wanted to be faster than himself. He wanted to run as fast as those imaginary beings who at full speed manage to pull away from their shadow. The invisible man did not have a shadow, though H.G. Wells never said his character was fast. In any case, he was fast in his invisibility. In the paradox of Zeno of Elea, the tortoise runs more swiftly than Achilles, but this is only possible because it is philosophy. Furthermore, the animal did not have a heel. Man accepts as normal the fact that he cannot match the speed of many creatures in the animal kingdom (anyone who has been chased by a dog or cheetah knows this), but he is convinced that he can be faster than himself. He has been trying to achieve this ever since he has had feet. The Greeks, especially those who distrusted the speed of turtles, gleefully justified the glory afforded to great runners of distances both long and short, those who today would be marathon runners and sprinters. They awarded them with a crown of laurels, as if to tell them, "Do with it as you will; put it on your head or use it to flavor your soup."

With their feats, sprinters demonstrated that the minimum time required to cover certain distances is part of a metaphor that is applicable to essential matters: in life, one can either go slower or faster; it is the fundamental question. However, as we well know, slowness is never rewarded (not even when it comes to satisfying instinct, which is always stepping on the gas). It may become possible someday, but not yet. Perhaps one day a gold medal will be given to the person who runs the 100 meter event in more time than anyone else. By that time, there will be those who cover the distance in days, others in months, and some in years. He who wants to break the record will have to take decades to complete the race. He will be born at the starting line and will end his life once he crosses the finish line. No tortoise will be able to defeat him. Fast men will be left without a medal and will allow the slow ones to beat them. The former will have their own race where their only rival will be speed itself.

Until this happens, we will continue to have the athletes of today, enemies of slowness and of turtles. They want to be the fastest in history, at least that history which began to exist when watches were invented and the hands thereof equaled the rush of days (and if not, just ask forgetfulness, which does not even need days to complete its work). In the times of Jorge Manrique, the poet, man knew that life flees by rapidly and that one must go with it. And while they run, the athletes of today seem to go faster than life itself. On such occasions, they are the tortoise and life is Achilles. As they go from zero to one hundred along the 100-meter distance with no turns, they seem to accelerate just like a Formula One car (and their rivals have still not found a formula to beat them).

They are black athletes trying to arrive first at the white target that is the finish line. Their aim is extraordinary. When they run fast they leave the world behind; when they run even faster they allow speed to admire them. They unleash the greatness of those race cars who dare others to catch them, knowing that they will always be out in front. They travel in first place; their speed does not know how to occupy any other number. These black athletes are as the Greeks were before them. Among the latter, though first chronologically, there were also sublime athletes, but their names have been lost in the distance because history recommends that the "publish or perish" dilemma be resolved, and no one did it for them. Because they were so fast, their footprints did not have time to leave written words behind, and forgetfulness was faster still (it spends its time beating records). They would have nothing to say about the present.

None of those athletes who today are anonymous, the ghostly essence of a slender figure, could have imagined what became of those conservative regional competitions whose greatest prize, all things considered, was nothing more than public respect. An applause and a few cheers were the only gold offered as a reward. Today, in contrast—and the contrast is great—athletes are expensive professionals whose stature as a person disappears with defeat. They do anything to reach the finish line first. Gérard Dine has stated: "The assembly-line champion is already on the drawing board. Soon we will even be able to intervene with precision on energy levels and mechanical, muscular and neurological elements." The athlete on the track will no longer be a point of reference of anything, except of a triumphant transition on the stage of the body: the duration involved is accustomed to growing shorter and shorter. Knowing this, Carl Diem said, "In the Olympic idea there inevitably develops [a] . . . conflict of the past with the future and of reality with the ideal." In this conflict, the ideal takes the, well, not even the bronze medal—more like the tin medal.

Even though the Greeks glorified the body and enjoyed sports in Olympic fashion, they possessed a celebratory sense of enthusiasm, of discipline, and of talent that surpassed the mere physical limitations of the outcome. Just as in the heroic stages of *The Odyssey*, man negotiated by pure muscle the hurdles of the event to arrive at the finish line with zeal. The process was just as important as the end result. Above all, the accelerated triumph of will and the enjoyment of the completed challenge served as the main avatar. Competition, that process of endowing the body with certain amounts of speed, took on various dimensions, one of which was its divine content. The gods also took part in the argument, favoring their chosen ones. They bet on the soul even before they had it close to them. Therefore, nervousness about victory or defeat was celestial, a trained performance that did not feel like it was similar to anyone.

Time has changed, and men have changed even more. The gods above have ceased to take interest in sporting events down here, but the athletes of today believe themselves to be divine, the deities of Adidas. The benefits of competition are no longer found in the immutability of Heaven or in the sole reward of victory, but rather in the immeasurable height of the ego: stars whose feet are in their own footprints. Fame, popular adoration, power, and quick riches are the longed-for prizes. Who would compete today for a crown of laurels, for immunity from paying taxes, for privileged seats in amphitheaters, for a chance to be honored in a religious ceremony as they were a sacred object, or for a laudatory poem and a statue, both crafted in their honor, as the Greeks did in the past? Surely no one (and no one need bother playing the lyre for them). The laurel, whose leaves are also known as bay leaves, is only appreciated in a good stew, though glory is no longer rewarded with food.

The healthy pessimism of Euripides led him to say that athletes were a breed without valor. Today it should be said that they are a breed without valor but with value, meaning with a price. The now defunct 20th century was marked by the drama of the Greek drachma, which is now green. The dollar removes pain. These are different times. The seconds on the stopwatch have become more and more insignificant, but seconds do not count; all that counts is winning. Only the gold brings the green. So reduced have become the times (though not yet time itself, fortunately), that 100 meters seem to have 10 fewer meters. If "distance is forgetfulness," as the song claims, sprinters move memory closer to the finish line since they cover the distance at the speed of the impossible in terms of human legs. What else can they not do? Under these circumstances, not even Zeno de Elea's tortoise would dare attempt it. Everything is very different now. Pindar would have very little to sing about, and Thucydides would not know what history or story to tell. But it would not be a tragedy: she also did not receive a medal.

Despite the disenchantments of reason and enthusiasm, the Olympic Games round off one of the great, massive courtships of the modern era. And since this era has not ended, neither have its annals, sports being one of the main ones: a panoramic festival where reality and reality alone is excluded. Every four years, for a few days that seem to have more than 24 hours, the world slows down to see the athletes pass swiftly by the television cameras spread out at all possible angles. Their movements, measured in thousandths of seconds, make it seem as though man has beaten speed, and some watches believe it. It is a strange paradox: go faster to gain time. To gain, to win; nothing else will do, because the important thing is to compete, and leave the losing to others.

DISASTERS WITH AN OCEANFRONT VIEW

AS UNADAPTED AS ALWAYS, every now and again water returns with a will to annihilate, reminding us that few things in this life symbolize as it does, and in such a harmonious way, life and death at the same time.[1] The water with which John the Baptist saved souls is the same water with which Noah had to contend aboard his ark full of living beings. Whether they came from the sandy promenades of the coastal resort towns of Piriápolis and Punta del Este—where the South and the end of the world begin—after the passage of two successive cyclones in 2012 (a pair of modest *tsouthernamis* that for a few days turned Uruguayan weather forecasters into media stars), from the streets of New Orleans and New York after the arrival of their respective hurricanes, or from Indonesia and Japan after they were hit by colossal tsunamis, all the images captured by the natural eye of the cameras displayed the same captivating power.

Worlds sinking below the waters, typical of the Age of Aquarius, present a fascinating picture. In these cases, destruction by water with postdiluvian characteristics was accompanied

---

[1]Even though the water of rivers, seas, and the skies has manifested itself excessively and indiscriminately under different names (floods, hurricanes, tempests, typhoons, cyclones, tsunamis, etc.) potable water is a scarce resource in the world. Nature is a great paradox. Some are now speaking of a world with "water poverty." According to information published in the March 23, 2014 edition of Madrid's *El País* newspaper, a total of 783 million people live without potable water, and 2.5 billion lack adequate sanitary conditions. If the current panorama is so unsettling, how then will it be in the year 2050 when there will be an estimated 9.5 billion human beings living on the planet? Water consumption today is 900 cubic meters per capita per annum, while at the beginning of the 20th century is was only 300.

by a powerful aesthetic fullness capable of affecting our way of interpreting reality with an eagerness of approximated understanding. As if it were something that bore its inherent originality on its shoulders, like a novelty exercising its highly *sui generis carpe diem*, we were able to verify that modern times are not identical to earlier times, not even in the way of perceiving the complex relationship that human life shares with nature.

We are going through the era of what was, of a world that ceased to exist long ago. We are traveling in the ship of retromania toward a future that will never be as it once might have been. The destruction of something, or of many things and many lives at the same time, due to a natural disaster with water as its protagonist, generates extraordinary collective interest. This interest is not mitigated by the fulfillment of earlier expectations, because at times, such as when a devastating hurricane hits (a wind suddenly begins to blow, one that seems as though it will be perpetual, a wind apt to be dedicated, and it continues until it blows itself out), the destruction comes preceded by a weather report issued in an oracular tone. This tone highlights a collective curiosity in response to an event that is about to occur in the unpredictable outdoors. Nevertheless, there is nothing new in the world that keeps things from appearing like those which happened at some point before.

Interest in books that recount wars, plagues, and destruction is ancestral. It has been around as long as eras that precede everything, when men were just learning to read and write, and to mitigate this shortcoming they scribbled animals on cave walls, even though this same curiosity existed earlier, when the illiteracy of human beings competed with that of gigantic dinosaurs, those unlettered creatures. Although intensified in relatively recent years, the tendency to feel in unison an interest that lies somewhere between lucid and morbid in the face of destruction and its catastrophic charms—which are typical of a good cataclysm—has always been present as a characteristic symptom of the human condition. Death, especially when it is someone else's, carries great attraction; it has a sort of bait-like power. With its unfinished influence, it synthesizes the infancy of a mishap, the disorder of acceptance going in the wrong direction (and without the countering influence of optimistic contrasts).

Seeing the death of others, through images and words that do not require much thought to startle viewers, witnessing all around us annihilations due to wars, natural disasters, and holocausts of all shapes and sizes, serves to remind us that life, day to day, is brief, and that on certain occasions it can go off script and be much briefer still, even more so than in much earlier times. This is the case in many parts of the Bible (Methuselah being an exception), a thick book in which massive destruction and natural disasters wrought by God—but let us not blame him for everything—receive special treatment. But again, what event in that book does not receive special treatment?

The story of the Great Flood, a peculiar occurrence in the nature of the planet which was presaged by Ovid's *Metamorphoses*, is, without a doubt, one of the events of greatest interest and attraction in the voluminous book of diverse ethics and teachings from which a religion and its faithful have sprung. There are other, similar accounts from those ancient times that contain morals suitable for the creation of fantasies, but it was precisely these stories, the most unfathomable, with their atrocious injustices and their passages of mass death, which caught our attention when we were required to read them in school. Surely this was because they spoke of devastation and miracles occurring simultaneously, and furthermore, because childhood is the ideal stage in life to be fascinated by, and even enjoy, the horrors that befall others, no matter the historical time period involved.

In our time, one which also has cataclysms but fewer and fewer miracles, interest in scenes containing destruction has an origin and a destination that is as voyeuristic as it is masochistic. The spectacle of death swapped its exhibitionism for the magnet of a nearly ritualistic desire; the modern eye wants to feel intimately associated with all that happens in order to be seen and rejoice in a gruesome tone over the horror that it sees there. No one wants to miss even one detail of death when it goes into action and exhibits its uncontainable character. It bursts uninterruptedly onto the scene with a precariousness that does not resemble anything seen previously, but it can be present in all that transpires afterwards as a consequence.

> *"It's going to be a great day for all of us; it could be something fun and memorable."*
>
> (Statement made by a resident of the city of Galveston, Texas, on the afternoon of September 8, 1900, as he hurried to the beach to have a front-row view of the approaching hurricane, not suspecting the plans that nature had in store. He was one of the approximately 10,000 victims, the highest death toll of any natural disaster to date in the United States).

The methods of visual reproduction that came with the first modern era have been at the service of the tale that has linked the different cases of destruction caused by nature with those acts brought about by man with the help of no one. Hungarian photographer Robert Capa (1913-1954), whose pictures appeared in *Life* magazine, among other publications, gained fame for generations to come as a result of his keen eye as a war correspondent. But he also garnered fame for having given the destruction caused by the Spanish Civil War and by World War II a touch that was as brutal and epic as they were: a ferocious visual transcendency with millions of victims. Modern man has felt a great fascination regarding the visual depictions of destruction (beginning with the hurricane in Galveston).

Nevertheless, this should not be considered as an exception to the rule, because it has always been thus. The only difference is that today we want to see cases of large-scale destruction as many times as possible on replay, from all imaginable angles, until we manage to make the sense of surprise become an attractive platitude. We want our gaze to learn what it already knows through a reiterated repetition *ad nauseum*. This illusion of vast panopticism seems to have reached its zenith on September 11, 2001, when two Boeing 767s pulverized the World Trade Center in New York and—more than just two tall towers of concrete, glass, and metal—they brought down an entire era. That day, and those thereafter for weeks on end, personnel at news programs worldwide grew tired of pressing the rewind button, revisiting the horrific images of progress laid low by progress. The image of that iconic instant continues moving forward, drawing the attention of future astonishment.

When nature becomes enraged and tosses its wind and water avatars out into the world, there arise unprecedented events that generate an extraordinary collective panic to inspire thought later on—later on because imagination also does not know how to work under the effects of fear. This thought tends to go into action with artistic or philosophic content after the dead have been counted and of course duly buried, thus becoming those who are able to find rest. Throughout history, practically from the time that human beings began to depict words with hieroglyphics and paint elements of nature on the walls of caves, literature and art have been nourished by the activity of earthquakes, erupting volcanoes, hurricanes, typhoons, tornadoes, and tsunamis.

Anglo-Welsh poet Edward Thomas (1878-1917), who died at the WWI battle of Arras, wrote in one of his poems (Thomas began writing poetry only three short years before his death): "My past and the past of the world were in the wind." He also wrote in the same poem: "I had forgot the wind. / Pray do not let me get on to the wind. / You would not understand about the wind." When it becomes less understandable, the wind accepts all names associated with its destructive eagerness in order to demonstrate in this manner that no collection of synonymities will be able to clear up the mystery of its blowings, of its lethal throbbings.

Allow me to elaborate. From Pompeii until today, out-of-control natural phenomena have, inevitably, been aesthetically startling in a way that surely must have been nearly the same during pre-industrial and post-medieval times as it is today (though without television). There are, however, specific situations that are hard to imagine due to the sheer excessive nature of what occurred and due to the precarious methods extant at that time to confront such a collective emergency. This is the case of the Lisbon earthquake of November 1, 1755, when a fourth of the city's 250,000 inhabitants perished after the hellish tremor that shook the ground between 9:00 and 10:00 in the morning and lasted several minutes, during which the wave that was created extended to other parts of the planet.

With its unbearable trajectory, and without stopping to take a breath, nature sent the people's expectations in another direction, the opposite one. As if playing to lose, it performed experiments with its idiosyncrasy. The damage, therefore, was widespread; the Spanish cities of Cádiz and Jerez were left in ruins. If photographs had existed at the time, we would still be looking at them to help our understanding, to make a truce with our desire to know. In these cases, we rarely can know or understand. It truly (and at such times life can feel truer than ever) must have been astonishing, like a dream, or rather a "hallucination," an apt word, with its varied meanings, to interpret with words the momentary lapse in reason, since for a short space of time, or for several such spaces in sequence, life ceased to think and to understand itself.

Testimonies from the time recount an indescribable event that destroyed most of the Portuguese capital's 30,000 homes. This explains the urgent need that arose to describe the democratizing effects (in times of monarchy) of the earthquake. The king of Portugal, José I, suffered the same quota of horror as the least of the Portuguese people, having been stranded in the street for an entire day. Such a situation is hard to put into perspective. In the mid-18th century, as Walter Benjamin reminds us in his essay on the Lisbon earthquake, Portugal was at its imperial apogee, and the type of reality imposed by the monarchy was ostentatious, with the solemnity of luxury being emphasized in the least important of details. For an earthquake to occur there was big news. The destruction it caused was unprecedented in scope. Immanuel Kant penned a brief account of this, which is considered to be the first treatise of scientific geography written in Germany.

Responding to the annihilating effects of the earthquake, Voltaire commented ironically on Leibniz' claim that we live in "the best of all possible worlds." (Susan Neiman's book, *Evil in Modern Thought: An Alternative History of Philosophy*, reflects on tremblers, which, according to the examples mentioned, inspired philosophers and writers to moralize nature.) Some of the images retrieved from words tell (with many tales) of a surreal, panic-filled day in the capital of Portugal. The city came to a standstill, and the memory of the day preserves unusual situations that summarize the unthinkable place that was occupied by life, a place between death and horror, among the screams and the silence caused by an absence of sense. A pamphlet from that time states: "In the same way that the magnitude of the disaster can only be completely appreciated when it has been overcome, one can also comprehend the terrible importance of this devastating catastrophe when one realizes that a great king spent the whole day in a carriage along with his wife in the most calamitous state, abandoned by all."

Natural disasters caused by land, water, air, and fire have always enjoyed aesthetic prominence. It is something to think about. It lends itself to that. Inspiration needs to be touched and moved by these elements to feel more alive than it really is. It awakens to their shakings and shiftings, as if announcing that something inevitable is coming. It is not without reason that art tends to imitate the exactness of death, especially when its aim is to depict the hours before death's arrival. During a moment in time like the present one, with more writers than readers— no one can deny that we live in original times—natural disasters have become great neutralizers of language. Faced with the images they leave behind, speech does not know what words to use or how to use them, and as a result it ends up avoiding the use of an incorrect one. It fears truths through approximation. Television reveals the resulting wasteland by utilizing a background of ambient sound, the sound track of inflamed elements of the outdoors that can lose its innocence too quickly.

Television cameras come up short. They also suffer the effects of a mirage. They are incapable of capturing, or allowing viewers to see everything. Their ambition of portraying a panopticism without pause is frustrated. A disaster presents so many optic angles that it falls outside the screen, the narration of technology. It is of no use to attempt to make additional sense of what is occurring. Rarely do adjectives feel more ineffective and metaphors more banal. "Seeing is believing," goes the old adage, but "seeing" a natural disaster does not mean that language can find an exact or even compatible expression to believe it and only then define it, if such a thing can even be done. Reality offers examples. Reacting to the earthquake-tsunami that struck Japan on March 3, 2011, a rescuer stated: "This time there was nothing to be done." This summarizes the soul of nature by demonstrating a metaphysical despair, a samurai-like condition, indifferent when faced with life or death, sublime in the face of evil.

The sea, the sea, perpetually renewed!
Ah what a recompense, after a thought,

A prolongued gazing on the calm of gods!
(Paul Valéry, "The Graveyard by the Sea")

In accordance with the mental conditions that prepared the way for the Old Testament, the excessive action of water can occur with gymnastic slowness. Even though at that post-Adamic time (a still premature time) there were no weather forecasts, the slow pace of the destructive work of rain allowed those affected by it in the future to prepare for the effects of water overflowing its normal course. As it was raining, Noah loaded animals into the precarious ark, until he managed to load them all, except for the fish. These fish were the only ones to celebrate the arrival of the flood. However, in empirical reality, when there is flooding, the water moves much faster through its natural channels than what we read in the canonical text.

Those who have been the victims of a flood or have seen one know what I am talking about. The destructive liquid movement does not allow for time to do anything once the consequences of its omnipresence begin to be suddenly felt. The water seems far away, as if to make one think that something can still be done, until, in no time at all, it sweeps everything away, and faster than the imagination had calculated. Destruction arrives of its own accord, in a deceptively docile fashion, without providing an alternative in advance to the unmasking of events. What then comes into view is the spectacle of a negativity without a shrug or reservation, a gesture that by then has ceased to hide its intentions.

Nevertheless, despite this ominous verdict, and perhaps because we associate water with life and for this reason use it when someone is baptized (when ships are christened we use champagne, since no babies are involved), we fear it less than we do fire and wind. We even go so far as to believe that in a flood there is more of a chance of being saved than in a fire or tornado, though reality often takes it upon itself to show the opposite. The ferocity of water in its various manifestations (rain, floods, tidal waves, tsunamis) can prove to be as devastating as it is deceptive and end up being far superior to other forms of destruction.

The human eye saw the television images coming out of Japan in 2011 and thought the advancing sea was moving slowly, at the same boring speed as that of a baseball game. But no; the tsunami's waves were traveling at some 600 miles per hour. No ball can travel that fast. This means the waves could cover the overseas distance between Tokyo and California at a speed greater than that of a Boeing jet. That explains the fascination caused by natural disasters; they are more powerful than technological advances with wings and the ability to touch down, and to touch off fear they do not need special effects.

The first great grammar lesson regarding gigantic aquatic issues is that it is impossible to escape from a place where no one can go. This phantom, which arrives full of horror, likes to surprise, concealing time and again the emergency exit. And it arrives without mentioning what we should do, because in the end, what we also fear so much is its impenetrable silence. Nevertheless, all of it together sounds like too much; to speak of apocalypse is hasty, though Hollywood has made a pet phrase of the term and repeated it altogether too often, and, as it turns out, very successfully. In any event, having watched dozens of Japanese houses burn as the water rushed by, obliging them to go along with it—submerged—for the ride, it would seem appropriate to make use of a literary cocktail to describe the scene. It was Dante's inferno mixed with the seaside graveyard of Paul Valéry. It was a great reality show. Access to this nameless, permanent place would only be possible on the raft of the *Medusa*. Destruction was letting her hair down. But, how does one narrate the journey? With what words does one refer to the disappearance that had been accomplished so long beforehand in the imagination?

"The car park at Tokyo Disneyland was drenched with water-logged segments from the ground following the 8.9-magnitude earthquake that rocked Japan's Pacific coast Friday," police said. It was earlier reported that a tsunami might have caused the inundation but police said the phenomenon was due to liquefaction of soil caused by the intense shaking of the tremor. There were 69,000 people at the Disneyland and the adjacent Tokyo Disney Sea, built on a landfill in Tokyo Bay, when the quake occurred, a spokesman at the local Urawa police station said. There were no injuries or property damage reported at the theme parks, he told AFP. "The visitors have been evacuated to safe places but there are many puddles due to liquefaction around the theme parks," he said.

(AFP news cable from March 11, 2011)

Those who were born near the water will always live with it close to them, even if it is only in the liquid country of memory. Marguerite Duras was fond of saying: "I cannot think of my childhood without thinking of water. My hometown is a town of water." For this reason, even the phenomenal destruction that water can cause is seen through a fascinated artistic eye. With its attentive beauty, the tsunamic water transformed the exotic landscape of the castigated Japanese geography, turning it into a storm out of a painting by J. M. W. Turner (1775-1851), a notable painter of tempests. For several days afterwards, from the liquid epicenter itself, we saw over and over live shots of the anticipated end of the world, with television crews flying above in helicopters to capture, right from the start, the newly occurred disaster, trying not to miss a single detail, since the worst catastrophes also bring the highest ratings. It is clear that when it arrives, the "end of the world"—the material apocalypse that has been announced so many times—could be covered on open television, which not even in these circumstances would transmit without commercials. Even those without cable or satellite television will be able to see it.

Japan is such a mysterious land that water wants to get in so that it can get to know it. A liquid ghost surrounds it. Japan is an archipelago of water surrounded by islands that do not suffer from thalassophobia (fear of the sea). This Nipponese territory is one of the ruins of the sea in all of its possible forms. It is water self-taught epidemic, like a force governed by uneasiness. During the Japanese cataclysm, and to show the ease with which the visual abolition of words can be achieved, the intrusion of technology with panoptic aspirations—aided by stationary cameras and the proliferation of cell phones (today every citizen is a universal witness, a thief of instants with visual posterity included)—allowed us to observe the gradual unfolding of nature's actions from different angles, with images coming from a vacuum in the making, images that were filmed both during and after the destruction.

They were images at the disposal of the remote control, but not to have them under control, since the visuality that they favored did not include explanations, or expiations. Dramatizing the results of its mortal crossword puzzle, the sea came forth, motivated by the fact that it was being seen in its roiling state through an electrode screen, angry with those who were about to die and who were in its movie. This film was in the horror category, not a B movie but rather a triple A, a blockbuster along the lines of a reality show. We learned, if we did not already know it, how fast, how very fast the transition can be from the indifference of agitated water's noise to the difference it produces when it is heard and seen.

This time, just like always, nature, in its renegade insanity, brought about a *locus* that, as might be supposed, was not *amoenus*. On the crust of Japanese territory, a salad of islands adrift, a physiognomy in movement felt good, just exactly as it was. It was a watery Hiroshima, a liquid atomic mushroom. Its

entry into reality was of a peremptory nature and there was
nothing to do but give in. During its coastal voyage, the colossal wave created kilometers of swamps as it went. The water did
not only make it to the river; it included it in its trajectory.
Given the seeping circumstances, it could not have done any
differently. The sea swallowed up all other bodies of water in
the vicinity. With its tide, which can be viewed as ironic, it
bested the technological advances that attempt to guess the
very thing that is about to happen. When it puts its mind to it,
water can do such things. From time to time, it shows its bipolar condition with wrathful brutality. It is even capable of being
cannibalistic.

The hegemony of the water arrived without a slogan, as the
stimulus and disorder of acceptance. Its genealogy felt spite for
everything around it. With its hypotheses in retreat, normality
did not really know what to do. When the earth turns into a
machine of insubordination, it accumulates liquid cracks, it
establishes mute speech in visuality that is always on the verge of
saying the last word, forcing the use of the logic of "save yourself
if you can." In these cases, reality cannot be blamed for not having done enough. After all, ignorance tends to make accurate
predictions; it comes to depend on "the certainty" of its mistakes.
Not without reason, as if the very life of the disaster had silently
been at stake, reality spread its effects, indications of uprooting.
It came to ask questions, all that which English speakers call
afterthought, the reflection after the empirical goings-on and the
coincidence of situations. The corollary was a posthumous cosmos, its war loot, which arrived without prior notice.

These phenomena "cannot be predicted, not even months
ahead of time; in this science has failed," stated a scientist,
implying that we are still at the mercy of the neurotic behavior
of nature. It was this same nature which fulfilled, exaggerated-
ly, the wish of certain people: "We lived 4 km from the coast,
protected by a forest and some rice patties," said Aoki Sekimu-

ra, an optician from Sendai, one of the most severely affected cities. "We always complained about not being able to see the ocean. After the quake, we walked out of the house, and instead of the garden there was the Pacific."

It was a case of *loci horribili*, and of a nature that was ignorant, Jurassic, sidereal, and telluric. It was also, therefore, sublime, a Godzilla of water and foam, capable in its untamable fullness of moving the world from its place, of introducing speech into that which does not appear like anything, and which was nothingness in full swing. In the disorder of acceptance, indications were imposed that carried a sensation of being uprooted, a sense of haphazard confabulations. That which remained to be said regarding this receding hypothesis, which was that of the waters returning to their deep natural channel, could only be said by inventing expressions and modes of intervention. So that it would not come up short, language needed to be helped, forced to exaggerate. In the end, everything exists so that words can express it.

When it wants to be, or when man so desires it, water—an artistic referent to greatest degree possible—can be literary, both within and outside of the page. With rocks in her pockets, just like a car filled with people, Virginia Woolf sunk into water of the Ouse River, leaving her ghosts to have to learn to swim all by themselves. The abbreviated existence of Percy Bysshe Shelley was even shorter in the water, spilling the dream of an unfulfilled resurrection over the scenery of Italy's Gulf of La Spezia, where he drowned in a storm. John Berryman, tired of fighting against the current, jumped from Minneapolis's Washington Avenue Bridge (his goal was apparently to be carried away by the icy waters of the Mississippi, but his 100-foot fall was actually broken by the river bank, his lifeless body then rolling down the embankment, nearly, but not quite, reaching the water itself). Hart Crane also wanted water to end the history of his life when he leapt into the shark-infested waters of the Gulf of Mexico from the deck of ship that was transporting him from Veracruz to New York. His body was never recovered. An inscription at the family tomb in Garrettsville, Ohio, states: "Harold Hart Crane 1899-1932 LOST AT SEA."

Hispanic poetry has taken up the topic of the sea. Pablo Neruda dedicated an ode to it, and it begins like this: "Here on the island / the sea / and so much sea / overflowing, / relentless." Enrique Molina, a maritime poet, wrote a fabulous poem entitled "High Tide," which features the sea as a background landscape and in which he speaks of the "crashing thunder of the waves." In his early period, Octavio Paz wrote the poem "Facing the Sea," the end of which proclaims: "The sea dies of thirst. / It twists and turns, by itself, / on its rocky coastal shelf. / It dies thirsting for air." In a poem by Vicente Aleixandre we read: "The vertical sea reveals the stone horizon." Another by Pere Gimferrer states: "The sea has its mechanical functions just as love has its symbols." I could go on. There is a wide inventory of poems that have been written about the place which is never still. From the sea, the horizontal Niagara, there also come legends. According to one, those who have survived three shipwrecks achieve immortality. Japan, after surviving so many shipwrecks, has demonstrated its immortality. It resists. It is one of those places that, come what may, will never be able to be changed overnight.

The visuality provided by the events in question gained access to a visually inaugural territory that became something more than a geographical area included in reality. An aesthetics such as had never before existed with these dimensions suddenly intervened, demonstrating that water did not need previous rehearsals, like a play does, to take the stage in a perfectly powerful fashion. The devastation was effectively convincing. It first dragged away all that it found in its path. Then, two days later, it returned to the shore thousands of bodies which it had carried off. Surely it did this so that no one could accuse it of theft. The dead that nature had killed did not enjoy good health.

Meanwhile, television continued returning images from the catastrophe to reality: it has the human eye trained for everything. Watching is a way of being complicit with the news that comes from the world on a daily basis. Due to so much insistence, sensitivity became accustomed to the whims of visuality. We are trapped in contrasts, prepared to see the end of the world from its beginnings, with the only condition that we be able to see it live. When its signs arrive, no one wants to look away, because indifference settles easily into our behavior with no one being able to notice it. Destiny holds us within itself in inexplicable ways, even on occasions when it wants to give an impossible definitive form to an overdose of water, water that, before dying, paid homage to the destruction.

Water, once again. So lively and fundamental in the paintings of German artist Caspar David Friedrich (1774-1840)—in which the Rhine River is more real—and of the Englishman with the initials, J. M. W. Turner, water now wanted to switch roles, acting as if it were the main artist and not the thing being portrayed. "Everything is possible in the water," writes Pedro Salinas in the poem "Reason for Love," where he explains the reason for the liquid condition of the principal human sentiment. Sculpting waves taller than 30 feet in height with its hands (thus revealing itself as a self-taught Michelangelo), the rebellious water painted an original and surreal landscape that included in its bowels automobiles, airplanes, and trains turned into scraps of metal. But it also contained boats, vessels that need water to know they are alive, as if water wanted to show that when it so desires not even objects invented to sail are a match for it.

Few times has a country shaken by an earthquake been left as immobilized by the mobility of land and of the fierce, brutal waters. The advance of infrastructure, turned by the circumstances into underwater projectiles, was a piece of news impossible to ignore. Enormous ferries were transformed into little paper boats; rivers and streams became epic land-based seas, good only for being seen from high above, in a helicopter. The sea and the bad weather played as if they were one and the same, and both won at this game.

There were homes made of wood floating by, on their way to forgetfulness, as if asking where their home was. They had ceased to know. Even malls were mauled. The fury of the water soon lost its anonymity, making of the complete destruction an act of beatitude unfamiliar with its content. It developed its erudition by traveling all over, without the need of cooperation from its surroundings to perfect a negative prosperity, a by-no-means down-in-the-dumps fervor at the level of the unimaginable. Death had reasons to be optimistic. But, "What is this?" reality asked itself, attempting to decipher the visual roar, a karaoke in stereo originating in hell.

Entire neighborhoods were destroyed and washed away without managing to realize what was happening, like boxers of precise shape and size defeated by knockout in an amorphous ring. Their independence from any and all utilitarian ends was inconsolable. They were all victims of a recombinatorial fit of rage which nothing then in existence could prevent. In several villages, houses went floating by without knowing what to do; they had been built for a sedentary lifestyle, not to go navigating about nomadically among pieces of junk, where thousands of automobiles, after having been submerged for quite some time, were rising to the surface to see how life was as seen from the water, not from terra firma where they should have been, on the raised embankments of the highways.

The infancy of the enormous disaster gave notice first. In the ocean that ceased to be Pacific (its name was not enough to keep the waters calm), and which drew near to the coast of its own volition, cars, trucks, motorcycles, tractors, and bicycles burned. Houses tried to swim in an attempt to avoid becoming islands flooded by the sea, which impetuously rushed in from behind with a desire to spare no one. I remember having heard that if something needs to be said, it can only be said by inventing it. Such a thing was unnecessary on this occasion. The world on that day, and the following ones, was born invented. In seeking out their content, these images of necrological futurology, victims of inhospitable furies, took control of the humans' disadvantage in order to favor a favorite situation, one which aesthetic eagerness—considering said situation to be non-repeatable—could have repeated over and over to the point of weariness.

Prompting the notion of soul in nature, there were heard in the subsequent images prophecies, noises emerging from the overdose of water and wind, arousing in the mind a dowry of resources that diminish empiric reality as we know it, confirming the *modus vivendi* of the operation of sight. Because, in such a time in history, with nature immodestly exhibiting its cannibalistic condition, its collapsed closeness, the following remains to be asked: how to establish speech and have it tell riddles of understanding? The world was exclusively that which could be seen.

It was a disaster with an oceanfront view. The post- and posthumous specter imposed a persistence dedicated to satisfying itself. And it fulfilled its plans in this regard. We saw and even heard the breathing of a secretive and catastrophic gesture that imposed the absolute lack of rational explanations, because there were none. In this overbearing way water showed its face. It abbreviated life as if it were a well-finished *haiku*. Composed of water jumbled together, ruining all in its path, the tide opened cracks and even ravines. With all that it undid in that tragic area of Asia, it made everything look new. It was a strange turning of the screw: the waves firmly swept along with them an erratic, longitudinal, and neo-expressionist collection free of cosmetic touch-ups.

Houses turned into boats with no course, and with no map or compass to guide them, while boats turned into houses of water. Amid the godless stammering—when nature speaks, it does so poorly—the gurgling of a waterlogged denial of life was heard. None of its insolent actions was child's play. The reports told the tale, such as this one in the Spanish newspaper *El País*, from March 13, 2011: "Bodies swept away by the tidal wave have now been removed with the coming of the dawn. The impressions they left in the sand remain visible. The epicenter of the tsunami is now deserted, silent, and still, draped in the smoke of dozens of still-burning boats adrift in the sea."

In a country as orderly as Japan, which is not used to paying heed to defeats dealt out by nature, even of the worst kind, the disorderly situation caused by a natural disaster is one of the few exceptions that can feed the delirium that in turn nourishes the arts that the Nipponese are so good at, as if they had never lost time. What a country! It is one where water seeks to imitate lightning, occupying the space of the ephemeral, as if it did not need witnesses to know in what time period it is living. This liquid history, however, the one in which Japan suffered disaster with the Ides of March, took the half-hearted gaze by surprise. In what little of the 21st century has transpired, other aquatic shows of sheer destruction have kept humanity speaking about the same thing for several days in a row.

This enormous painting is regarded as one of the key works of the 19th century. The dramatic scene is based on a real-life event that occupied Théodore Géricault greatly. On July 2, 1816, the Medusa, a French frigate, was shipwrecked off the coast of Senegal. The 150-plus soldiers on board, who had been sent out to colonize Senegal, tried to save themselves by constructing a raft that subsequently drifted at sea for thirteen days. The fifteen survivors told of massacres and cannibalism.

(Description by www.inkling.com of the painting *The Raft of the Medusa*, which is housed in the Louvre Museum, and which is accompanied by the following information: Théodore Géricault, 1791-1824; ca. 1819; H: 491 cm, L: 716 cm; Oil on canvas; Denon, floor 1, room 77; INV. 4884)

With the arrival of the 20th century, in different parts of Earth's aquatic geography, and without giving any advance warning, water became a cadaver factory, perhaps to demonstrate that in nature there also may well exist the "liquid modernity" to which Zygmunt Bauman alluded. The names given to water based on the circumstances lost their importance: tidal waves and tsunamis are, for all practical purposes, the same thing— anonymous, malformed creatures. The beast, without face or fingerprint, has displayed different behaviors, but for some reason we do not christen it. Why do we keep waterspouts and the like in a state of incognito? Is it because we do not believe that water can be baptized with water? Is that why? We name hurricanes as if they were newly born babies, using male and female names indiscriminately: Andrew, Mitch, Rita, Katrina, Wilma (though without last names).

Tsunamis, on the other hand, with their unexpected swells, are left precisely as animals in the jungle (except for Dumbo the elephant and Tarzan's monkey pal Cheetah): exactly as they came into the world, wild, freed from the presence of language outside of epithets, without being named—synonyms of anonymity—or even given a nickname. This is surely because their birth and growth are so sudden that they do not leave time for anyone to find a name or moniker for them. A traditional Japanese poem could say: "Between life and death it snows incessantly." The reality of certain natural occurrences characteristic of the first part of this century could have its own paraphrase: "Between life and death water enters incessantly."

As is normally the case, the visual arguments regarding the recent liquid catastrophes (the earthquake/tsunami in the Indian Ocean, 2004; Hurricane Katrina, 2005; the earthquake/tsunami in Japan, 2011; Hurricane Sandy in New York, 2012) included an anomalous swell that set adrift the damage it caused, as if the world mattered little to it. But destruction matters to the world. Historically, it has always been thus. The attraction that art feels for the horror produced by nature is surely due to the anomalies it expresses, to the fact (in no way circumstantial) that nothing which falls into ruin can be replicated with identical intensity, not even through the most ambitious cinemagraphic montage. In this daemon without rest, where no one knows beforehand what this fury can express as it moves from one place to another, the ocean, accompanied by an emboldened wind that knows how to fulfill its obligations, gobbles up all in its path and leaves as a legacy the originality of its annihilating manifestation.

So strong is water, that all-powerful queen of its condition, that it can move shores, drag them inland, and arrive at that embankment after which the probable abyss begins, that nothingness that no one ever knows. Showing itself on a spiral-shaped liquid plain, the solitude of the water, with its impartial fatalism, is only matched in the appearance of its destructive power by that of someone about to commit suicide. The difference is that such a person—unless he is a Muslim fundamentalist in the cockpit of a commercial airliner—does not take others along with him or her, forcing them to visit the great beyond before their time. Earth cannot resist water. Through its devastating action, water does as it pleases, taking its power into safe harbor. Throughout history, the song of the water swan has remained encapsulated in words and images that take part in a material universe that functions as an enigma and as an inaccessible escape from reality. If this were not the case, it would not be what it is.

Art, in its different manifestations, has found inspiration in
the disasters associated with water when it overflows. In the
history of painting, both East and West, several portraits have
brought to the attention of thought and of the eye the asymmetrical relationship between man and the liquid world that
surrounds him, and which on occasion tends to show a particular hatred toward living species. The tales told by art about natural disasters refer in countless examples to ghosts dressed in
agitated, violently moving water, issuing ineffable predictions
that will continue to be valid even after they become reality.
They are variations, visual stimuli caused by all that from the
real world which provokes thought and which lends a more
productive task to curiosity.

In our relationship with nature when it is attractively sublime, whether it be for its destruction or for its way of allowing
itself to be seen, we continue to be romantics. We look with the
same eyes as with which Friedrich looked at the landscape that
dazzled him. On the map of water and wind, which at times carries us to "the horizontal vacancy" of the sea (*Moby Dick*, Chap-
ter 133), we see reflected the vulnerability of life. Water capti-
vates vision with its magic spells. It comes to wash the routine
of life, to tragically award reality, as if nature in a liquid state
were—because it is—an empirical imagination. Here and there,
but also farther away, rain, with its vertical gymnastics, falls in
chapters. Its monotony is different from that of sunny days.

Romanticism, that aesthetic tidal wave from which we have
not yet entirely emerged, saw in the waters overrunning river
banks and flooding in from the sea a suitable place for the gaze
and the imagination to swim together, and even share the sinking of an indiscoverable beauty going against the current. The
paintings of Friedrich are no exception. Earlier, in *The Ship-
wreck*, another admirable work dated 1772, Claude Joseph Ver-
net (1714-1789) combined earth, sea, and an overcast sky as
they never had been before in those colors. Decades later, in

The Raft of the Medusa (1818-1819), Théodore Géricault portrayed the life of the ocean water after the shipwreck, and to
highlight the emotional magnitude of the hours of survival, he
used an enormous canvas and an extraordinary volume of color,
tremendous portions of visuality. He did this as a testimony to
the fact that nothing can be ordinary after water overflows its
ordinary course. It lends itself to exercising its freedom freely.
Discovering an isolated incident of maritime tragedy allowed
the artist to rescue the emotional influence exercised by nature
when it shows itself indecently and forces one to pay attention
to its excessive disorder in action.

After Géricault, water was never the same. The eyes of the
world needed frog legs to reach it another way. Nor was it the
same in the yellow seas of J. M. W. Turner, seas with anguish
included and which invite the splendor of fury to take refuge in
one's gaze, the only available life preserver. Modernity, from the
20th century forward—contrary to what naval engineers
thought for a time—did not make water more vulnerable to
human control. Just as before, as if it were nothing, life continued to be shipwrecked in unthinkable depths. In 1912, Max
Beckmann painted one of the best depictions of the sinking of
the Titanic, one that continues to be the first. No one among
the great triptychs managed to capture as did this German the
agony occurring in the invincible, cold water of the North
Atlantic. This is because the death suffered by the hundreds of
tourists making the maiden voyage was not a romantic death,
not even the part where Leonardo DiCaprio looks out from the
bow of the ship. It was a death that came hurriedly to the world,
to be portrayed as ice frozen forever by the human eye.

Life also predicted its very mortal condition in the visual
quantity of this marvelous oil painting. Nothing is free, not
even nothingness. When visitors enter the enormous hall of the
Saint Louis Art Museum in Missouri, where the work hangs
(the best art tends to have the magnificence of the hanged),

they exhume that which was lived earlier by others in worse, liquid times, translating with the instantaneousness of this bloodthirsty beauty a unique empathy regarding certain mortal appearances that have gone out into the world in search of a description of someone who in some way represents them. *The Sinking of the Titanic* is a metaphysically imposing painting, like those that one would like to see daily but cannot because the piece is in a museum, and in which, to make matters worse, they do not sell a poster of it, like one of those that hang in the living room alongside a René Magritte or a Jackson Pollock, also reproductions.

The Saint Louis Art Museum is one of the best in the United States due to its refined physical space and the magnificent works it houses. In this same museum with an air of open sea—although the only water nearby is the Mississippi River—there is a little known (actually very unknown) realist painting by John Steuart Curry (1897-1946) entitled *The Mississippi* (1935). The painting screams out to be recognized, especially by people's gazes. I found it by chance, as these things tend to appear when one least thinks of or expects them. It hangs near Beckman's *Titanic*. There is an extraordinary Zurbarán, *St. Francis Contemplating a Skull* (1635), and a Gauguin, *Madame Roulin* (1888), worthy of the same adjective. The museum has it all, if exaggeration allows for such a thing to be said. It is a journey to beauty that has just recently begun, when it is still full of enthusiasm. Turned into a promise, it looks, unexpectedly, to be an expert in itself. But let us return to the work by Curry, an American painter forgotten today, although in truth he was always forgotten. His fame, if he ever had any, was fleeting, the type that goes unnoticed.

The Mississippi—the painting, not the brown river—is about a flood, a Goliath of inevitability. Reality mimics art. Whoever said that before me was right. The New Orleans flood in August of 2005 due to Hurricane Katrina was a life-size replica of what Curry saw before the CNN cameras did. This is because the floods of the Lower Mississippi, a river that empties near this coastal Gulf city, have, with their enormous power, been a common occurrence, having happened in the past, ever since the planet had images and water. "Poetry is the journal of a sea animal living on land, wanting to fly in the air," said Carl Sandburg, the Chicago poet. In the case of the stranded inhabitants of Curry's painting, they would have liked to have been able to fly as high and far as possible.

In the painting there is a black family (a man and woman and their four children) that has climbed up on the roof of a precarious hut. One of the interpretations could be that on this particular day it seems that the water wanted to be where everyone else was: at the height of the circumstances. Could its excess of sociability have been the thing that made it seem destructive? What irony: liquid water turned into a stone-faced interloper. The waters are rising, and seeing the angry undulations of the waves that Curry depicted so well, as if he had been there (perhaps Curry is the father, or one of the boys in the painting), everything indicates that the end is growing near, in the form of water swallowing up people. It is coming, even if it is already there.

The man is praying, pleading, and he is looking at the deaf heavens, which offer no protection whatsoever, as if seeking impossible answers. We do not know if he received them before being overcome by the waters. The woman, with her head bowed, has a look of resignation on her face, the same one that boxers have when they have fallen to the canvas and remained there as the count has reached ten. The children, meanwhile, with sad faces, appear to have accepted that this unfolding scene of horror is not some fun game, even though there is water involved, like the water in puddles to be jumped over and in the summer swimming pools to be dived into. All of them, collectively and individually, are up to their necks in water.

Will death come, or will it pass them by? Or, did it already come and this roof with people on top of it is all that it left alive?

Between resignation and desperation, life in Curry's painting is portrayed in its exaggerated extreme, in this case a wet and sweeping extreme, beyond which death reigns intolerant, intolerable. Those who are there but who at any moment could be us, have arrived at the imperfect edge of reality that separates the living from the dead. It separates those who tell what is happening from those who will not tell the tale. That is what we see, and that which our eyes imagine and hear. It is the music of mermaids being heard without pause beneath the high tide. It is music that sings to the dead, to the voiceless who have drowned. That which is about to occur reminds one of John Keats's headstone: "Here lies one whose name was writ in water."

> There are these two young fish swimming along, and they happen to meet an older fish swimming the other way, who nods at them and says, "Morning, boys, how's the water?" And the two young fish swim on for a bit, and then eventually one of them looks over at the other and goes, "What the hell is water?"
> (David Foster Wallace, graduation address given at Kenyon College, May 21, 2005)

Water is symbolic. This is the case in the Bible. It is a symbol of life and death. It is a symbol of nothingness that is more potent than anything and everything. It is a symbol of other things, if there are other things. John the Baptist baptized with water, and it was perhaps the same water that existed during the soaked era of the great universal flood. The water, therefore, was neurotically chameleon-like, with different purposes, one destructive and the other baptismal. It was the water of life, of spiritual rebirth: it marked the entrance into a totally new existence. Christ turned water into wine and also walked on water.

In his poem "La saeta," or "The Chant", Antonio Machado penned the following words in his honor: "I cannot sing, nor do I wish to do so / to that Jesus of the cross, / but rather to Him who walked upon the sea!"

In Spanish, the word for 'sea' is most commonly masculine ('*el mar*'), but in certain set phrases, and at times in poetic use, the feminine article is used instead ('*la mar*'). And these enormous bodies of water can indeed be masculine or feminine, and can even be, when they so desire, masculine *and* feminine (the sea is androgynous). It was upon this extensive oily marine surface, covered at times by foam as if it were make-up, that the bearer of good news walked, perhaps to demonstrate that whenever he wanted he could swim in such a miraculous way: walking as if it were nothing, just like Johnnie Walker. Even then they did not believe Him. Water is the province of miracles. Earlier, however, in the Old Testament, it was also that of death and purification. The world was destroyed by a flood which, to be completely true, became, as wine, universal. We come from the survivors, from Noah and Naamah, not from Adam and Eve.

We emerged from the wetness (something stated by Thales of Miletus, a pre-Socratic, post-Flood figure). We, like seahorses, dolphins, and sharks, are children of the water. But despite all of this, we do not know how to live underwater, not even for a little while. We were not born to live among the liquid and the non-solid. Those who attempted it wound up buried in water, sinking with Atlantis, a mysterious land impossible to find whose landscape took a nosedive similar to that of Géricault's doomed frigate. There is only one Agua Man. Noah was able to stay alive in the water, riding on an ark, but his is a Biblical story. In the Bible, which marks the beginning of many things which, just like water, will never have an end, water makes innumerable predilect appearances. Water, which has a deceptively meek appearance, is one of the book's most famous stars, even if it is not in the infinite cosmos above, which is where it is most needed. Mars would be a beach resort, a touristic hotspot, if it only had water on its surface. There are countless stories and parables in which water has a role, perhaps not always an exclusive role, but at least a main one.

The stories of Noah and John the Baptist are the before and the after, the alpha and the omega. Water is synonymous with the source of life, that which we drink, that which is used to baptize. Water is a source of endless death: that in which we are capable of drowning and of finding a soluble death to express it. In water, we see the beginning and the end as they have ended up being. In water Narcissus saw his reflection in the best way possible, precisely as he wanted to be answered by the echo of his own image, because water is also a mirror of the realities that we desire to achieve. It is the reason for our desires, the intermediary that helps us arrive, but arrive where and at what kind of sensations?

Every now and then, turned into a machine of insubordination, capable of turning human life into something as intense, animated, and brief as a *haiku*, nature approves its disproportions and places itself at the service of an illumination, a *satori*. The need for words is obviated. In such cases, should something be said? To whom? To what? When? Where? And how or why? The death that nature carries with it leaves one groping blindly, preventing a reconstruction of the present. It is only possible to see as far as one is, even if incompletely. Cesare Pavese said that "Death will come and it will have your eyes," but death, including when it comes swimming or flying through the air, like a bird of fire, does not have any anatomy, not even eyes. If it does have anything it is, and then only barely, the intention to hide in that which sight cannot see and which is not exactly the sight of others, not to mention that of a previously existing "you."

So similar in this regard to love when it ceases to be so, water kills little by little, as if it were something that took considerable time, as if it really were difficult. Water and fire destroy quickly; they have the velocity of a sigh. Water lives by its patience. When it arrives, it stays. It seeps into pores and cracks, demonstrating that no wall is strong enough to resist or dam high enough to stop it. Taking possession of the closeness that moves in on it, it becomes a ghost dressed in destruction, emitting unspeakable prognostications, without correcting anything. It does not even give off signals of having done it for the last time. Is there some great natural destruction that serves a purpose, aside from captivating reason when it feels the lack of moderation in full proportion and desires to keep watching, and living?

It is the world as a majestic liquid sepulcher. The welter of water from the Indian Ocean, that of Japan as it shook, and that of New Orleans on that Monday, 29 August 2005, entered in as would someone into his or her own home, though it did not enter just one home but many, as many as it could. Just as in Curry's painting, the people, having climbed up on their roofs, which looked like unbreakable horses, saw the water rise. It rose and rose some more, until it left nothing, or rather nothing premiering an image, and barely that. The transformation of fragility into an instant devoid of words caused the unknown—we do not know what—to be even more incomprehensible, since death never reasons. It only offers images as the complicit part of a silencing on the verge of vacillating. One's gaze felt obliged to readjust amid a landscape of accumulated occurrences gorged by an attempt of enormous totality. An unrelenting randomness—but no one can know which one—put them in this place, dedicated to eluding the very thing to which they were alluding.

Here he lies where he longed to be;
Home is the sailor, home from the sea,
And the hunter home from the hill.
(Epitaph on the grave of Robert Louis Stevenson, 1850-1894).

With its introductory and autobiographical language, water does not deny admission to any example. It is contemporary water, with its routine of colors and sounds in order to not feel lost from sight. It is water that swims better than anyone. The world today is Venice, surrounded by water that has come from everywhere. Even the movie industry has gone back to water, just as it had done with *The Ten Commandments*, in which Charlton Heston, playing Moses, gave water orders in such an effective way that it has never been equaled, neither before nor since. Catastrophe as entertainment has a very old history, though not as old as this Jewish prophet was. Floods, infinite rain, overflowing seas and rivers: they are all an overdose of water.

Because nature has been so insistent, we have learned to be contemporaries of Noah. And to illustrate to us what the world was like the days of the universal flood—when nature carried out its own special effects, unassisted—in 2014 Hollywood frivolously and expensively refloated the history of Noah, his family (there were eight survivors), his ark, his array of animals, and his struggle against a determined rain that forgot to stop and through which nature turned Earth into a liquid house, drop by drop. Humanity and animal life were changed into inhabitants of wetness. The overflowing borders beautified the world's foreign beauty, though something in its symmetry was definitely altered. The waters returned to their source and the flood disappeared, as it always does (as the saying goes: "Every time it rains it stops raining"), but neither the land nor life looked the same. They still are not.

With their rhythm of self-taught ferocity, water catastrophes dispense disproportion, opening a range of consequences. A Japanese proverb affirms that there are four truly terrifying things in the world: earthquakes, thunder, fires, and parents. Water, the mother of so much destruction, can, without even trying, be as horrifying as all four of these things combined. Nature has taught us that everything that happens in the imagination happens first in reality. But this occurs without seeing signs of it beforehand; abnormality still cannot be predicted. Nature is non-submissive (from this condition spring its hard-to-accept actions, the soliloquys it performs for itself), and it places reason before the enigma of all "that" which cannot be stated ahead of time, and even less the manner in which it will be stated. Perhaps it is for this reason that it possesses such enormous power of conviction when it is invited to make an appearance with its gamut of obituary spirits in art and literature, concerned about everything, as if the very life of disasters were at stake.

In *King Lear* (Act III, Scene II), Shakespeare described it with poetic precision: "Blow, wind, and crack your cheeks! rage! blow! / You cataracts and hurricanoes, spout / Till you have drench'd our steeples, drown'd the cocks!" A similar titanic struggle was waged against adverse weather conditions by Robinson Crusoe. On his remote island, he was forced to deal with tormenting rains that turned him into a solitary gladiator against the forces of nature, a human umbrella. (Indeed, the power of torrential rain in our era has rendered the umbrella an obsolete invention.) Today, more than before, we live lives passed through water. Soon, if things continue this way and the neurotic atmosphere continues to show its worst states of emotion, we will go back to measuring time with a water clock capable of keeping track of time absolutely, including that of earlier times, when moments of bad weather, particularly in Christian mythology, were considered to be punishment for man's sinful behavior. The current era is hardly saintly, so perhaps the weather is sending similar messages. Or might nature, with ferocious water, be getting its revenge for man having disobeyed its laws?

Whoever said that "the sea is a language" was not mistaken. Art and literature have established in their surroundings a nautical tradition that babbles in its own tongue, assuming the idea that water, a liquid muse, is a lighthouse of stories born to be told. There are stories to which imagination periodically feels obliged to return. We find literature with an aquatic homing instinct in Herman Melville; in the great Robert Louis Stevenson, who died listening to the high tide of the South Pacific; Ernest Hemmingway, a fisherman of the high seas; and Álvaro Mutis (Maqroll the lookout demonstrated that an estuary is not part of the nature of rivers, but rather a territory where words come to overflow). All these authors wrote of the sea as an apt place to perk up one's ear and listen to the other tales that up to that point land-based confabulation had not taken into account. In the water, imagination rows against the current. It has no other way of doing it, since water, like no one or nothing else, can signify the excess of nature when it wants to be that and only that: the specter of a persistence changing the prognostications of reason.

Made wobbly most likely by geisha girls who the oceanic depths turned into murderous harpies, the sea, a dune of water, shows its claws every now and again. This phenomenon is brilliantly portrayed in *The Great Wave off Kanagawa*, by Katsushika Hokusai (1760-1849), that progressive Asian who seems to have seen before anyone, as if for the first time in this way, enraged waters lying in wait, and in animated form, which is not the usual image. In *The Great Wave* we see the water, a nightmare taking shape, which is being watched from afar by Mt. Fuji, that great declaration of principles in the Japanese landscape. If it had a mind to do so, the entire island nation could fit into that mountain, or at least the imagination of a country in unison. All manner of things fit into the world's water, including happiness and horror, hope and resignation, peace and fear. It all depends, just as in life. Water is birth and destruction, tranquility and spectacle, life and death. I will let Wallace Stevens say it best in *Ideas of Order*: "The water never formed to mind or voice."

THE MUSIC OF COLLECTING

THE PICTURES HAD NOT ARRIVED BY THEMSELVES at that place full of people. Life pays more attention to them than to phrases that are about to be spoken. A picture is worth a thousand words, but at times there are two or three thousand (these pictures at least, with so many origins that they ended up not having even one, had the good manners to know how to go unnoticed). The place—a must see—was full of things and beings to see. If reality tells the truth, and at times it does, the locale in question, based on its expanse and purpose, was an enormous traveling flea market, although the day I visited it the most evident creature was a different one: there were more human beings than fleas. All sorts of things were being bought and sold, not people like in the busy era of slavery, but rather objects and various types of fetishes by no means anonymous. Some of these articles had a nearly incalculable value, especially for those who lacked the money to buy them. But many people do have the money.[1]

To have (the same as *to love*) is an unjust verb. I saw wealthy people pay small fortunes for a baseball card, for a stamp that was once stuck to a letter, or for something that among collectors is not any material thing, but the sound track of an obsession. And then there was me, who had gone there out of simple curiosity. Well, actually it was not so simple (but it also was not like the cat's curiosity and therefore could not kill me). To the contrary, it was in fact a complex curiosity without an inferiority complex. I wanted to know what it was all about, this monstrosity of a market where, although there were some people who were ugly on the outside, none of them seemed completely monstrous to me, only certain portions of them, in separate anatomical parts: head, stomach, extremities.

For weeks I had been finding out from regular visitors to these booths about the pedigree of those who frequented them. I did not find out about all of them, which would have been impossible, but rather about the main ones, those collectors of greatest celebrity, who were members of international clubs, some of whom could even be found in the *Guinness Book of World Records*. I had read that in this market, which was unlike any other, there came together prestigious collectors seeking (a redundancy, for sure) the costly fetishes that they collected. They were after the object of their desire, which could be something dark, just like the brilliant movie by Luis Buñuel, though in truth not quite that dark, since they might only be looking for, as I was able to confirm, a stamp, a baseball card, cigar boxes, post cards, sepia-colored photos of people who at one time or another passed through this world, first-edition books completely unknown to me, brooches, or perhaps a table made of expensive wood with a view to the past, because some people collect furniture that they do not use to sleep in or sit on. It was one of those places, not at all immaculate, where the word

---

[1] Interest in the novelties that objects from the past can bring is confirmed by the solid and sustained audience of the program *Antiques Roadshow*, which has been featured weekly since 1997 by the Public Broadcasting Service (PBS) and which is the American version of the British show of the same name, which debuted in 1979. *Antiques Roadshow* has been nominated for 11 Primetime Emmy awards. The program is recorded every week in different parts of the United States, almost always in small towns, where the most incredible and costly fetishes of memorabilia go up for sale, some more select and attractive than others. The stars of the program are the objects themselves, but so are the prices paid for them. For example, a complete collection of Charles Schulz's Peanuts comic strip art was valued at $450,000. A Navajo Ute First Phase blanket from the mid-19th century, which purportedly belonged to trailblazer and Indian fighter Christopher Houston Carson (1809–1868), better known as Kit Carson, was appraised at nearly half a million dollars. Besides the objects and prices—the latter being exorbitant at times—the other great stars of the show are the appraisers, whose judgments regarding the relationship between the "object's value" and the "price to be paid" for it tend to be unappealable, even though such judgments can often seem incomprehensible to neophytes.

all is never too much or enough. Anything could be found there, though none of the experts could give me an answer about how to collect ideas.

There were throngs of people, hundreds of human beings crammed together as if on a Hong Kong street, all of them speaking in their surrounding language, with a curiosity predisposed to finding their discoveries. Among this purchasing hoard I found some who seemed to be beings dedicated to collecting. They had strange faces, very strange, some of which were like those that Hollywood creates with special effects. They were special faces, but it was impossible to collect them; their owners were the only ones who could do that. They were their very own album. There were lots of collectors and all of them were very much alike. It is the mimicry of collecting. The market was so big that it was impossible to cover the entire area at one go. It was like an anthill, except these ants spoke and paid in cash.

Besides, it would never occur to any ant to get emotional over a toy soldier made of lead which, because his feet were made of this metal, could not walk, or over a vinyl record with a whole in the middle. I thought for a while about returning the next day, which was a Sunday, but since I only thought about it for a while, and not two or three whiles in a row, I never went back. I got partially stuck in that nice Saturday for which they had forecast rain in the afternoon, but it was still morning.

What I saw around me left me surprised without leaving me. What I saw were somewhat exotic objects for sale, and the prices which were being paid for them, both high and low, as if they were a collectable extension of the human race. Amid so much enthusiasm for the same things, which in the end were different, I had a desire to start collecting things immediately. Something, I do not know what. Something that could be anything important at that precise moment and which would make it so that someday I would get interviewed on the Charlie Rose show on

PBS as the greatest collector of useless objects. It could be something like used napkins, burned matches, empty bottles, candy
wrappers, dull nail clippers, some tire stolen in another state
(and which had not gotten there on its own), or a pumice stone.

Like I said, I do not really know. Anything that was cheap
and at the same time easy to collect. Bus tickets, especially
Greyhound, whose numbers were palindromic, a fancy way of
saying that they read the same forward and backward. Nevertheless, I realized right away that for good collectors nothing is
cheap or easy, just like that. It takes them years to find the
object of desire that they desire to buy, and for this reason they
are capable of paying developing fortunes for this thing, a thing
that is costly because there is not another one in the whole
world that is just like it or even similar to it. The deceptive cap-
tivations with which objects surround their immortality can be
exaggerated.

Of all the available sections, the one that interested me the
most was the one dedicated to baseball cards, as it took me back
to my elementary school days when I collected them and could
spend hours on end playing *sapito*—a game in which coins are
thrown into the open mouth of a metal toad—with the goal of
completing my album as quickly as possible. In such albums, life
was frozen, even if baseball cards are not cold. I recall touching
them lovingly, as if they had belonged to me since their creation and as if they were my contribution to the paltry household belongings. That was so long ago. One day, however, I
grew tired of using my hands only for that and began to use
them for other important work beyond ringing the doorbell and
holding the toothbrush the right way. I also began to use them
to do that which adolescents of that age tend to do. I do not
wish to be explicit on this point. Besides, baseball card collectors over the age of 18 do not play *sapito*, at least they were not
playing it the day that I saw them in the market, though they

did use their hands to greet people and to pull money out of their pockets correctly. They knew how to pay well.

For a small piece of paper with the printed image of someone less famous that George Washington, Abraham Lincoln, or Brad Pitt, and which was merely a used stamp (some unknown lips had passed over the aged surface), a woman no taller than 5' 7" took out enough money to buy a round-trip ticket to Jackson, Mississippi, passing through some insignificant town in Louisiana. There were other philatelists of similar height, but men in this case, one of whom carried a magnifying glass for the purpose of enlarging—enlarging the size of the stamp, that is, not his own size. The fetishes on display attracted different kinds of visitors. For a card of one of the baseball players on the winning team of the 1982 World Series, a card on which appears the smiling face of Ozzie Smith next to an expressionless baseball bat, I saw someone pay a sum equal to two hamburgers and a six-pack of Pabst Blue Ribbon beer. I could see that in the mind of the buyer, the amount paid was not great, because after the purchase was made he exclaimed wildly: "I got a deal!" I asked him to please let me see it up close, but he would not let me touch it: "This is mine forever," he said, referring not to the hair-dyed woman, whom he had collected some time ago and who was there beside him, but rather to the baseball card in question. He had bought one of those hard-to-find cards, and since life does not want repeated baseball cards, the acquisition meant a resounding success. He considered his obsession to be perseverance, and his home, wherever it was, a mini-museum of national heritage.

The area dedicated to the baseball cards was spectacular. It was the nerve center of a strange lack of conventionalisms. People who had ceased to be children several childhoods ago were still acting like children. However, unlike true children, they did not need to ask their parents for permission to squander $100 bills with the imperturbable face of Benjamin Franklin, the man behind the lightning conductor, or to buy a baseball card with the picture of an outfielder who was famous many years ago, someone who nobody would recognize today, even if they saw him in the same short pants he had been photographed in next to a ball and an inexpressive bat. Even though human beings in general—women included—are strange by nature, in this type of massively attended event one can see, grouped together in the same place, the strangest humans of all, collectors, who are every bit as odd as that which they buy.

In the post-20th century world, the eagerness to collect things seems to go against the apparent data of reality. Unlike what one might think, interest in collecting has increased. Habits of reality do not answer to precise mechanisms. Given the historic circumstances, collecting seems to be an appropriate hobby for another era, not this one, which is characterized by deleting and a favoritism of forgetfulness. In a time when the most-used key is the *delete* key, there has been an increase in the number collectors in whose mental computer the most popular key is that of *save*. It is evident that many need to drop anchor in the past.

It would seem that children who grew up accumulating Chinese toys that last less than a week should not have a notion of an object with posterity, and yet they do. Collecting also abounds among them: miniature cars, keys, dolls, little toy soldiers, an infantry of Pokémons (collecting has evolved). Current memory lives in the present. It is a reality of paradoxes: the latest and most recent things have today become anachronistic. It is a history like that of vinyl records. At one time they were the latest song of fashion, a fashion they still carry with them. Today, however, they represent the fixed periphery of the past. Music no longer travels through black grooves. It is just as before but different; the radicalization of difference defines our era and its occupants. Millions now collect songs on their nicknameless iPods.

In a time when disposable goods are the epitome of the ephemeral, all varieties of things are welcome in the accumulating plan. Nothing should surprise. Science tells us that all human beings have the tendency to collect things. For this reason, the hobby of collecting is as old as humanity itself. The almanac of history provides examples. The Romans collected slaves; the people of Sodom and Gomorra collected the most easily committed sins; the biblical Sara collected children (the descendants of Israel come from her), and Noah collected animals: the ark was his album (would he have let the mouse on board had he known it would end up becoming a computer component?). The continents also collect. Europe collects African and Arab immigrants; Africa collects poverty; Asia collects followers of Buddha; and Latin America collects dictators. Countries do the same. Mexico and Colombia collect drug traffickers; Bolivia collects altitude; Ecuador collects the changing extension of an extensive line; and Uruguay collects holidays. Even the objects in a collection collect something: dust.

All collecting represents a watershed moment. At a certain stage in their not-so-passive existence, objects cease to be amateurs. This intermediate time is made possible by a rite of veneration through which materialism is freed from its condition, yielding, paradoxically, to material objects. Exhibiting a doubtful empiric imperative, collecting sponsors a ritualistic practice of renovation, because when objects change hands they are reborn. In the hands of their new owner, they feel as if another name were being attached to them to add a sound to their earlier meaning. Objects come to feel rich, important, indestructible, protected by a certain veneration. Enthusiasm for their value collects pasts in such a way that the present forgets that tomorrow will be another day. It is not surprising that there are people who become famous for collecting rare items that at a certain point in their material life ceased to be useless. Many of them are millionaires who defeated anonymity by demonstrating their exalted consumer idiosyncrasy through an act of collecting.

On the horizon of accumulation there arises a certain exclusivity, and the privileges of indifference and disdain show their
elective affinities. Objects' belated secret is revealed when they
say only half of what they are. They arrive at this moment by
way of an abandonment of usefulness, putting their ecstatic
movements to the test. Collected pieces inform the stoicism of
those who yearn for them in their incomplete, resurrected state.
This is because, unlike what is gathered by the hunter, the collector's pieces are alive and outside the designs of taxidermy, and
to stay this way they accelerate their non-embalmed immobility. Memory and experience merge, and from their synapsis the
illusion centered on an accessible phenomenon materializes,
entering the region of an object that has only recently been
found, though a search for it has been going on for a long time.

In the habitation of habits, as anyone can see in the markets dedicated to these activities, collectors instinctively place
in order the seemingly arbitrary reasons of their behavior, the
subliminal vicissitudes that point to a fortuitous devotion that
does not end with the purchase of the most recent object. The
wounds of persistence are healed, although just temporarily,
until another promise of well-being discovers a new objective.
Trinkets, no matter what their value, show that they have not
considered abandoning life as long as it remains. Collectors
have the sensation that their obsession will never expire and
that to be able to extend out better, real experience must first
be imagined. They are obsessive creatures who feel shackled
because they cannot gain access to their emblematic possession
when will demands it of them. Desire continues to be enthusiastic about its plans, postponing compensation.

In this evolution, this becoming, a showing of accessible fantasy generates the energy that motivates one to take possession
of the object. It would only remain for collectors to change the
destiny of these things which, based on their names and their
magnitude, cause them to become obsessed, and which are the

synopsis of an indemonstrable explanation. At some point in the process—a trance?—objects cease to be "really" objective. Subjectivity adopts them, turning them into guardians of an unprecedented dependence, of a symbolic perseverance. It is fervor vis-à-vis a promise that through any and all means will remain incomplete, since collectors rarely let objects out of their grasp once they have had access to them. Their urgencies of continuity go against the grain, because it is in this way that the narcissistic adherence to certain referents of behavior functions. Sooner or later, the seducer will be seduced by his conquest.

"Ownership is the most intimate relationship that one can have to things" (Walter Benjamin). Objects, then, become mute pets with which collectors speak each time they appraise them, reconciled to the credibility of their ego. Objects are substitutes of a tangible symbolism; they invent satisfaction, making it less invulnerable as they do so. The voracity of collectors transforms the usefulness of the object into a compulsive obsession fed by extramaterial reasons. It is an obsession that will only be complete as long as it continues to know that it is not complete. The answer arises without explanations or any way to find them.

The traveler returns from the long journey with a material *souvenir* (a French word rendered *recuerdo* in Spanish; *meibutsu* or *omiyage* in Japanese; and *memorabilia* in Latin) that bears witness to his adventure and which will be given—each imported object is an object in action—to those who did not travel but who, rather, become the final destination of the newly arrived. Collectors, after all, are a different type of traveler. The things which they collect testify of their earthly transit, to the journey of their mind on the map. They incarcerate objects; they have an altruistic relationship with their own curiosity. They take possession of the pleasure of collecting. They exercise a perplexity that cannot be dismantled, not even after its value has been identified in more than one way. They build their own museum where memory receives the lending of earlier pasts. Nostalgia becomes memorable because it does not know to be anything else.

There is an Australian rock group called Hunters and Collectors. Hunters and collectors (gatherers) are alike, but the latter do not have to kill objects to own them. Without the need of taking the life of that which they supposedly love, many collectors engage in an intrinsic learning of the objects that keeps their obsession up to date, in the state of a devotional relic. Through his verbal curiosity, the poet collects apt phrases and the novelist collects stories that can be told. Others stockpile material objects which it is impossible to make talk. They alleviate their pathology in a way less connected to the transcendence of language.

They collect the experience of objects. They perform the taxonomy of an ownership of property that cannot be shared, of an intimate museum without substitution. In it, objects use their form to provide security and to entertain on the basis of a usefulness replaced by a random value. So then, the externalization of intrinsic desires updates the slogan which states that some things exist only to be kept, that is, preserved outside of temporality. Wherever they happen to be, they become connected lives which, for a determined price, have found the way to keep their posterity entertained. In hundreds of thousands of the world's basements there are countless objects in their earliest forms that were stored there and fell asleep and many cannot see them.

Each collectable item bears record of a moment preserved as an out-of-use existence, as a spatial category turned into a temporal one due to its backward-looking interest. In them, time does not actually stop but rather slackens the speed of its pilgrimage. These objects thus become museums to the reminiscence of usefulness, promoted by the complicity of a motivation that is valid beyond their importance. In the same way that the mind collects memories, there are those who, while they can still remember, collect objects. Collectors exist because there are things out there to be collected. And people collect them for different reasons, almost always irrelevant (the grammar of life lacks logical laws). It is a passion with motives, but not always, and in fact almost never, with a method. Collections are sentimental copies of an indefinable category, except for the material things that they contain and which can be classified.

Collecting, which for many is a great waste of time, seeks to once again find time—the least collectable commodity that we find in this life—where it has not yet returned because it has never left. A pastime becomes a referent for the passing of time. Each piece in a collection is a water clock that marks dry hours on its liquid minute hand. Originality based on a nostalgia for the various lives contained in an object is accompanied by a dissected temporality. These are minutes that in comparison have been miniaturized. It is for this reason that collecting grants to the person who practices it an artificial control over time. Some people are redundant and collect watches or clocks. It is a metaphor of the life they would like to eternalize, since collecting can be interminable: there is always something missing or which has nothing similar to it. Sentimentalism is never complete, no matter how much reality is capable of imposing a limit on the expansion of inventory. How many Stradivarius violins or Vermeer paintings (37 remain, only one of which is part of a private collection) that still exist can be collected?

Collectors belong to a community that shares common knowledge about objects whose material and symbolic relevance is not always evident or given away by their age or origins. They engage in this activity simply because they want to, but they might also see an omen for the long-term results of such determination, as if they truly believed that one day the collection will be extraordinarily valuable. There are those who have indeed believed this. One John Jay Pittman, for instance, worked as a teacher his entire life and in 1954 put up his house as collateral against a loan to travel to Egypt and buy a collection of rare coins that had belonged to King Farouk. He worked for decades to stockpile more and more coins, spending all that he earned to achieve the same, addictive objective. His family thought him mentally ill, the victim of a cruel obsession. Perhaps without ever having planned it, in the future that Mr. Pittman never knew, such great interest in the past yielded its reward in the present. In 1996, shortly after his death, his numismatic collection was sold at public auction for $30 million dollars.

In this life we all collect years, and some purchase the remains of earlier years held in the objects that belonged to the past, and which due to their price and exclusive nature will always have a future. Collectable fetishes are the soul of an example and their influences, incalculable, return to themselves. They have a refractory character; being animated presences, they perpetuate moments that oblige one to take possession of their magic, because there is a great amount of such magic deposited in the desired object. Such a fetish becomes a good luck charm with an immediate response; in this way it is turned into something that bears record of its insistence, into the justification of a legitimate whim. In collecting there is a renunciation of obviousness, since a precarious fiction and a way of life transition into enjoying the comfort of a material equivalence: a crystal or porcelain vase cannot be seen merely as a jug, a baseball card ceases to be just a piece of paper, a stamp is no longer the intermediary of a love letter that arrived at its first destination.

Observation in a possessive state lives in its affections without being able to understand them, let alone explain them. Why do we buy books knowing that we can read them for free in a library? Why, if very few of those we purchase will ever be reread? What reason activates passion when the process of obtaining an object of selective value is fulfilled? What sense of pride or superiority begins to justify this irreparable passion? What anxiety is articulated in response to the incomplete state of a reality that favors the sense of unreality? Just as some children sleep with their favorite stuffed toy, collectors feed their insomniac activity with their own affections. The acquisition of the object partly alleviates their anxiety, though only to a limited extent. Collecting is the radicalization of the purchasing act: the mechanisms of acquisition lead to a cause that is resolved through buying, including by chance.

Above all, collecting is a mental experience, an act of psychological recreation, one in which happenstance finds incentives to augment its striking repertoire. Possession stimulates the activity of certain unknown feelings that discover their facilitating nature in the strictly non-symbolic moment when a collector takes possession of the object and of the past as an uneasy relic. As a result, the emphasis is not placed in the meaning, but rather in the motives, which remain elusive, without revealing themselves, and which represent the excuses offered by patience to feel up-to-date. In each object, which is the victorious victim of the transaction, the valuable lessons of perseverance are put into practice: lessons of emotional persistence with regard to the admired objects. *Connoisseurs*, consequently, collect feelings in the form of objects that are nothing but encapsulated time. Infatuated with a habit that is incomprehensible and reluctant to accept substitutions, they externalize the assessment of their enthusiasm, the premeditated capture of the preferences that characterize said enthusiasm. The vulnerability of existence is replaced by a desire for possession.

In a culture such as that in the West, which more and more is oriented toward what we have or could have, an artificial preterite is created. Each collection is an individual museum that tells of an alternative yesterday through its personal objects. Memory, just as collecting highlights, is a fiction under control. In the experience of that atemporal pleasure (which for that reason is valid), factors without explanation are exhibited, since the value of the market, in the end, is the only empirical evidence of the past in question. Duration goes into a dramatic trance, even if all collectables are not identical or have the same value. Don Juan collected women, but they were freer to leave the collection than, say, a Chinese vase made of crystal or of porcelain, or a dissected butterfly. Not all collectable objects share the exact same intelligence or the same desire to exercise their freedom at a later time.

Collecting is the art of remembering with objects. Curiosity regarding the background of these articles implements a methodology with its own merits and benefits. Everything has value, and this value goes beyond the symbolic. This may include china, crystal, desserts, out-of-circulation bills, coins, miniature pieces of art, empty perfume vials, super hero magazines, seashells, butterflies, lighters, staplers of all types, ribbons, buttons and banners, containers (one man has a collection of 3,000 beer cans), and even toasters (at toastermuseum.com one can see a collection of 600 toasters from around the world). Obviously, it is more aristocratic to collect antiques than, for example, match boxes or empty wine bottles, which can also be found at the carnival of illusions liberated from the dark that are associated with the flea markets of collecting. In the wide expanses of such markets, the pilgrimage of collectors is indiscriminate and scorns the circumstances, as if they had nothing to learn from the previously evaluated things they find. But what does that really matter? In any event it only matters to them.

The sociology of collecting is a zoology. There are predilections of all kinds, an innumerable variety of material bestiaries. What cannot be collected? In Spain, there is a fan who owns the world's largest collection of recorded soccer games. He has game recordings from nearly all the countries and leagues where this sport is played and the games are recorded. This fan spends his life dedicated to a collector's zeal that surely has led to having fewer savings in the bank than he currently does. The game recordings are his personal assets. He wasted a fortune on them.

He has thousands of games, the great majority of which will never be watched again by anyone for the simple reason that they have lost their currency, if they ever had any. Furthermore, could there be anyone interested in seeing again, or even the first time for that matter, a game which, to offer an example, was played 30 years ago in India's professional league, between two unknown teams who played soccer very poorly and whose efforts ended in a scoreless tie? Who could possibly find interest in rewinding and rewatching the plays that took place between minutes 30 and 45 of the first half of this obscure game and whose fruitless results foretold the inevitable 0-0 ending? Collecting, as this case highlights, is an insanity that includes the very real possibility of not only wasting time, but of knowing beforehand that there is not much noteworthy in life.

Included in the *Guinness Book of World Records* is Mr. Plastic Fantastic, the person with the most credit cards on the planet—1,208 cards, which would permit him to make purchases valued at up to $1.5 million. A man in California is the owner of more than 42,000 keys from 16 different countries which he accumulated over a period of 50 years. Would this allow him to open the doors of perception? And to close those of the past? The dilemma of retrospection lacks one single formula, but it has at its disposal several different names: philately ("the collector of stamps corresponds with the past," according to Gómez de la Serna), bibliophilism, numismatics, arctophilia (teddy bears), deltiology (postcards), copoclephilia (key rings). So then, would a compulsive collector of shoes, like Imelda Marcos, be a shocophile? And what about someone who hoards light bulbs? An illuminophile? Should we call someone who collects perfume bottles a vialophile?

I go back to the beginning paragraph. That trip through the flea market brought back memories to me of the time I visited a similar market, but one that was far away from this one. Among various other things, some venders were selling clothes turned into a collectable fetish since they had belonged previously to famous individuals for whose autographs people pay with checks that they themselves have autographed. It is a redundancy of interest. I curiously made my way to a black leather jacket that looked familiar to me. I thought I had seen it long ago in a photograph or on the body of someone who was standing right there smiling, the way people smile when there is a "cheese" and a click.

There was a picture next to the black jacket, and besides the jacket itself, the very photogenic person in the photo also had (though he was not wearing) a microphone. Nevertheless, the jacket had not belonged to James Dean, as I had first supposed, but rather to Elvis Presley, as I soon learned. Icons illuminate their myth with dark clothing. I made the mistake of asking the owner if I he would allow me to try it on, but he responded angrily: "This is a collector's item, not a motorcycle jacket." I do not know what he meant by that, as I have neither a motorcycle nor a scooter, and when I ride my bicycle I never use a jacket. In any event, it would have been impossible for me to buy it. It cost $58,000. With that kind of money I could have bought a furriery, so I continued on. Besides, I was not really so cold that day as to bundle up.

A few steps beyond, but without yet entering into the Great Beyond, they were selling objects that had also belonged to famous dead people. And what strange and expensive things I found there, not to mention the many strange faces. "I know that strange things will come," says the tango, and the majority of them could be found in this place. People who appeared to have less money that I did were able to afford the luxury of paying several thousand dollars for something that I could never manage to buy, not even in easy monthly installments like the poor of the world do when they are tired of always being poor. Maybe that is why they were able to purchase such things and I was not. For a scarf that allegedly belonged to singer Janis

Joplin, the one she was using when they photographed her with it on, someone who was not cold but with enough money paid $18,000. He signed a check, and with the same hand he affectionately touched the wool scarf which, due to its ancestry, had been turned into a bundled trophy. What will he ever do with it except keep it stored in a place with no necks?

Among the fabulous inventory that was for sale and which invited one to believe in gradual paganisms and to invent better realities—in case such things exist in this world—there stood out a pair of basketball shoes that had belonged to Michael Jordan, a cowboy hat that Gary Cooper used in a movie that was not *High Noon*, the cloak of a gay pianist whose name I forget, a purse once owned by Greta Garbo, a pair of gloves whose only owner was famous, though I cannot quite remember why, etc. Oh, and there was a towel from a five-star hotel that John Lennon supposedly used one night to dry himself, because the stars, when no one is watching them, also bathe. The list of "memorabilia" was interminable. In its unrepeatable expanse, the inventory list was longer that the average human life.

I returned home wondering about something that I still cannot understand. How did the expert buyers know that those highly expensive fetishes for sale had truly belonged to those it had been said they belonged to? I do not know the answer. It should be noted, however, that I did not see anyone arguing or protesting that they had been sold a pig in a poke. And life compensates with its asymmetries, making itself evident where it is not so, because in these markets of obsession it never can be. Since I had time to carry out this activity, on both occasions (the one that happened on an ordinary Saturday and the other which also took place a day before Sunday), I reflected on the fact that human beings are strange by nature: they can spend a fortune on things that matter only to them.

PANIC IN THE PANOPTIC SCENES

I *(The home of a devalued ego)*

THE DROP IN VIEWERSHIP RATINGS of "traditional" television programs, meaning of those still structurally based on a situation plot with a resolution and on the orchestrating work of a screenwriter, gave rise to the proliferation of reality shows. These shows enjoyed their moment of glory during the 1990s on network television and with the turn of the new century have found an apparently unending niche on cable. The alibi (and strategy) of this type of television format seeks to make us believe that humans are actually and unbearably like that, all the time, precisely as they are portrayed by their own acts in front of the camera.

Behavior that is too implausible to be implausible passes before our eyes, to the unbelief of reason and the satisfaction of the *yearning* for entertainment, but only when the expectations do not go beyond mere nosiness into a nothingness in full swing. We stand before a mirror where the reflected image is that of all of us acting collectively. And for far too long, more than a decade now, a large part of humanity has accepted being reflected in this mirror, which is at once both concave and convex; the perspective matters little or not at all. Given the circumstances, there is something at first glance that forces one to reflect, but from a point of view of skepticism. This much reality desiring to pass as reality cannot be true. It is, furthermore, a reality that has set out, it would seem, to force us to believe it.

The tastes and preferences on the entertainment scene changed radically as the door closed on the 20th century and opened on the new one, though few were capable of foreseeing the shifting of priorities that would put these preferences at the top of the share and ratings charts. The ratings, as we know, make no demands and allow for an existence free from responsibility. If the numbers go up, as they did, it means life has found an order to adhere to. Success depends on figures, with no one and nothing to decipher. Reality TV proliferates because a winning excuse was needed during prime time, when traditional programs—comedies, series, and soaps—had ceased to possess the power of attraction.

"Generalist" television was in crisis, and the zigzag of impulses foretold a collapse of the traditional way of doing things, as well as a surge in new expectations identified with the immediacy of the product. Like a last-minute fill-in, almost as a transitional vehicle, there arrived on the scene an audiovisual experiment without any known precedent in the world of television. With its massive reach, the idea turned out to be a novel one and immediately fostered a diversifying marketing supply. A defective but very effective style was established. In keeping with the days in which we live, television changed because people no longer watch it the same way: the Internet and the proliferation of cable channels altered the dimensions of the supply of instantaneous entertainment, spurring the collective desire to want to see ourselves on a screen with our entire range of emotional weaknesses.

In an era that appears new, when the talk of the world is that of genes (due to the Human Genome Project), there appeared a new television gen(e)(re): reality shows. The globalization of expectations led to an ill-advised example, one comprised of sleep-inducing time devoid of narration, one that invites weariness. The majority of reality shows attempt, with varying degrees of success, to impose a dangerous and deceptive premise of inclusiveness. This type of television is a bastardized species of television docudrama in which boring people try to be fun and aspire to celebrity through their persistence in superficiality. The protagonists are people who feel comfortable in the observed setting, since no talent is necessary there. They are not as insects that must pull off an unbeatable show while under the microscope. They must only be as they are the rest of the time, when no one is watching them. The program's formula seeks to appear in nature as a completed act, but it inevitably remains unfinished.

In stores, people are watched as they shop via closed-circuit television. These are individual shows with mini-intimacies. Here the eye enters another type of domain, because the circuit is open. One click with the remote control allows for the abolishment of privacy. One authorized click is all it takes. It is strange: we can turn on the television and find ourselves in the middle of someone else's life, something that did not happen before. Private domestic affairs become collective matters with no other reason or justification than to waste time, turned into the residual expansion of time itself. What irony: the spleen trusts in the narcotic power of technology. Prose and Prozac. That is the state of things: the public is obsessed with banality, and reality TV represents the latest reward for its omnipresent superficiality. It is the cure for an insanity that does not exist.

The first format of this kind to have a worldwide impact was that of *Big Brother*, and the idea came from Holland. In a matter of months all humanity came to have the same pseudonym. The mass exploitation of its generalized content established easily assimilable commonalities without regard to borders, and its success caught on worldwide, Africa and Asia included. It extended from miniseries to mini-intelligences. The concept could not be more basic: 170 technicians, cameramen, producers, and directors, tracking 24 hours a day for 112 days the domestic activities of the 10 participants trying to win a determined amount of money while being shut inside a bunker under surveillance.

It is a reverse metamorphosis: the insect of Kafka awoke having been turned into 10 humans. "We created a new genre where we proved that ordinary people can be very interesting," said the creator of the format, Dutchman John de Mol (Endemol Entertainment International), upon releasing his product. It was not an invention; it was a "discovery" (a bad fall into the freewill of a major find). From there on out it was tediousness as a hobby. In no time at all, *like* the result of a fast-moving and fatal virus *like* the many we see in actuality, television viewers felt possessed by the stupidity of others and by the desire to exist also incompletely. It is *like* an audiovisual anthrax. And yet there is no real comparison, because to speak of *Big Brother*, it is necessary to use the term "like" another way. The show is only *like* itself. It is the height of *like*-ness: how can it be *like* that?

A veritable taxidermy job on a collective striptease, *Big Brother* worked from the start as a curiosity. It brought to viewers around the world an extraordinary number of recent examples of earthly behavior for which members of the audience felt an immediate empathy, no matter where they were from. Strangely (and one of the tenets of *Big Brother* is that nothing in human nature should strike us as strange), viewers tuned into the program out of curiosity and remained faithful to it due to a sort of unthinkable mimetic coincidence. With its burst of dissected but active symbols, *Big Brother* spread the globalization of taste toward permeable spaces. The popularity on screens the world over of an imported format confirmed the cloning of a collective experience. The program's success was unparalleled. Even the extreme south, which Charles Darwin equated to the end of the world, brought the geography of the living room out of its ostracism: television brought the same end, also as a finality, to all.

Some 20 odd versions of *Big Brother* were created around the world, and it is calculated that more than 1 billion people—a neighborhood or China Town as populous as China itself—saw the program at one time or another. If this says anything, it is the following: 1) people still watch television; 2) human beings can perceive an attractive additive for television programs of easy consumption that give priority to the homogenization of social behavior in exchange for their simplification; 3) *Big Brother* is an international fraternity that does not place excessive demands on those it accepts as new members. Furthermore, the numbers are astounding, and can even be considered alarming. An example from the South: on Saturday, June 30, 2001, when *Big Brother* ended in Argentina, nine of every 10 television sets were tuned to the program. This is a ratings record unequaled even by man landing on the Moon or by any World Cup soccer final.[1]

An unusual scenery spoke to the sudden collective national eagerness to feel befriended by the interpersonal play of conflicts and affections: weddings postponed until the end of the final episode; parties held to celebrate the consecration of viewers' favorite contestant to be the only occupant of the house to not be evicted; bars and restaurants who set up television sets so no one would miss the show. The decay of popular taste was populist in nature; the property of privacy took to the street: "Big Brother is watching you" (George Orwell). The participants, in the house of the watcher, did not know what was going on outside (the cameras did not act reciprocally), but the audience thought it knew what was going on both inside and outside the house: each spectator felt like a distinguished part of the eye belonging to *Big Brother*. A public corporation of spies facilitated the non-reciprocal game of looking without being looked at. For that we have to blame (or thank) the intransitivity of the television mirror.

In the different versions of *Big Brother*, or rather the same version but in different languages and with different actors, the cameras captured an average total of 5,040 hours, perpetual action that then underwent a process of editing. To manipulate viewers' attention, the strategy was to use the falsification of art-

---

[1]Nearly a decade and a half has passed since that day, and the format continues to be news in various parts of the world.

ful devices. The proliferation of cameras reinvented, with noto-
rious ease, a sure fact that was not difficult to access. In this way,
the unthinking attraction to the paroxysm of the trick turned
out to be tributary to a sensationalist privacy that sought to
make the controversy into a subversion and which, in distorted
fashion, imitated a reality with its own modes of verification.

In a pact of exhibitionism, the participants allowed the spectators into their accelerated desiring. The objects of their desires
had specific names: fame, popularity, and money (some people are
capable of killing for these things, or, even worse, they are capable of acting the way they really are). They trust in success and
find benefits in the ruins of behavior. In front of millions of gazes,
they begin to crumble ethically and aesthetically, with no compassion for themselves. Life continues to have the consent of a
precarious situation and delivers itself up to this condition. Examples enter and exit the screen, tracking the ephemeral site of a
story and its behavior. If television continues to function normally, as it has until now, within a very short time it will be rewarded with a more violent *Big Brother*, a mixture of gladiators and
human fights instead of bull fighters and bull fights. It will be like
kick boxing without rules. By then it will not be a bad idea to
leave the participants inside, and without food; the only ones to
survive will be those who behave like Hannibal Lecter. The main
prize for the winner will be life, the life that he has managed to
keep, while the rest will remain confined to the house forever.

In the curricular accommodation of the contents and symptoms of reality by means of polyfocalism, the farce of the avatar
was established as the product underwent a pre-selection and a
post-editing. It was the perfect conspiracy in the service of an
imitation unlimited by a repetitiveness which, invariably,
ended up rendering the surveillance banal, turning it into an
episode of its consequences. The complicity—not rewarded—
of watching and of feeling watched, of participating in a deper-
sonalizing tactic from the strategic venue of the living room,

captivated and reduced demands. On this shining surface (the brightness has nowhere to hide), viewers felt as if they were participating in a universal addi(c)tion of data and behavior that do not require any specific qualities to carry out their function. In this live reality show, emotion was also given short shrift. It was for this reason that no one could feel like a foreigner in this shared lack of will and the rise in instant notoriety.

From their comfortable domestic passivity, viewers shared the quick glory of people with no artistic attributes, who they celebrated for a nearly simple reason: since the emerging media star lacks talent—except for the one acquired by allowing him or herself to be sniffed and pried without reservation, all in exchange for the mere chance, with no guarantee, of winning the prize—the viewers themselves might actually be the new stars. These viewers, identifying with what they see, may say: "That's me." Since its appearance, this peep show has dissolved the limits of the human game preserve that is a house and of that which was considered unseemly to be shared outside the walls of the home. In these auraless hours, collective complicity with indecency was exercised with a minimum of blushing. It was not without reason that the inhabitants of the bunker acted with indifference, as if they did not feel watched, as if the cult of appearance were not a necessary evil. There they were, tending to become absorbed in themselves. And the audience looked with a magnifying glass at the center of the absent labyrinth, since there was nothing complex in that cathodic place opposed to common sense.

So then, empathy came at the level of gregarious deficiencies. We ought to speak of the solidarity of these deficiencies: the observed specimen was of the same lot as the audience. And this is worth remembering, because in this entire matter of reality TV there is an implicit pathology—or at least nearly—that is shared voluntarily. Dramatic viewing turns fellow men and women into informants of that which the spectator would like to be. In this manner, the impact of immediacy can be verified by the voyeuristic actions of the TV viewer. The lack of weightiness in the behavior seen in the *Big Brother* house (which was later that of *The Osbornes* and *Jersey Shore*, as well as of other productions of this type), became, in the end, a self-portrait (in no way scandalous) of the TV viewing public located outside the fake mansion, a public which was even in agreement with the brief, spasmodic condition of lesser achievement. The craving for the instantaneousness of fame lives off of unrecyclable lapses.

Just as with the emblematic recording at the beginning of *Mission Impossible* ("Your mission, should you choose to accept it, involves [fill in the mission], and should any member of your team be caught or killed, the Secretary will disavow all knowledge of your actions. This message will self-destruct in five seconds"), the tape of public recognition is destroyed—against its will—in a span of time that is as short and self-destructing as it is prudential. The building of low-cost celebrity need not wait long either to be activated or to be diluted. As soon as the participants begin to live life before the camera, the dividend of glory is at the mercy of its reach, as well as its final grandiosity. The key of the convening is the offer of notoriety accompanied by money.[2] And, since things are so bad . . . It is the multi-exploited fame that lasts only briefly, but which also takes only a short time to build, and even less to codify: it is the paradigm of a new form of exhibition included in a fleeting content.

Week after week, movement was seen inside the panoptic human cage, a garage of behavior (not to fix it but rather to view it), a shortcut to extreme apathy along which there appeared emotionally needy people seeking attention. The effects of interference, and the harassment of others who dare confess without concealing information, crossed the instant barrier of the fore-

---

[2]In the 2014 edition of Big Brother in the United States, the prize for the winner was $500,000.

seeable. Even though the cage was as transparent as newly made glass, the bottle was thrown into the sea awaiting an answer that arrived with no signature: the television set protects busybodies at least. The screen was a balcony from which to verify destinations, but with mistakes. It was a mirror of behavior where contemporaneous civilization could be seen in a barely popular state: it was a deteriorated image. During that time, no plants grew in the populated house. What did grow was the need for fame among uncultured people brought together by the same objectives, or rather without any objective except for that of winning the prize and awarded with an ephemeral notoriety. During this agreed-upon lapse of time, they lived a transitional phrase which they never abandoned, and it never abandoned them. Since none of what they said was important, all of it had validity.

In this conversational conflict, the *lingua franca* of oligophrenia served to remove indifference. No one avoided a lesson in tedium when it arrived punctually with all of its elements predisposed to engaging in flattery. The noble responsibility of training (to make one forget that time passes the same for all of us) was ruined before the imperfect future came to fruition. Who can be concerned with other people's happiness when those involved boast, without knowing it, about their lack of purpose? There is still no antidote against such inanity. No one in the viewing audience came away moved by these humans without human characteristics, and those who left (kicked out) will have a hard time experiencing the same Prodigal Son ending in reality. Once was enough.

During the time in which these people lived under the microscope, these legionnaires of banality were coherent in their deficiencies, boring language itself with their conversations. Since they no longer had anything to say, they wanted to be incomprehensible all the time. They went from a lack of captivation to disinterest, making impossible the act of words. The words were victims of nonsense adrift, and of a performance within this drifting that sought to make an impact on the most insignificant things that define this nonsense and which, in this case, were the majority of things. Faced with the evidence, doubt asked itself the following question: if they are this stupid in "intimacy," in this intimate setting, how will they be in "extimacy," in daily life outside? Turned into microcelebrities, with their personalities worsened by the obligation of delivering high ratings, that is to say made dopier, the protagonists of reality TV seek, first and foremost, to be considered for that which they have not yet become. It is a strange way of being in one's being before being.

Years ago, in the apogee of the modern era, the invisibility of illusion was the victorious sign of a liberty liberated from suspicion. Being invisible meant eluding being watched. Not now. There rules an exhausting visibility, an accomplice of the obsessive manner of feeling superior in the act of public exhibition, knowing beforehand that the detectives have been detected. Unlike Truman Burbank (from *The Truman Show*), the participants on *Big Brother* "act on their own," knowing they are being watched on the other side, where they also are.[3] We witness an asymmetrical but authorized observation, which makes the observers feel more alive, exultantly alive, since they submitted to a constant and unedited observation by the public, that

---

[3]The European, Latin American, and U.S. versions of *Big Brother* basically varied in one fundamental way: the behavior of the actors in front of the cameras. According to Paul Romer, the producer of the U.S. version of *Big Brother*, the participants never forgot that they are in front of a camera. In contrast, he said that in Europe they quickly forgot that they are in front of a camera, but this was not always the case. A female participant on the British version of *Big Brother* confessed that it was not reality TV but rather a dramatization. She said the truth is that they were all so bored that the producers had to find stories that were not really happening. In the Argentine version, the actors resembled their U.S. counterparts: throughout the different editions, they were a theatrical imitation of themselves; they were intent on building their feelings and on being the center of a totalitarian attention.

anonymous and collective neighbor who accepts them for that which they have not yet been able to be and yet aspire to do. Left defenseless against welcome invading forces, the ego feels accompanied, chosen to join the mutually perverse association that results from nosiness and which gets visible results.

In short, this panoply of exhibitionism is a parody of the favorite childhood game, hide-and-seek. Even if they are behind a door, or behind the mask that they invented so well for themselves, sooner or later all of them will be discovered by the omniscient gods of the remote control. Until not so long ago, in the contemporary era, individual privacy was an obligatory demand. In this post-contemporary era (or whatever post you like, including a musical one: "Wait, Mr. Postman, please, Mr. Postman"), the phenomenology of this exhibitionism swept away the atavisms and anomalies of timidity, fostering the desire for celebrity as an extreme form of exercising the survival instinct. The indifference of others is what brings discontent and causes a hierarchical rupture with the masters of self-satisfaction. Faced with this panorama of reality ruined by routine, there are those who seek to be the exception, meekly joining an unexceptional collective theater.

II (*Insects close up: the camera as microscope*)

We daily pass by obsessive television cameras: at work, at the supermarket, at the library, at the convenience store, at the laundromat, at restaurants, any place a body goes. We pay the same attention to them as we do a chair, or an ashtray when we do not need them. As with other objects in their still itinerary, cameras became part of the routine. According to a survey, in the United States 74 percent of those polled are not opposed to being monitored by closed-circuit television as they work. Freedom was gained and privacy was lost. In the past, busybodies and snoops were pointed out, fingered, to show their disrespectfulness. Today, one's thumb attentively pushes a button to begin the espionage. All of us are the spies and we are proud of it. Voyeurism, like in the film *Monsieur Hire* (Patrice Leconte, director), is no longer considered an illness. Or, at the very least, it is a contagious ailment from which no one is immune: there lies in wait for us the virus of a diminished condition.

Television, demonstrating its current lack of inventiveness, resorts, in emblematic reality TV shows, to the mediocrity of daily life as the star of an entertainment format that is popular the world over and which sums up some of the negative virtues of Western civilization. Years ago, there was a program in Uruguay called *Venga y cante* (*Come and Sing*), and people went on this show to sing without having the slightest musical talent (the attraction was not rhythm or melody, but rather involuntary humor). *Big Brother*'s slogan could well be "Come and do in front of the cameras that which you dare not do in public." For money in dollars, people of varying ages (though no senior citizens and no children) dare to let themselves be seen without adjectives. No emotional alibi provides enough protection. The public relates to snippets of intimacy observed in inverse proportion with its understanding. The premise is to share vulnerabilities in an interactive fashion. Before one's eyes circulates confidential information regarding the protagonists, who do nothing to hide the repeated disorganization of their behavior.[4]

Within the fictitious house, everyone lives an abnormal situation in splendid happiness, as if in front of the camera life

---

[4]Commenting on the proliferation of reality shows in Spain, television critic Javier Martín, of Madrid's *El País* newspaper, wrote: "Thanks to the *Big Brother* generation and to other versions of reality TV and their sequels, Spaniards have been shedding their modesty in front of the camera, especially since they have realized that their moral loss can redound to their financial gain. Being ridiculous—whether it be by jumping off a diving board or by becoming romantically involved with a "freaky" couple—is the first step in a career of media fame" ("*Millonario anónimo, donativo-anuncio*"/ "Secret Millionaire, Donation-Commercial", 31 May 2014, p. 57).

were much easier to endure. Thirty cameras capturing the action in all manner of languages—*Big Brother, Gran Hermano, Grande Fratello, Grosset Bruder, Grand Frere*—have served to portray the latest in fun. The tangential ubiquity of the cameras has severed the fine line between reality and entertainment. The negligence towards the evidence of intimacy magnified the eye's experience, transferring the place of persuasion from suggestion to proof positive. This visual experience is prolonged by the insistence of those things that never completely finish being fulfilled, since non-fulfillment defines them.

We enter into the private space of strangers who in a brief amount of time begin to become familiar to us, although this entry—which is free—is never completed; something is always missing. Or rather nothing is missing but there is too much of everything. The great reward of reality TV shows is not the final prize in dollars, but the days lived in front of the television cameras in the house with transparent walls. The time of fame is somewhat more than 15 minutes, the amount calculated by Andy Warhol in an era when being famous was more difficult than it is now. Today fame can last for several weeks in a row, the amount of weeks that a reality TV show lasts. For the ego, these weeks represent a trip to the stars, the easy embarrassment of condescension, a proposal of indecency *ad infinitum*.

Nevertheless, due to the shortage of original ideas and behavior, the staged action ends up causing an unbearable monotony. The repeated situations desensitize the content in direct relation to the foreseeable way in which the circumstances unfold. Appearance is left unprotected once the televised intimacy becomes common place, trampled by the gaze of millions of viewers. The prison of the mind acquires an alienating visuality as private anxieties lose independence. They soon cease to be anonymous, and their response to the intrusive practice is very simple: there is nothing complex beyond that which can be seen in the here and now freed from any and all possibility of a future. It is physiological television, since it parts ways with the allure of fiction to insert itself into a realistic future (which is its new way of creating fictions) where each scene attempts to become a record of something unexpected that does not manage to come to fruition but threatens to do so.

In the preservation of the simulated confinement, the residents of the house replace outside life with an intimacy issued in installments. The bait of curiosity turns them into heroes of an insufficient act that overcomes the calamity of the show. What is in play is the definition of a person through the efficiency of the group. As in *The Three Musketeers*, they are all for one and one for all (or rather, all for none), until the "all" ends up erasing the single person, the unique attitudes. Even names are useless, being inexact data of a behavior that is not at all mutual and even less exclusive. The process of loss of anonymity has an erosive quality, since the fiction is created that no motive remains hidden or can even be hidden. Identity is recorded with all its inconveniences: life is captured live on a tape from which there is no escape, not even when the action is rewound, because there are those who tape each episode of the show—incredible but true.

The residents become known through an accumulation of details that establishes an autobiographical process that is carried out over several weeks in a row of scrutiny. The impunity of the invisible being is lost in the precarious and disjointed model of an open-door identity. They are authorized autobiographies that get mixed up with the constant flowing of accumulated information that originates, at least in appearance, in the normal places of life. But do such places exist? As an effect of a tyranny exercised with the consent of the parties involved, the gaze enters into the expected responses of the human repertoire as if it were an animal laboratory. The group becomes an abstract entity divided into different names, whose dynamic seeks to construct a purpose. The alibi of the panoptic exercise has an asymmetrical destiny: it makes observers believe that by watching they "know" the actors and that this demiurgic observance—as it is happening at the same moment in which is it seen—changes the knowledge or ignorance of those being watched.

A social/anthropological experiment that projects a sense of verisimilitude, reality TV presents evidence that is contrary to the characterizing fiction of television programs, since it is a format that lacks a script and developmental guidelines. The driving force of entertainment is no other than the unedited behavior of the characters, the work of their uninhibited performance. Therefore, if said characters are not interesting—as has occurred, for example, with all the international versions of *Big Brother* produced to date—the show fails. The episodic interaction between ideas and attitudes becomes fossilized in an unoccupied gap, on the fringe that leads from anticipation to that which is foreseeable.

In this conventional emotional reality, which aspires to be considered as a witness, the spectators' imagination is freed with regard to things foreseeable, removing from it all responsibility for what might come next. Anyway—though the show moves forward in one single way—the only things that happen are those that are expected to happen. By way of consecutive routines, of large doses of "every day the same thing," boredom becomes ritualized. This is due to the fact that tedium, when it demands behaviors aimed at making people believe that things happen in nothingness, acquires a semblance of validity and complicity. The large amounts of time that pass in the house activate the inactive side of nothingness, and this nothingness, despite its insistence, will never be able to be an art form. In any case, it will be a shock damaged by the predictable path of its illusions.

The expression "civilized society" finds in the adjective an excuse, because not all societies manage to become civilized. Or can it be considered "civilized" to spy on incomplete human beings who, due to a lack of greater interest in life, allow themselves to be spied on? In Spanish, the words *espiar* (to spy) and *expiar* (to expiate or atone) are similar, but the expiation of the spies that we all are is never carried out. Life as a performance became the motor of a monitoring at the bottom of which the participants defeated sensibility with their childish way of relating to reality, with behavior that is adrift. We learned nothing. (It could be argued with all validity that, out of a sense of decency, they were less idiotic in front of the cameras than was their normal custom; it is possible.) Inside the screen there were people, and inside the characters, nothing. It was a vacuum with the form of an appearance.

The ritual followed the steps of a gradual frustration. The techniques of survival employed by those involved included the exaggeration of nonsense, self-parody (involuntarily), and neurosis over having been, uniquely and exclusively, marionettes of an unfinished pretension. As could be foreseen from a mile away, they ended up being ignored with exuberance; the move from nobody to somebody failed. It is clear: for this era, privacy is no longer a refuge of secrets. The pipe dream of anonymity has been lost. A pathological exhibitionism and a centerless narcissism have changed the notion of private life. Millions of volunteers want it this way. Privacy has another meaning. It is not the same as before, when the greatest intrusion a person could perpetrate was entering a neighbor's garden.

In 1936, Federico García Lorca finished his masterpiece *La casa de Bernarda Alba*, and during the second act of the play he has Bernarda state the following: "I was born to have my eyes open. I will now remain watchful, closing them no more until I die." In *1984* (a novel from 1948), George Orwell imagined a hyper-technified society in which the government apparatus exercised totalitarian control. Its permanent monitor, called Big Brother, dominated even the most private hideouts of the mind. This sharp eye dismantled the possessions of privacy, allowing silent vandalism to take control of behavior, as if a hacker had entered into the portal of an extreme secret to make it his own, like a substitute appropriation.

Movies, which tend to get to everything before television and after literature, portrayed exercises of totalitarian scrutiny: *The Truman Show* and *EDtv*, as well as *Body Double* earlier, and even earlier Alfred Hitchcock's masterpiece *Rear Window*. The premise of them all, with minimal variations, was the same: spy on others all the time to dominate them through the remote control of observation ("Hell are the eyes that look at us," said the poet, and here the gaze constructs its polifocal limbo: only indifference can save it).

Omniscience is also the aspiration of reality TV show producers: to film from beginning to end the life that fits into a television program. We witness the fiction of scattered interests that sacrifice their continuity in exchange for another that pays more attention to them. As if they were astronauts in a space capsule seen simultaneously by the rest of earthlings, the actors submit to the police-like surveillance that finds them at their most vulnerable. They are dissected while the activity continues uninterrupted. For cameras there is no such thing as limits of distastefulness or dissatisfaction. The bathroom is just as good as the living room; the evening is as satisfactory as the morning. If they represent the human race, the spectators, seeing them so close, feel like they are snooping on themselves.

Situations are brought about that are similar to those we feel when we see our face reflected in the mirror. The fiction of immediate recognition urges us to observe our neighbors, or, what is more, to feel like we are living with them, as if we were spouses of a compatibility that is too easy to be completely or incompletely credible. It is the great entertainment of the future (even if it is no longer like it was before), the entry into the great collective meddling in which no one is safe from the snooping periscope that lies in wait. The remote control exercises its neutrality; it goes unnoticed as if it did not know what it is all about. It is television without lasting images, galvanized for the comfort of the circumstances. Through numerous attempts and by dint of repetition, nonsense legalized its procedures. The readily apparent moral turns out to be as poor as the underlying proposal. Seeing that others have a life that is more miserable and boring than our own, we feel redeemed by television. We think: "We're not so bad off after all."

III (*The infraordinary*)

In France, the adaptation of the format was called *Loft Story* (the reference to Erich Segal's 1970 novel, at one time a bestseller, is evident). The first season lasted from April 26 to July 5, 2001, and it was promoted in the following way: "Eleven single people isolated from the world in a loft measuring 225 square meters, filmed 24 hours a day by 26 cameras and 50 microphones." It was also said that none of the participants would be able to escape the permanent vigilance of the cameras, and that to follow their movements during the night infrared cameras would be used. This confirms that the great gimmick, the intrinsic novelty of *Big Brother* (and therefore of telesurveilled society), is the number of cameras utilized to "see" the different versions of the phenomenon from all possible angles, as if the participants were soccer players trapped in constant replay.

The overwhelming number of cameras generates the perception that television viewers are accomplices, committed with their "infinite" gaze, capable of paying attention, or at least of taking into consideration an event that in truth—or in its true appearance—is not one but many. This dissimulating dislocation without authorial control—whose only rhythmic pattern appears to come from the movement of the cameras, from the suspicion that things can be seen better from another angle, and so on and so forth—highlights the exception of an excessively ephemeral instant, one that lacks long-term projection. The exclusive snooping of others' passivity produces impressive results.

Between the furious motion of gestures and actions without interest or justification, there begins to emerge a very basic central premise: everyone can be anyone. Each tenant in the house is a replica, instant copies that do not advance in their motivations. They share the genome of oligophrenia. Amid IQ bankruptcy, an act of conduct cloning is applied in accordance with the circumstances. It is with good reason that one of the show's premises is to explicitly suggest that this banality was already present there before filming began, and that it will continue after the season ends. As if it were a modern poem with no beginning or end, the show establishes a deceptive mechanism, manipulating the idea that the history of the participants begins only when they arrive at the Big Brother house, and that only there does it continue and receive attention. In his 1973 essay entitled "The-Infraordinary," Georges Perec made reference to narrations of life without a story, to a description of events absent a linear narrative: "What's really going on, what we're experiencing, the rest, all the rest, where is it? How should we take account of, question, describe what happens every day and recurs everyday: the banal, the quotidian, the obvious, the common, the ordinary, the infra-ordinary, the background noise, the habitual?"

So then, how does one take account of it? Question it? Describe it? The "infra-ordinary" is that which serves no purpose situated within the easily recognizable visible, amid the vampirization of irrelevant behavior with no supplementary value. What we are witnessing, it turns out, is a poetics of abnormality, of a spectacle dependent on the fact that there is no spectacle and that the result reaches the spectator in pure form, without having gone through the cutting room. In this regard, reality TV is further from cinema than the theater, even if it lacks a script. These are not results seen every day. Those residing in the house give the idea of characters seeking a point of view. And more than being a point of view, or a point of departure, they are a point of warning. Subtracted from reasoning, theirs are histories whose only existence is verbal. Soon the audience discovers that the actors are not actors, that they are "there" without ever becoming anything more than what they already were, and which television, with all its technology, cannot change.

The vision of the ordinary is inscribed not only in the context of a search for celebrity and of an economic reward for how it takes place (even resorting to an exhibitionism of its degradation), but also with regard to a make-believe profoundness (the relationship with the world ceases to be abstract: all the characters, or participants, are recorded by the cameras just as they are). It is as if the transparent *Big Brother* house had come to an agreement with language in order to see, like a forensic scientist, "what is on the inside," where none of what happens is innocent. The result highlights an interest that is manifested by the down times, by the desire to document nothingness when that which is happening is happening to others. The participants are that and nothing more: mere residents of a way of existing in a certain place. It is a very peculiar way of substituting reality with a whole that is divided into segments of ruined behavior.

Bad ideas cannot be imposed on images of reality. *Big Brother*, however, seeks to impose the idea that what viewers are seeing is "really" happening. As prisoners of the webcam, they are witnesses to a lasting duration, one without interruptions. And the rest, all the rest, where is it? What happens each day in the "house," and which each day is also repeated— "the banal, the quotidian, the obvious, the common, the ordinary, the infra-ordinary, the background noise, the habitual" —suggests the probability of a continuous beginning, one that does not require previous information in order to be perpetuated. The goings-on are proportional to what we cannot say with certainty about them, being illustrated by a large dose of information devoid of an objective. Nevertheless, this dose manages to lure the habitual out of its apparent neutrality. In this continuous encore of the unforeseeable, we see the affirmation of a Dadaism bereft of aesthetics in the sense that nothing can ever completely become an explanation. Like someone without a desire for something specific, reality is content to simply be watched.

Just when it seemed that everything that could be said about existence had been said, this comes along: in telereality there emerge incomplete accounts of language that are more concerned with speaking than in telling a story. Just when it seemed that nothing new could be invented to break the daily routine, non-inventing came to replace inventing. And in this case there is a documentary purpose, as audiovisual material is disseminated in a single take, without going through any editing process or a variety of test runs. It is "true," since everything comes out precisely as it was hoping to be seen. We verify the presence of an intention desirous of becoming structural, a representation that replaces another. Following the temporal logic of "one moment after another," of a temporality with no intermediaries inside, reality transforms into one that is placed on the stage without having rehearsed and without relying on the beautification provided by the scenery on set. And it is as if precisely this absence of a subsequent step in which the original version is touched up were the bait aimed at generating interest. In nothingness, everything is possible, and possibility disguises itself behind a double paradox. It is a matter of interfering as little as possible in the ways of seeing the world. Furthermore, the duration is accelerated by a process of slowing down; since nothing takes place, all is left for later.

The passage of the foreseeable, of nothingness in a state of lethargy, in short, of that which cannot change or be transformed from one moment to the next (except for by remote control), focuses viewers' interest, which skews toward that which could be called "the empty zone of events." Facts that language sets aside without specifying them seem to be screaming out for the lack of interest in the subject (which is never able to be determined) to continue, to go on expanding a visuality with attributes. The tactic, in any event, is to warn beforehand—as is clear—that nothing is going to happen, and that this is precisely the only thing that is happening. The participants seem to be in a nexus-type situation, one of being a link to emptiness in a state of development, and within the confines of this they seek to relate their unnecessary story. These cornered pop stars, with their worst codes of conduct, and with very few minutes of notoriety, are at once exposed and protected—though not exempted—by a paradox: in the nomadism of their behavior, they prolong their presence toward anonymity. We are not really meant to know anything about them, but rather only pay attention to what is happening around them, which only requires minimal effort. They are simple, inoffensive intermediaries of a torrential emptying of expectations. Without much effort at all they turn into the only data of their own statistics.

In order to feed high ratings and to make changes on the fly in case such ratings decline, the viewers also feel as if they are being surveilled. Audience measurements can tell what viewers are doing with their televisions at the time that *Big Brother* is being broadcasted. The show provides a thousand reasons not to watch it a second time, but it has managed to achieve repeat viewership and hold its place on the world's marquee listings for more than a decade. A considerable majority have adapted to the inadaptable with deliberate intentions, in a situation where one might even invoke the statement made by Charles Baudelaire in the mid-19th century: "No one uses their imagination anymore. Imagination is dead." *Big Brother* has become its obituary.

IV (*Don't cry so much for yourself, Argentina*)

Argentina rang in the third millennium seated in front of a television screen. If not for the fact that in Europe television viewers feel a similar empathy for the nothingness that is a synonym for entertainment, it would be easy to conclude that the most characteristic image of developing countries comes from the television content of mass acceptance preferred by the people. There is emerging a deteriorating landscape, with behavioral acts that could only be justified in the name of ratings. That which takes place before one's eyes, like an uncommon fury, prevents lying. A slender young lady born in Buenos Aires starts crying inconsolably because they tell her she has been nominated. She cries as if left by her future groom. How strange: in Hollywood when people are nominated for something they laugh and celebrate. I immediately thought that the Argentines, at least those who fit in a television set, are in truth sad people, like those in a tango, and they celebrate a nomination by crying.

I later came to learn that it was not a nomination for an Oscar, but rather a different kind of nomination, one that did not come with a statue. It was a nomination in which the one chosen is thrown out of a house where there are more human beings living, all of whom cry when nominated. There are evictions. What could there be in that house that no one wants to leave? The young lady was crying because she wanted to stay, and they did not let her. I have seen people in similar situations, some of whom cried even more because they were being evicted from their little house because they could not make the monthly mortgage payments. But *Big Brother* is a game. In any event, it is a game in which those involved have to guess what type of game it is. For those who think, it is not fun, though perhaps it is fun for those who are able to remain in the house without being nominated. Through the art of multiple cameras, the residence of this fictitious fraternity is turned into a gutter without enigma where a flock of humans isolate themselves from reality, and, above all, from thought.

Within this intrinsic improbability are heard conversations on the edge of anemia that illustrate the worst possible tedium, that in which language is worn out and words do not refer to any feeling or decision. These words float about like a noise, like an end without finality. Words in this place have lost their turn forever. There is no possibility of replication. The only metaphysical concern of the dwellers is that no one nominate them: a physical goal. They congratulate themselves and demonstrate a lack of intellect by continually refuting any act of thought, or even anything slightly resembling it. It is a degradation of contretemps.

The situation is not a bad one by any means. These people are given food and they live without working or having to pay the rent. All they have to do to not be kicked out immediately is act like developmentally impaired people 24 hours a day. This presents no problem as they also act this way in their own homes (where they do have to pay rent). In all they spend several weeks, expense-free, showing viewers—free of charge—how to be just as stupid and without having to leave home, not even for a moment. Home, boringly sweet home. It is an extreme and fictitious sedentary lifestyle in an era of nomadic lives. The leading characters chose this confinement as a tactic to escape anonymity: theirs is an opportunism within hand's reach.

Despite being a bad example for intelligence, the different versions of *Big Brother* have been a great public success. People have seen it, they have even been moved to tears by the imbecile behavior of the characters, and they have even felt that there are absolutely useless situations that cause dependence. Since nothing happens, all feel protected. This type of occurrence should surprise no one. In imperial Rome, the multitude fought to enter the Coliseum to see the gladiators tear each other apart. They celebrated the winner deliriously, a winner who sooner or later ended up dying. Victories do not take pity on mortality. Those were pagan times, and these, which are none-too-sacred, are paying times—the last to be evicted is paid money in dollars.

The game has a basic premise: the cameras perform a vampirization of (outside) intimacy. On top of AIDS and the bird flu, we now have an epidemic of voyeurism. It should be pointed out, however, that a farce is introduced, a simulation of spontaneity. Because the characters in the show had to go through casting auditions beforehand, they know they are being watched, and they modify their behavior to gain the favor of the public, which will end up choosing the winner. They vote against and kick out the others. When this happens, those evicted cry because they do not want to say goodbye and leave. It is the same as a reprehensible television drama series without a script, which is to say, much worse.

These actors, protagonists of their limitations, have nothing to say, therefore there is no drama or emotional performance. It is a tournament of clowns in which the public must choose the idiot who was most pleasing to them (they cast their votes by phone). It is a perfect democracy: everyone is able to feel committed to an imbecility belonging to someone else. And the one who wins is the one who is the least different, since no one can be more real than anyone else. George Orwell imagined a controlling superior identity, but here, in the frenzy of interactivity, we are the busybodies. No one is saved from it. The paradox completes its cycle: we spy on the lives of others, believing that we see ourselves from outside. We are all strangers in the process of being so.

Seeking some interesting phrase that would redeem us/them, I tuned into the program for an entire week. I could find none. I turned up the volume on the television set several times, but that was not the problem. I went back to it the following week and discovered the same number of useless sentences, but fewer people: one person had been nominated and thus received the prize of expulsion. This person was crying, looking like Gwyneth Paltrow when she won her Oscar. But this was a male; he too was crying. I changed the channel. I saw more programs, including one in which there were also people. I turned to a sports show (I saw more than just three or four goals, and one of the ones I saw was excellent). I kept watching different programs, and I saw yet another, on another channel, in which there was a shootout and nearly all those involved were either cops or robbers.

A long time went by, as in several minutes in a row. I returned to Big Brother and the one who had been evicted was still crying. How could that be? I was afraid that something would happen to him before a commercial break. Those who remained in the house were laughing their heads off as if they had managed to rid themselves of a case of dandruff. Another person gone; what joy. Strange brotherhood. The fewer the better. The host asked the person who had been kicked out: "How do you feel? Are you sad?" The questions were at the level of the participants: no one had to think to be able to answer them. Television without priorities (in a trivialized medium, the messenger is not always connected to the message).

For the moment, the majority feels content. The boredom of the current format is entertaining enough so that one need not change the channel. Going beyond the in-no-way strict limits of mental deficiency, idiocy and comfort act simultaneously as those involved agree not to think more than they are able, though they do not even attempt it much. Proof arises of cooperation between beings contrary to reality even though they remain in said reality. In this diagnosis of situations, the group feels and speaks in front of the cameras with no other novelty than that of the passing of dead time. There is no trickle of intelligence. Even those who try to please *Big Brother* fail: in the house there are people without life inside. They have nothing to say, nothing to say to themselves or among each other, and they do not know how to say it. In short, they are Mr. and Ms. Nobodies with the mental coefficient of no one. It is nothingness on the verge of being complete. Time without action—the lyrical dullness of thought, which Andrei Tarkosvki and James Joyce turned into the slow pleasure of beautiful things—is, in this case, an accomplice to a nothingness with different plans. Its purpose is emptiness, and not even later on can it be justified.

In front of the cameras, the cast of *Big Brother* feel that they can do whatever they want with what they are. They invent themselves without realizing it, appropriating data from reality that cease to be at the service of what is real. They have come to television in representation of the insignificant, determined to coincide with themselves in the least significant manner possible, or something like that. Showing their outdoor self in an indoor fashion, they manage to demonstrate the hypothesis that life is much better the less attention is paid to it.

In this vacuum of common sense, eyes are incapable of discovering the circumstances of the behavior shown by beings who are being observed in their outer temperature, in the mechanical show that they put on by feeling observed as if they were superior entities, at least in their compulsive imagination. We are witnessing (and it occurs with impunity), an operation of emotional striptease (egocentrism explained to those with brain damage), as if, facing the mirror of the multitude, the cast members were asking: "What do you think of me?" And they would know that the answer would not be flattering. Nothing happens in their lives, therefore nothing is resolved.

In a closed space, the transparent house of *Big Brother*, the participants reveal all the versions of who they would like to be at the very moment when the world is seeing them and generating the illusion, or rather, the question: "To what extent can they be completely unreal?" We, the world whose remote control activity is in remission, are on this side of the mirror, giving permission to what is irreparably occurring in a very bizarre fashion. The action takes place in the time-space continuum, situated between what we are seeing and those who feel seen, in a sort of interactive reality without anything completely specific on which to base itself.

In a theater of reflections and layers superimposed on the surface, life takes twists and turns to demonstrate that it is the same as always, and that rarely can it choose for itself (*Big Brother* is no exception). In this territory occupied by panoramic intimacies, in this simultaneity without surprises, we see occurrences of discontinuous reality. There is a televisual alteration of reality that turns lies into a place inhabited by the truth and by a permanent doubt. What certainty do we have that reality really occurs, or that there is a reality less unreal than all the rest? We feel like a kind of god who contemplates the boring state of the human condition while trying to climb the ladder of celebrity, though it is not a matter of fame for the sake of fame itself, but rather it is a matter of obsession with fame.

At the beginning of the first episode of *Big Brother*, the host stated that all the participants were normal people. What an ambiguous definition of normality. The neighbors of serial killers also say that they all seemed normal and they are incredulous when they learn of the aberrant acts they committed. When Orwell wrote *1984*, the world was showing the first symptoms of a different abnormality. This English author arrived early at the premonition of a fear that was spreading from everything to everyone. He imagined that power, to be maintained, needed to spy on the ideas of a civilization that was growing more and more intelligent. He was wrong. There is nothing to be worried about, nothing to spy on. Only a demented person like North Korean leader Kim Jong-un could still believe that there are interesting people in the world to spy on.

According to the premise of reality TV, human beings are the recipients (and senders) of their idiocy, and as such they live, either in their own home or one that is loaned to them. To spy on such people, therefore, is an unnecessary exercise. What we are is enough to constitute complete futility. Among dilemmas, pauses of lasciviousness, theatricalities, and impossible romances, there appear on the screen jabbering indistinctly souls tormented by the lack of promises. These are people who cannot be reduced to a single adjective. What is there to spy on where there are no ideas, or difference, or sensitivity, but rather monotonous behavior keen to alienate and at the same time not leave anyone alienated? What?

Reality TV—a dilettantism in-no-way episodic—creates the enormous fiction that all limits are violable. Spying on someone taking a bath in front of the cameras cleans away boredom, and evicting this person from the house becomes a miniaturized exercise in power (a form of exiling someone). Everything can be violated, absolutely everything, excluding, that is, certain exceptions that occur in the act of reception, exceptions that are skeptical and disillusioned by the ingredients of negativity belonging to a bevy of supposedly human behaviors. It is a lodge without ontology. We are witnesses to the grandiloquence of oligophrenia.

As if they were turtles that leave their shells to go out and die in the elements, these obvious candidates for forgetfulness exposed the shortcoming in their personalities daily and nightly in exchange for being able to do that which they longed to do: be seen without having anything to show. It was a virtual exhibitionism. They proved that the gaze can also suffer from amnesia. To be able to survive, the actors were only obliged to be what they are, even if they still do not know it. The first response exhibited was to speed up the intangible conflict with the others, to participate in a confrontation, as if they were gladiators with rubber swords.

Without a superior idea that would turn them into fiction, they accepted the inferior charm of appearances, moving outward, toward the incomplete "fellow being" who the entire time preferred to remain in that state. And faced with the failure of expectations, spectators quickly felt distant from that which the actors could not show because they lack it. That is to say, at the beginning no one knew what was going to happen and later we all knew too much. Things went from expectations to disinterest in a brief lapse of time. If this is entertainment, waiting in the dentist's office must also be entertaining.

In the reality TV format, *Big Brother* especially, indolence becomes an inexplicable ill. It is indolence as apathy, as the height of insensitivity, as the diagnosis of an obsessive reality where the interaction between nothingness and its presence is the only genuine thing. It is indolence in order to satisfy the curiosity that ended up killing the cat but not (yet) the human being. Television is capable of entering a hypothetical but recognizable home seven days a week. The same as with midgets, idiots can be recognized from afar. Whether they be in Madrid, Sidney, London, or some U.S. city, they can still be observed up close from a living room sofa in South America.

They become famous for reasons that no one knows; the ratings offer no such reasons. And they come out of the event without anyone needing them. They can have several synonyms: stupid, idiotic, imbecile, or with minds in a precarious condition that away from the cameras could belong to another species within our own. Perhaps it exists—a society without satiety, a strange case of redundancies. The television facelift takes years off their appearances: each one of the actors looks to be some 30 years of age, but never do they rise above the childhood stage, as their behavior proves. In this regard we see retrogression. We see bodies whose mental age is younger and that have learned (this is their great merit) to exist without having to think, which is to say that their actions do not depend on intelligence. In their sickly adolescent version, with voices, gestures, and perspectives battered by the gregarious deficit, they seem, in the end, like people safeguarded from adulthood. The name of the idiot today is Dorian Gray.

V (*Reality, a cameo appearance*)

We enter a movie theater to see—in a dark room—life in technicolor. With reality shows the opposite occurs. Inside a colorful house, we see life in black and white, as if intelligence and emotions had lost their chromatic diversity. We see the television

cameras acting as if they were at the service of the National Security Agency (NSA), creating massive espionage, an intrusion
into private life for which we did not have to pay admission. The
computer is not the only modern machine useful for exhibiting
intimacy without modesty. The television is also a means to this
same end. On the other side of the screen, television viewers are
drones flying over someone else's privacy. How ironic. In times of
cyberwarfare, when fear of having frequent secret visitors into our
privacy abounds, we feel like accomplices of a vigil of vigilance,
using the back door to enter another's life.

And we do enter, but at the end of the experience we are
overwhelmed. "Whoever invented the idea of privacy, of a private home, was the greatest genius of all time," stated Jonas
Mekas in much earlier times, when privacy was not traded for
anything, least of all for its exact opposite. Today privacy feels
powerful, showing itself off, placing its privileges at risk. Has it
perhaps ceased to be important? Could the loss of privacy be the
point of departure toward a new way of occupation of human life?
It appears necessary, therefore, to define what reality TV is and
its relation to empirical reality might be. What is real, what is an
illusion of reality, and to what extent does a hybrid of both lack
intentions? The old question is repeated: "Is it me or is it real?"

Popular and cheap, the reality show genre has made popular that which is most indefinably basic. In 1961, Newton
Minow, who was the chairman of the Federal Communications
Commission, said that television was a "vast wasteland," coining a phrase that will never be outdated: "When television is
bad, nothing is worse." Given the great ease with which human
beings enjoy television when it is "worse," interest in reality
shows is unlikely to die any time soon.[5] Different formats feed

---

[5]Reality TV continues to be very popular the world over. In some countries,
such as Australia, U.S. reality shows get high rating, meaning they continue to make lots of money, since they are cheap programs to produce (an
hour of reality TV costs half of what an hour of a drama series costs). It is
not surprising, then, that Fox announced in 2014 that it plans to debut a
cable channel that will air reality shows 24 hours a day.

its continuity through the representation of situations unusual
in appearance. The premise is to generate the obvious beginning with what is now inexistent. It is a matter of presenting
human beings in their most inappropriate behavior, people who
are showing themselves as they want to be known. Television
viewers are reflected in them, satisfied by confirming that there
are worse people in the world.

In popular television shows of the past, such as 'Candid
Camera," the premise was that participants did not now that
they were being filmed. Today it happens in reverse: they know
that they are being filmed, but that is not the important thing.
What is important is to generate among the audience an expectation, a desire to know how much the cast members will dare
to do in front of the camera, to what point their deliberate
impulses will reach, and to what degree the irrational and the
rational can act together.

Voyeurism, morbidness, exhibitionism, and narcissism burst
onto the scene like effects without a determined cause. Stimulated by simulation, the amorphous characters believe that by
accumulating fame they will also accumulate money in short
order. But reality is characterized by not easily pleasing everyone's illusions. There is more fame than money at stake here for
them. They are exposed at the same time that they are exploit-
ed, since not all of them receive remuneration, though the
broadcasting company earns a lot of money from their presence
and because they have thousands of hours of programming
without having to have paid neither script writers nor actors.
We see them speaking, laughing, bathing, being friendly, and
eating, and we desire to know what else they can do.[6] The *pane
et circuses* generates unrealistic expectations capable of rendering the remote control inactive. Who would have said that
such a thing would be possible?

The participants in reality shows act out as conspicuously as
possible to feed their exhibitionism and exacerbate the audience's dependence on what it is seeing, without being able to

believe it at first, only to later grow used to it without much difficulty and with a minimal investment of intelligence. It is an
effective way to validate entertainment that must entertain
based on the scarcest possible conceptual or dramatic development, depending only on certain episodes of human behavior—
when its presentation is at its least developed—to establish the
plot, to weave the thread of the story. Men and women who
have voluntarily become guinea pigs dream about attaining
residual glory, living under the illusion that people will recognize their faces on the street—or on another program—once
they leave the house. That is the collateral effect of reality
shows: they create characters without anyone knowing what
they are good for or good at.

They all fantasize about making a career in show business,
but very few reach their goal (the only TV life they have is on
Big Brother, and they are not able to get another one, not even
later on DVD), or ever manage to be accepted into the traveling club of world celebrities. Some, however, do make it. Paris
Hilton is the most emblematic case. As if she were someone
truly important, she visited Uruguay at the beginning of 2014

---

[6]There are those who are capable of almost anything to be on *Big Brother*,
just like the character in the 2012 Italian movie *Reality*. For example, Josie
Cunningham, a 23-year-old woman from Britain, announced in April 2014
that she was planning on terminating her pregnancy of four months to be
considered for a place on the latest edition of *Big Brother* (UK). Her decision came with an explanation that is dumbfounding to any person with
common sense: "I was excited at first but as soon as I noticed I was getting
bigger, that was it . . . nobody wants to see a naked pregnant lady. People
will disagree with my actions, they always do, but I don't care . . . this is
something I have wanted for so long. I can't give up my big break for
anything." Fortunately, a week later she announced that she had decided
against going through with the abortion: "I just couldn't do it. I really
thought I would be able to but I couldn't. I'd felt the baby kick for the first
time 24 hours earlier and I couldn't get that feeling out of my head. I'd
forgotten what the feeling was like. It was magical. It was like the baby was
telling me not to go through with it."

for the first time and only for a few short hours. They paid her a fortune for allowing herself to be seen live and on the scene. A group of young people idolized her out loud, shouting: "Paris, we love you! Paris, look at us!" (but she continued on, without seeing them). They yelled this as they saw her appear on high in a pair of expensive Italian shoes with extremely tall heels, from where she sees the world as if it belonged to her. The only talent of this woman with a hotel name is having appeared on the reality show *The Simple Life*, between 2003 and 2007. She has been good at adapting to reality, including after the TV ratings ceased to be in her favor.

The Kardashian clan, "another reality" that is the product of reality shows, has also shown no signs of wanting to disappear any too soon from the public radar. Bearing their uselessness on their shoulders, they have now spent several years under the spotlight and still manage to attract attention. In 2013, Kim Kardashian was the second-most-searched celebrity on Yahoo!, behind only Miley Cyrus. According to *Forbes* magazine, between June 2012 and the same month in 2013 she earned $10 million. Some, such as Hilton and Kardashian, lack talent but possess the ability to garner attention. Could that be the definition of "talent" in the 21st century? They synthesize a symptom: they are faces and names that circulate over the artificial surface of reality, wooed by a great tribe of faithful followers who think they are talking to God each time they communicate with their idols through a Twitter account. Social networks have consolidated their power of attraction for longer than expected.

It is precisely on social networks that videos go viral, videos containing transgressed intimacies (*Big Brother* entered the bedroom because the door was open). Documentation of private matters seen up close has become fashionable. People unhappy with their lives seek to give it new and different dimensions by publicly exposing details that cannot be postponed.[7] This practice is also a good way of disassociating themselves from reality, from being victims of moments lacking in lucidity that have portrayed them as protagonists of their own indiscretion. The public feels like an accomplice at a time of shared nosiness, synthesized by the so oft-repeated phrase "Look what I saw." A visual state lacking words is imposed, a simultaneous alteration of the public and the private, which mix together indiscriminately, exchanging reputations.

In *Reality* (2012), the character Luciano, who owns a fish stand in Naples, competes to be a participant on *Big Brother* (*Grande Fratello*) and ruins his personal and family life attempting to achieve his objective, becoming the first victim of his obsession. Just as this Italian films allows for a glimpse of, it may be that the "Big Brother" phenomenon has lost its impetus, but not the desire of the masses to be in front of the television camera one day, in front of the invasive eye that would open the doors to an extraordinary reality where fame and money would complete the ideal of happiness within reach. Fifteen minutes of fame are not enough: it should last longer, become a dream prolonged by vigil.

The 15 minutes of fame are only the beginning of the long road toward nothingness wrapped as a gift. By gaining entrance into the bubble where everything can be reality, Luciano feels that he has passed exam of the collective gaze. He wants to turn into a figure without existence, but with fame. Like Paris Hilton and Kim Kardashian, he desires to feel recruited by celebrity, which no longer means being on the cover of a magazine, which was the goal of the rock group Dr. Hook & the Medicine Show with its 1972 song "The Cover of 'Rolling Stone.'" Today, any promotional space will do, including the smallest section of a gossip magazine like the ones people read with curiosity in the dentist office waiting room.

---

[7]Byung-Chul Han, a German philosopher born in South Korea, opines: "Today, one's being is no longer of any importance. The only thing that lends value is appearing, showing oneself off. Being is no longer important if you are not capable of showing off what you are or what you have. An example is Facebook: to capture people's attention, to be recognized as having value, you have to show yourself off, place yourself in a display window or showcase."

A surgically applied glance marks the beginning of a disin-
tegration of privacy and also of objectives. The walls of privacy
are crumbling down. Former spy Edward Snowden, who surely
knows something about all this, said that "a child born today
will grow up with no conception of privacy at all." Characters—among whom no one was born the day before yesterday—
go on *Big Brother*, and on other substitute shows, to do precisely that: to sacrifice their privacy in public. In the beatification
of a performance under strict surveillance 24 hours a day, with
cameras throughout the house, they become different versions
of themselves, devaluated versions that do not seek the recognition of an active intelligence. They already accomplished a
lot just by passing the test in order to live cooped up for a period of time, like birds who have decided on their own to enter
the panoptic cage to have a place to show themselves off. In the
refutation of content, omniscience helps to project an extreme
realism in which there stand out trajectories that lead to
nowhere. Maybe one day nosiness can be absolute, with cameras implanted in people's minds to know what they are dream-
ing about. More than one Starbucks customer will say, "What is
this camera doing in my cappuccino?"

Until this hyper-panoptic scenario arrives, we will continue
to witness the ritual of shows defeated by urgencies that are much
too obvious to contribute interest to events. It is an effective way
of destabilizing reason, but without a point of view or narrative
structure being imposed. Since it does not know how to ask for
itself, reality ends up being interrogated by human behavior in an
environment that portrays such behavior as having subdimen-
sions. The promiscuous and rarified tone of an ambiance where
the last remains of finesse have been embalmed is shared by the
drugged vertigo emblematic of a place open to the public. In this
place, human beings—or so they seem—come to comprise the
final casting list of reiterative subjects besieged by their superficial ambitions. It is as if with their actions they were saying: "We
are what we want to see on the screen." For them, reality is not
real, nor is there only one. It is for this reason that it is hard for

the world to recognize that merger of personalities and hypothetical psychologies, which, as a result of not knowing what to do with their lives, have ended up on a television screen.

The public will soon tire of seeing intimate matters played out before/inside the camera and will want something more, just as it wanted before, when millions enjoyed public executions in town squares, mass killings, and ideologies. Without being forced to do so, they took to the streets to cheer Hitler or Stalin, with the same shouts of jubilation as before, when, at the foot of scaffolds and guillotines, they were accomplices in delivering their victims over to the executioners. We want to believe that we are not like these other people, but it has always been too easy to follow the example of others. Only one slight change has occurred: today the comfort of the show requires less remorse.

LIVES IN THE SUPERMARKET

EVEN BEFORE READING ALLEN GINSBERG'S POEM, "A Supermarket in California," where watermelons appear and Federico García Lorca is hiding behind them, I liked supermarkets. My grandfather worked in an enormous one, the first supermarket in Uruguay (he is the only one in our family to have been first in anything), and the first time we visited it, I felt the same goose-bump emotion that I did when my first American girlfriend (a blonde named Sally, or Sue, I believe) took me to Six Flags in St. Louis, Missouri. The only difference was that at the amusement park there were hot dogs, candy, and french fries everywhere one turned, in addition to an elongated roller coaster, a giant Ferris wheel, and a lake, which was artificial, just like everything in those plastic places. But nowhere did I find toothpaste, toothbrushes, or anti-dandruff shampoo, articles that are more necessary for staying clean than for staying entertained.

Walking down those friendly local aisles of American life, I found numerous edible products that had deserted and ended their days in a kind of collective cemetery for items which, in function of their obligation to utilitarianism, could not be in another place or change their destiny (not to mention their destination) at the last minute. I felt as if I were in the midst of a battalion of volumes that produced empirical results and were the continuation of a project benefitting household economies. The supermarket was a phenomenon of capitalist philanthropy where the occasional discounts on prices are the alms vaguely similar to the assistance received by panhandlers in the street or those who ask for help at the door of a church.

The allegory of a usefulness that serves as an example to reality, the supermarket, as I realized prematurely, was not another

245

colonialist naivety of the U.S. Empire. The "American way of life" had arrived in the most extreme reaches of the south in order to popularize cellophane, the shopping cart, plastic bags, the multiplication of canned goods as if they were fish multiplied by Jesus Christ, cans and boxes of rice that the customers could touch without having to ask an employee for permission, as I used to have to do in the small stores in my neighborhood, where the owner grew angry every time I approached the bananas, as if he thought that I was capable of doing something with fruit other than caressing it and buying it. In supermarkets, where we can touch the merchandise, we feel as if we are interacting with it. We feel as if it is we who are giving service to the products.

With its orderly variety of goods placed in an orderly fashion on shelves that must be full at all times, supermarkets have always seemed to me like places of very entertaining usefulness, a sanctuary of convenience and bulk sales. They are a true representation of the everyday in its exact dosage, if there is such a thing. They are also a literal translation of consumerism applied in equal quantities to a dozen bananas, a bunch of chard, a pound of potatoes, endless bins of junk food, high in sodium and preservatives, or any other thing considered useful, but above all that which is most suited to be showcased in that bunker so very well lit from on high.

That first visit to the supermarket where my grandfather worked seemed like a dazzling slow-motion scene played out near the cold storage, where the meat of dead animals spends its final hours before being turned into puchero stew, meatloaf, tacos, and hamburgers (which are so delicious with ketchup and mayonnaise, items found in the next aisle over, among the edible goods in sealed containers). I should have had a camera with me. I should have had more eyes. That way I could have better taken in all those disciplined fruits, those rows of tuna cans standing there so still, those superb armies of 1-liter bottles of cooking oil. It was a world of varied names, some from outside, like me, who had only just now entered into this expanding sphere of useful magic. All of this, including soaps with their varied aromas and plucked and packaged chickens (rare birds, indeed), seemed to me to be indispensable, part of a canon, part of a liturgy. And all of it was happening at a necessary speed: a hedonism of no particular brand and yet of all brands, decorated with time in its best slowness in order not to cease continuing to arrive in a punctual manner. Peace and quiet—a paradox of free time—could wander down aisles that did not run the risk of entering the paths of extinction, at least not as long as humans are hungry and need to practice good hygiene. Subjectivity is pleased by the repetition of abundance. It is difficult to leave such a place and very easy to return, and soon. In capitalist life, waste is a habit that is not so easily annihilated.

There was something magical and preponderant about that many shelves stocked full with products for all uses and tastes: some for disinfecting the kitchen, others for brushing teeth and making them shiny, several ready to fry and eat, and others to be placed in salads. I was very excited to discover that the Fanta bottles were not all alone. Unlike the one I was accustomed to seeing cold, alone, and vulnerable every Sunday at the family table next to the pitcher of rosé wine, in the supermarket where my grandfather worked the Fanta was accompanied by other bottles just like it, all of them just like it, dozens of them, as if they were happy, very happy, in the place which was full of them, forming a platoon. For all products, despite their type or origins, supermarkets are a kind of motel where bottles are with their (glass) family or significant other, even though at any moment a human hand, of which there are so many, could come by and leave them orphaned.

Uruguay entered the modern era on the day the first supermarket was opened in Montevideo, November 1, 1963. It was the month and year that President Kennedy was assassinated: finally, the American president's ideas about progress had come to pass, at least one specific one. In the light of the current era, the results stand out, as if on that date long ago life had transitioned from one age to another and only now has come to say so. Since then, a universal trend has been radicalizing. People want to live close to where they can buy anything and everything, that is to say, where the needs of the body and or reality can be superseded by convenience. Lives within view of the supermarket. I have not been to that first Uruguayan supermarket in years. I should go back sometime and try, along those refrigerated aisles, to recover part of my childhood when it was still the best part of that childhood, that fortunate period when one feels like his or her own master (but let it not be in the memory, which is the supermarket of recollections). To recover, if possible, the uncommon nature of that moment in time full of surprises and expectations, until the time comes, if it does come, when there are no more doubts, since by then less absolute truths will, at long last, have been placed in order.

Visiting supermarkets is one of my favorite pastimes. I have been in all the ones in Montevideo, and there are more and more of them all the time. In some of them, I have gone so far as to buy something not on sale. I prefer to walk through supermarkets over museums, where the works are not canned or frozen, which is why they must be hung on a wall. Any Kroger excites me more than New York's Museum of Modern Art. I would not trade any real can of Campbell's soup for the lonely one depicted in Andy Warhol's painting. I am certain that I would prefer to be in a Kroger than in the MOMA. There are supermarkets that are better than museums. Besides, they do not charge an entrance fee, and there is a greater number of pieces in the collection. If art is edible, as Salvador Dalí said it was (and I really do not know what kind of condiments I would put on one of his works; ketchup or mayonnaise?), then supermarkets are the true museums of our time. For this reason, in good supermarkets a can of tuna is worth as much as a painting by Pablo

Picasso in which there is no fish, and much more than one by
Edgar Degas containing only scaleless and unfrozen ballerinas.

The supermarket is a marvelous place to engage in tourism.
The first time I traveled to Paris, I asked the concierge at the
hotel where I could find the closest one. He told me to go to one
on the next block over. I went, but I did not like it because it
was too small. So small, in fact, was that miniscule supermarket
in the City of Light that it could have been lit by a single can-
dle. It was, more accurately, a neighborhood convenience store,
a French-speaking 7-Eleven, and I wanted something more on
the (edible) level of my expectations. It had no aisles. The next
day, instead of going to the Louvre Museum, I drank some coffee and then rode the Metro to the Denfert-Rochereau Station.
When I got off I found an enormous supermarket that excited
me much more than the Mona Lisa, which I saw the next morning, but not without considerable difficulty because it was surrounded by a group of Japanese taking photos of it. They were
not tourists; they were kamikazes. So disturbing was the infernal
noise of the clicks that La Gioconda was no longer smiling.

In the area around the painting, there were as many people
as there were products in that Parisian supermarket I had visited the day before. I spent nearly five hours in that store surrounded by products, checking to see from what varied places
they had come and what they contained, enjoying the very particular aroma of the country cheeses before removing their
packaging. I was a tourist among cereals and sausages. I am fascinated by canned goods, and I also love the name, as if it were
meant to indicate that due to being canned, they are good
inside of there, that they are well behaved.

Many containers said "Made in France," but they said it in
French. These included jams, sodas, beans, and, of course,
scrumptious Camembert cheeses, all of them identified, for
their own good, in the language of Flaubert. It was, without a
doubt, a fabulous literary experience (temptations of the tongue

need no dictionary to know what to demonstrate and what to say). It was also a trip through the history of the present. I took photographs of myself with the wines and the *foie gras*. I am smiling in all of them. I spent so much time there, surrounded by mute merchandise, that I forgot to visit the Arc de Triomphe and the Eiffel Tower.

In the supermarkets of the First World, which are rated suitable for all audiences, temptation wears the face of discounts. The scarce words used on signs to promote products prove to be extraordinarily effective. There are phrases that possess great powers of convincing. Typical examples are: "Strawberries half price"; "Buy a pound of cherries and get another half free"; "Two-liter Coca-Cola on sale for $1." People navigate their carts down the wide aisles surrounded by shelves, and there are signs painted with vivid colors to help the consumer decide to buy one product instead of another which is also there waiting to be liberated from its motionless position within reach of the world. Quality and origin serve to grab the attention of willing pockets.

When customers who are adrift find a label stating, "Organic lettuce; no chemical products have been used," they feel the immediate desire to buy at least one head, even if the price is higher than that of lettuce that comes saturated with chemicals designed to enhance their texture and flavor. These latter heads were picked 15 days earlier but still retain an enviable green color (it is enough to remind one of the line, "Green, how I want you green," from García Lorca's poetry), the same color that dollars always have, even though they contain no preservatives and perhaps for that reason are not fit for consumption. And it is a shame, because the tendency today is to eat all that which has not received any chemical treatment—"organic" they call it. Lettuce, plums, carrots, asparagus, leeks, celery, arugula, tomatoes, etc. Today naturalness is the preferred currency in all regards.

On the way to the beloved meat section of a supermarket in another place that was not California, I happened to find a sign sticking out of two pieces of ice whose purpose was to keep fresh the fish that was already cold—what a paradox. There were many types in this veritable rally of fish, some pink, some a shade of blue (surely they had come from a melancholy sea), others white, and several that were a little blacker than the rest: the racial melting pot had also made it to this fish and seafood display, which was about the same size and dimension as the goal area of a soccer field, also sometimes called the "six-yard box." The sign, in Spanish, said: *Salmón fresco*. Since *fresco* can mean both "fresh" and "cool," I was able to touch the dead creature and verify that the latter meaning was indeed accurate: it was cool. Actually, it was quite cold. The dead, including those on sale, are cold, and this salmon was at the freezing point. It had come from a journey through temperature. If it had been clearly marked as frozen and placed in a frozen food section, it would have been just that, "igloo" fish, but this fish, according to the sign, was *fresco*, and even though I knew this meant "fresh" in this case, it nonetheless presented a case of undoubtedly ambiguous terminology.

Supermarkets use a different logic, one whose duplicity is exquisite (depending of course on the recipe used). How can fish be fresh and frozen at the same time? What would be the answer, both grammatically and rationally? Is there such an answer? I looked at the fresh salmon, which appeared healthy in its posthumous pinkness, and it did not have an answer to the dilemma of its condition, though it continued in this condition, keeping a cold-blooded silence. As soon as a man appeared wearing a white smock that made him look somewhat like a doctor of dead fish—a supermarket forensic scientist—I took the opportunity to ask him, because I just had to do it:

"Why does the sign say the salmon is fresh?"
"Because it's fresh."
"Does that mean it has never been frozen?"

"It means it was caught very recently."
"How long ago?"
"I'd have to check on that."
"Can you assure me that it's fresh fish?"
"Absolutely."

I bought a piece of this creature that appeared to have been anesthetized, imagining that it had been caught with loving care (and with bait) on the high seas by brave fishermen who defied storms and sharks to catch it, as if it were a fryable Moby Dick. I pictured it in my mind's eye entering the ship's clean and healthy nets, just like a soccer ball enters the goal and finally comes to rest, nestled softly against the net, then having its scales removed and its head chopped, and being carefully cleaned, just as pets are washed in the backyard. In short, I envisioned a process that, despite its painful appearance, was elegant and immaculate. We always have the idea that the flesh that comes from the ocean is cleaner than the meat that comes out of a slaughterhouse, because the days of these latter animals, both before and after reaching this place, were bloody, and because they met a cruel and bloody end.

However, just like a lover disillusioned with his love prey— in this case the belle would be the salmon and I would be the beau—I discovered a very ugly fact. And I only found this out after having devoured it completely (I never liked half-done things), thinking that this creature turned fatal victim had been caught two days earlier on the windy waters of the North Atlantic, where fearless sailors risk their lives to please the dinner guests. The fish, a witness to its motionless situation, did not come from the vast, wild sea, but rather from a tame, waveless farm without shipwrecks where the fish confined therein eat their own feces several times a day.

Furthermore, it was not a normal fish, like those seen in *The Little Mermaid*: it had been genetically modified to be six times larger than its normal average size. It was nothing but an obese creature with scales. So that it would weigh more on the supermarket scales, they had altered the solicitous proof of its genealogy. The geographic origin of the creature was despicably falsified. A frigid fraud had been committed against my palate, but also against the palate of all humanity, because no man is an island (nor do all fish come from places where there are islands, waves, and seaweed).

That fish, in a state similar to porn stars who inject silicone into their breasts, was more plastic than the plate it sat on later, just before its visit to the oven. It was a fish created in an aquatic laboratory, a Frankenstein with scales, a sort of mutated carp (though not a porn fish). It had spent its childhood and adolescence in an artificial nursery where thousands of its species, in a state of hybridization, fight rowdily, just like piranhas, for a small space where life swims, modifying its trajectory. Supermarkets are an ocean where life walks with good manners in order to take home the immobility of things that know how to be still without being forced to do so. On aquatic farms, where fish receive injections similar to those of athletes who engage in doping to reach the finish line faster, reality swiftly manufactures its tricks, causing us to believe that all that exists and is able to be rounded up can be natural, or become so one day. In the life of this test-tube fish, which ended in good company surrounded by potatoes and yams, the only natural thing was my transitory astonishment, one that for different reasons has been repeated time and again during my daily and nightly tours through supermarkets, those fascinating and photogenic places.

In *True History of the Conquest of New Spain*, Bernal Díaz del Castillo (1492?-1584) mentions a great street market located in Tlatelolco (it had been moved there from Tenochtitlán in 1428). For the Aztecs, this market was just a market. However, for the visitors with metal weapons, accustomed to European underdevelopment, it was a super market. Montezuma had servants who would go to the market and bring him the best food available, a pioneering advantage of the recently discovered reality. In this regard, we were First World before the Europeans. In his own words, the great chronicler speaks of the effectiveness of that unprecedented open-air space, diversified by the variety of products offered for barter (gold for cocoa, fruit for copper, bananas for slaves, etc.). Bernal Díaz recounted with accumulating prose the moment when the Spanish entourage, accompanied by Montezuma, visited the Tlatelolco market. Due to its meticulous richness it is worth citing the passage in its entirety, taken here from the 1928 translation by Alfred Percival Maudslay:

> Let us begin with the dealers in gold, silver, and precious stones, feathers, mantles, and embroidered goods. Then there were other wares consisting of Indian slaves both men and women; and I say that they bring as many of them to that great market for sale as the Portuguese bring negroes from Guinea; and they brought them along tied to long poles, with collars round their necks so that they could not escape, and others they left free.
>
> Next there were other traders who sold great pieces of cloth and cotton, and articles of twisted thread, and there were *cacahuateros* who sold cacao. In this way one could see every sort of merchandise that is to be found in the whole of New Spain, placed in arrangement in the same manner as they do in my own country, which is Medina del Campo, where they hold the fairs, where each line of booths has its particular kind of merchandise, and so it is in this great market. There were those who sold cloths of henequen and ropes and the *cotaras* with which they are shod, which are made from the same plant, and sweet cooked roots, and other tubers which they get from this plant, all were kept in one part of the market in the place

assigned to them. In another part there were skins of tigers and lions, of otters and jackals, deer and other animals and badgers and mountain cats, some tanned and others untanned, and other classes of merchandise.

Let us go on and speak of those who sold beans and sage and other vegetables and herbs in another part, and to those who sold fowls, cocks with wattles, rabbits, hares, deer, mallards, young dogs and other things of that sort in their part of the market, and let us also mention the fruiterers, and the women who sold cooked food, dough and tripe in their own part of the market; then every sort of pottery made in a thousand different forms from great water jars to little jugs, these also had a place to themselves; then those who sold honey and honey paste and other dainties like nut paste, and those who sold lumber, boards, cradles, beams, blocks and benches, each article by itself, and the vendors of *ocote* firewood, and other things of a similar nature. I must furthermore mention, asking your pardon, that they also sold many canoes full of human excrement, and these were kept in the creeks near the market, and this they use to make salt or for tanning skins, for without it they say that they cannot be well prepared.

I know well that some gentlemen laugh at this, but I say that it is so, and I may add that on all the roads it is a usual thing to have places made of reeds or straw or grass, so that they may be screened from the passers by, into these they retire when they wish to purge their bowels so that even that filth should not be lost. But why do I waste so many words in recounting what they sell in that great market, for I shall never finish if I tell it all in detail . . .

The words, even coming as they did like fired from a machine gun, were insufficient to describe the fabulous content of the great Aztec central market circa 1521. Bernal Díaz expressed his perplexity over the spectacle of abundance; this tradition was interpreted from the perspective of a hierarchy dominated by the wonder caused by that which had never before been seen. A market of edible products had caused the conquistador as much aesthetic amazement as a religious temple full of gold and jewels. The written tongue first spoke through the eyes of the stomach.

The Aztecs had moved several centuries ahead of modern customs. With the passing of eras, the traditional market transformed into a supermarket and, in turn, into a hypermarket. Life came to depend on prefixes for a place to get its food. Lovers of initials and abbreviations, Americans dehyphenated the combination, which is to say, they joined the prefix (super-) to the noun (market). They also turned the super market into an interior and walkable supermarket under artificial lights and air conditioning. Inside this panoramic space, the consumer surely feels the same way the butter must feel in the refrigerated section.

Besides coining a new word with the combination of "super" and "market," Americans implemented the concept of self-service, something developed by Clarence Saunders in his Piggly Wiggly stores, the first of which opened its doors in Memphis in 1916, long before Elvis Presley built the mansion in which he died, looking rather obese: he liked supermarkets more than gyms. Saunders patented the concept, but in 1933 the Albers store in Cincinnati was the first to use the word "supermarket." However, the first supermarket as such, King Kullen, did not open until August 4, 1937, in the borough of Queens, New York. This was the same year that the shopping cart made its appearance. With the opening of the first "official" supermarket, the practice of the seduction of convenience and of voluntary slavery was established, because in supermarkets shoppers are also employees (of themselves) as they must take charge of the entire process, from beginning to end: choosing the products, filling the cart, paying, and carrying their bags to their cars. All of this has a positive side: one saves money by not needing to pay a tip.

Supermarkets are the inhabited representation of a global multi-instantaneousness. They make omnipresence possible: they allow one to be in several places at once. That is why when we go into a supermarket we do not know what country we are in. Are we in Mexico? Because if not, why are there so many bags of Doritos and so much picante sauce? Or could it perhaps be Italy, due to the quantity of spaghetti and fettuccine packages? In this UN of aromas, shapes, and flavors where aisles are horizontal elevators that move people from one place to another, my loyalty to the canned sardines and jars of honey cause me to return weekly to its ethnic neighborhoods, which are only barely separated by long rows of well-ordered products.

Supermarkets are public spaces where human beings quickly come to feel inseparable from the things in them, in the most generous possible use of the word 'thing.' They are morgues where the cadavers of chickens, cows, pigs, and fish are in view (but without headstones), waiting to be buried at a later date, not under the ground, but rather in shoppers' bellies. Inside a supermarket, we feel kidnapped by variety, by that phenomenon which is impossible to simplify, even if there is nothing simpler than supermarkets. Everything is displayed in an easily accessible way, suspended in time, ready to be taken somewhere else after having enriched the customer's experience.

Recognizable for its permanent functionality, the supermarket is one of the protagonists of modernity that seems to change the least, even if its products change, especially those that pass their expiration date. Like a Disney theme park where the amenities are meant to be taken home and the fantasies come in containers that invite shoppers to reimagine that which exists, supermarkets cannot change the original form in which they were conceived, because otherwise they would become a different entity. They would still offer food and drink, yes, but without the characteristics unique to a market where the mode of purchasing stimulates the free will of the customer.

Supermarkets are emergency rooms. They are open 24 hours a day and willing and ready to give service to the human body. But they themselves can be injured. When there is looting, the first places to suffer the consequences of the violence are supermarkets, where even those who are not hungry go in to steal anything they can. The generous hospitality of supermarkets is unlimited. In Argentina, the supermarkets preferred by looters are those with Chinese owners. Could it be because they are cheaper even when there is disorder?

A supermarket is a place where close encounters of all kinds occur, the meeting place of urgencies and appetites, a place that allows in its interior the fusion of expectations and verisimilitude, which permits the contents of experience to be emptied. In that asymmetric universe—where crackers peacefully coexist with salami and cabbage, with all that happens to be nearby, creating a cosmic fraternity of products—one feels represented upon entering into the action. We are chance visitors to this place on which we cast no doubt, and we are the pets of these products that have been patiently awaiting us. We are like characters in a Chagall painting, but situated in an ambience that could be considered artistically degraded.

Perhaps more precise is the case of U.S. artist Brendan O'Connell, in whose paintings the advantages of the artificial at the service of functionality are abhorred as he seeks to capture, like a taxidermist, the activity of supermarkets and hypermarkets (Wal-Mart is the model). He represents such stores as if they were a territory filled with zombies wandering up and down inhospitable paths, and he reveals dehumanized gestures that have discovered in these places the opportunity to express themselves before disappearing. No one seems happy or content in O'Connell's paintings, and yet they do not feature dull tones but rather display a gamut of intense colors in which visually alluring blotches expand to affirm the physical nature of supermarkets, with their bombardment of shapes and colors.

Supermarkets are an Amazon.com where all that is for sale is within view and, for our convenience, we do not have to wait several days for the items to arrive. There is an underlying reason inviting people to visit a supermarket: the illusion of a permanent beginning restarts as soon as they change aisles. Everything can be found under one roof. And that is not the only reason. We can go to the supermarket for the simple pleasure of parking the car for free and then driving a vehicle that is not ours without having to pay like we do when we use a car from Hertz or Enterprise. Shopping carts are the only vehicles, besides bicycles, that we can drive without having to think about the high cost of a barrel of oil.

In the supermarket, all the individual egos that roam the universe appear alike, as if its deceptive neutrality could effect the disappearance of any presumptuousness of celebrity that shoppers might have. We enter the supermarket to be just like everyone else, something that is not too hard to achieve. We are more accessible to ourselves there, and we even think of ourselves as less interesting. We go to achieve an objective and we try to achieve it as soon as possible. We cannot go to the supermarket to escape; we have been chosen to fulfill an initiative without being able to exercise invisibility.

People do not go to the supermarket to go "shopping"; they go "to the supermarket." Though it may not be sublime, it is a "functional" aesthetic operation that enriches the experience. The *flâneur* of which Baudelaire and Walter Benjamin wrote, the great modern stroller, the vagabond with no real place to go, finds in the supermarket the ideal place to eliminate his ennui, his boredom, without needing a remote control to do it and to tell life there are many other things to do. The supermarket is an invention that radicalized individualism. Since its first appearance, no one on the consumer end wants to be served, not even when making purchases.

People prefer to enjoy all the freedom in the world to spend their money and waste their time, which they think they are gaining. The metaphor of usefulness is used specifically for consumers, who, during their wanderings, perceive a repetition of abundance. It is perhaps for this reason that the cumulative addiction experienced upon entering a grocery store multiplies if the shopper arrives on an empty stomach, feeling in a recalibrated way that everything for sale is necessary to alleviate their hunger as they walk down the aisles, because life can always be satisfied with more and more.

Without rules of interpretation, the trip through the supermarket occurs asymmetrically, allowing one to skip from aisle A to aisle F, passing aisles B through E, as if this place of travels were a library of products that can be read as well as used, though few people pay attention to the indications on the labels. Who has stopped to read the information regarding the chemical components used in a Polish sausage, for example? Or the instructions about how to use correctly dandruff-combatting shampoo for dry hair, which recommends that the hair be wetted before use, as if some people used shampoo without first wetting their hair? And who reads the instructions about how to open a can of tomato sauce, which actually surely does not have such instructions about this process? It would perhaps not be a bad idea (though I also do not know if it would be a good idea) to create a "universal anthology of instructions" listed on product containers, a taxonomy of all of them. However, I am unaware of how many people might be interested in such a book, considering the fact that they do not pay attention to such indications when they are attached to the products themselves.

Instructions for use may or may not be important to the consumer (we should acquire such knowledge before we purchase the item), but there are more transcendental things on the shelves than words printed in such detail and tiny letters, words which say, in short, what the user already knows. One goes to the supermarket to buy (or at the very least to walk), not to read. It is a treeless, birdless park with paths that do not fork any more than is necessary. The supermarket is a theme park where everything is for sale, except the cars and the employees. Oh, and the cash registers.

On one aisle are the noodles, while on another is the Nugget shoe polish, though it can also be used on boots. The sardines await on the next aisle, and farther down is the bathroom tissue and disposable diapers. The utilitarian and the edible live together without discrimination. All of these are tolerance areas, ideal for moving from one section to the next with the pleased invincibility of a zombie. Supermarkets are a democratic arena where racism among the products is unthinkable. Even though there is a universal code that organizes the supermarket aisles of the world in similar fashion, there is no one and only correct method of exploring this implicit labyrinth whose entrances are invariably where the exits should be.

Due to the way in which the aisles are arranged, the "lettuce and tomato tactic"—to give it one possible name—universalizes the systematizing practices of capitalism, because as soon as shoppers enter a supermarket they come to the fruits and vegetables, that recently picked life. Before the preserves there appears that which is still present in its natural state (though far from its home in the ground or on trees), inviting shoppers not to ignore the rest, as if to say, in its healthy exhibitionism: "The best has just begun." This trip is going to take a while.

When shoppers enter, they are not given a map of the supermarket and its sections, or a pamphlet with instructions about how to get out the quickest. Nothing is prearranged, since the very order of supermarkets is random rather than precarious, something refuted in practice by empirical reasons that do not stand out as so easily predictable. The hypotheses regarding the layout of a trip through the supermarket have not been completely established, since the present existence of useful items is not easy to put in order, even if it is there explicitly, causing concern. An immense peculiarity can be seen, but one thing is certain, and it is the great certainty that we have: those who enter supermarkets can leave sooner or later. If, as stated in the popular expression, "all roads lead to Rome," in supermarkets all aisles lead to where the exit begins. That is where their universe of enjoyable difficulties concludes. Just as in life, we pay at the supermarket as we exit. It is literature and excessive reality. We move from Pandora's box to the box we call a cash register.

In the movie *The Day of the Dead*, the dead walk down the aisles of a supermarket thinking, perhaps, if they are thinking, that there they will find the door to return to the earlier reality to which they had belonged. They walk the aisles of indulgence the same way that most people walk through supermarkets, with a somnambulistic and routine face, as if nothing mattered more than buying only that which is necessary before leaving as soon as possible, as if the products were on the verge of waking up. They walk among prices and discounts just like zombies, disciplined only by the territorial organization through which they must travel, absorbed in their utilitarian purpose. In this state of alert and transit, they pay homage to concentration and then to concentrated products.

In the capitalism of light and fit greek yogurt and chicken with hormones (edible Lance Armstrongs), in the polytechnical culture of the shopping mall, the supermarket (a cousin to the mall) continues to be a democratic place where everyone wanders down its aisles giving the impression that they can buy whatever they might want, interacting with their consumer fantasies in order not to forget the reality that follows their footsteps. In supermarkets, we travel through a new global dictionary of easily digested words. It is for that reason that there are so many products with brief names (kosher, sushi, tofu, soup, ketchup, salt) which, despite their short names, can be eaten slowly. They are the antidote for junk food. In this expanding eclecticism, any consumer can feel like an archaeologist surrounded by a proliferation of useful goods, capable of remaining catatonic when faced with the abundance of priorities. Marco Polo must have felt something similar in his journey to China, even though he had to walk a greater distance, and without air conditioning.

In supermarkets, reality has something more with which to entertain itself and gluttony has another option for gratifying itself, with or without dignity. To be precise, due to their kaleidoscopic condition, supermarkets go against the designs of our era. In an era of anorexic and bulimic beings, they feature an overpopulation of products, a state of reality without comparison. What do they not contain? The food is never the same, and in its mutant condition it transforms the world's digestion, beginning with that of those who live in the neighborhood. There are foods that are frozen, pre-cooked, organic, and dehydrated. They all provide sustenance, at least that is what they claim, but to what extent do labels tell the truth? What is the truth about a food? Is there one for the flavor and another for the nutritional value? Without taking the time to seek an answer, people still go on eating, and nothing indicates that they will stop any time soon. This is why today a greater (and ever-increasing) quantity of things is sold now than in the past, which is why supermarkets are on the verge of experiencing their own Babel, which would not be without its benefits. The products know it better than anyone.

The transformation of these products before our very eyes makes us believe that we are witnessing the metamorphosis of Ovid or Kafka, or of both at once. Seeing the butcher move as a living entity among so many pieces of dead and still cow (both of these states being against the creature's will) produces a strange sensation. It leads shoppers to believe they are in a museum looking at paintings of dead nature scenes (I love those of the Flemish School because it features a lot of pheasants, and also those of Chaim Soutine), but then suddenly something starts to move as if to say that not all hope is lost.

A similar phenomenon is caused by seeing the baker appear among the recently baked loaves of bread as if he too were a croissant, but with a vocabulary and a white uniform. It is simply exciting. It is . . . it is like being there. It is as simple as when something happens and a person is distracted to make a break from the totalitarianism of will: "The logic of the supermarket," states Michel Houellebecq, "leads inevitably to a dispersion of the senses; the supermarket man cannot be, organically, a man of one will, of one single desire."

With so many new grocery store products from other countries around it, the bath tissue feels less alone, as do the people who need both of them. The long linear shelves found in supermarkets are called 'gondolas' in South America and other places, just like the Venetian boats that transport newlyweds along the canals of the sinking city. Though less romantic than Venice, supermarkets are ideal for coming into contact with something or someone. Some people have found the love of their life (or of a week) walking (and not on the shelf) in a supermarket. These are good places to meet people who are either there by themselves or are poorly accompanied. There are those who, buying a dozen oranges, have found their half-orange, with a navel. This is much like the artificial salmon that have fallen carefully into nets (though in the case of humans the nets belong to Cupid). These produce-section couples may share their love of carrots, chard, chickpeas, horrendous broccoli, docile blood-red beets, and other products from the vegetable kingdom with more anonymous reputations that are a good idea to buy at least once in life.

Supermarkets were created precisely for this purpose, so that people can try everything. Their aisles are a pedestrian walkway of obligation for consumers. Their carts are full, all the items on the shopping list are checked off, but they continue sauntering about, lingering, cruising. There is room in their shopping plans for the unnecessary. The desire to buy produces consumer sleepwalking, and this desire feeds itself. When the shoppers reach the next set of shelves, the previous desire will be obsolete. The volume of products gives rise to the necessity of buying something unexpected. The power of the purchasing desire increases with each inch of floor covered. When one leaves the store, the ideal is for the cart to look like an 18-wheel semi-truck with an oversize load.

Supermarkets show that life is all that exists to be purchased. They are part library and part athletic tracks. They are a school of languages where one can learn other languages: French (Camembert), English (light, diet), Italian (spaghetti, pomodoro), Japanese (ramen), Chinese (noodles, dumplings). Disciplined in their designs, they represent a doubtful systematicity of consumption. Due to the way in which they are arranged, they are a travelable metaphor of life as it is lived these days. Satellite transmissions have brought remote corners of the planet closer, and something similar happens in supermarkets. Uses and tastes are communicated. Canned goods for humans, as well as those eaten by dogs and cats, are separated by only two aisles that do not take into account genetics but rather the convenience of shoppers, busy beings in that congregating ark of different appetites on the zoological scale. It is clear that only humans can enjoy the fashion parade of labels dressed up for the marketing party, since animals, perhaps due to the fear that they might leave without paying, are not allowed in supermarkets.

Everything in the supermarket was conceived exclusively for customers and their wallets, designed in such a way that both of them spend as much time as possible inspecting the variety of goods on hand. Walking in company with a metallic cart of large cubic capacity, visitors feed their consumer frenzy, even if they do not need quite so much to feed their bodies. In the random order of things, of apparently arbitrary sequences, it still makes sense for one to wonder: "Why is such and such a thing close to that other thing but farther away from the rest?" Just as happens in the world (because they are their own worlds), supermarkets also do not provide answers regarding the secrets of their identity (all I leave with from Kroger are questions and full shopping bags). In any event, they are as indispensable as the diversity of items they sell. The universe is their branch. They are everywhere, including in the imagination.

I have an album full of photos taken in supermarkets, including in Spain, France, Germany, Mexico, Ecuador, Colombia, and even in Montevideo's neighborhood of Pocitos, close to the apartment where my parents lived. They are pictures taken in different sections: by the canned beer, the bananas, the soft drinks, the bread and cookies (several shots from this aisle), the bags of flour and sugar, and I even have a Polaroid photo that I had taken of myself with a beautiful blonde cashier (at least at that moment she was) in which both of us are smiling, though I do not really know the reason why. In this collection there are other, equally venerable pictures, and one that stands out was taken in a huge supermarket in Washington, D.C., not far from the White House. I went in with the hope of running into the President of the United States, because I imagine that the presidents of countries also eat and practice hygiene. I did not see him, but I did buy a very good shampoo for dandruff.

The enormous supermarkets of the United States are as comfortable as the one featured in Allen Ginsberg's poem, although I have never been able to find García Lorca there, despite the fact that I have looked for him for so many years behind the watermelons where he was allegedly hiding (he must be very well hidden), as well as among the other fruits a little farther down. I checked the cantaloupes, the pears, the plums, the grapes, the kiwis, the grapefruit... the ripe blueberries! . . . but García Lorca chose to remain hidden behind the watermelons, in that visual inexistence. What was back there? And the same thing always happens: when I get there, he has already left. But what are still there are those magnificent lines by Ginsberg, which I tend to remember each time I get bored, especially of a Sunday, when one gets older than on the other days of the week, and I go and spend a good long while in the supermarket to keep the half oranges and whole cantaloupes company: "Where are we going, Walt Whitman? The doors close in an hour. / Which way does your beard point tonight? / (I touch your book and dream of our odyssey in the supermarket and feel absurd.)"

Several times, supermarket employees who have never read Allen Ginsberg have said to me that hackneyed phrase which the beatnik poet transformed into poetry by combining it with other, less common ones: "The doors close in an hour." In fact, many times they have had to kick me out, drag me out, because the doors "close in one minute." If I add up all the minutes that I have spent floating from one aisle to another, I arrive at the calculation that I have spent entire seasons in supermarkets, the equivalent of diminutive lives. "Eight days passed, and they were like eight centuries," said the character in Jorge Luis Borges' poem "The South." I have spent days and centuries among aisles.

My record for staying inside a supermarket came in one located in St. Louis, the birthplace of so many poets who could have hidden behind the watermelons like García Lorca (T. S. Eliot, Marianne Moore, Tennessee Williams, William Burroughs). I went to that supermarket twice with my late mother and we spent four long, memorable hours there, plus a few more, walking down aisles, looking at labels and origins in a supermarket the size of an airport. In that place imagination could soar on its own, and even with the engines shut down. There were so many things to examine that we would have needed two extra legs each in order not to get so tired and to manage to make it to the soap and detergent section without the long delay that we experienced in doing so, which was not necessarily the fault of the nonexistent stop lights.

The aisles were the boulevards that led directly to several products that we ended up buying even though we did not really need them. Finally, when it was very late, we returned to the hotel, but because we were tired, not because we ran out of aisles or products to continue looking at. It was a day of epiphanies in more than one regard. For example, I discovered in that supermarket the importance of canned herring, almost all of which comes from Finland. Since it was during the 1980s, there were still no Russian herrings available due to Communism and the Cold War. Today, on the other hand, there are too many former Soviet herrings, which are inexpensive but not as refined as those from the Netherlands, a country which also gives us good cheese and friendly tulips.

I never go to the supermarket for a precise amount of time. I do not even do that when I go to the dentist's office! That is why no one wants to go to the supermarket with me; everyone says I spend too much time just to buy half a dozen eggs, and that I waste valuable minutes of life looking at motionless jars of black olives to figure out where they came from and how much sodium they contain. I like to taste them first by touch. However, that gratuitous monotony of chemistry and origins inspires me. I feel like García Lorca and Ginsberg. I am my favorite poet when I am there. Furthermore, even though the jars are not crystal balls, I see in them things in the future, and I see all of these things on a plate. I see muses with protein achieving their best roundness (supermarkets are the ideal libraries of Alexandria for ball-shaped culinary boluses).

Most people go to the supermarket with a list of things they must buy and then leave quickly. I, on the other hand, go without a list and leave later, much later. I buy the things that happen to occur to me during my march (including in reverse), and many such things occur to me in the supermarket. I once went to a Kroger in Chicago and I bought a cheese. My significant other at the time was angry because that dairy product, with its crater-like holes, was so big that we were eating cheese for a year. We did what Mickey and Minnie did, though the cheese was anything but mini. We ate cheese in the morning, at siesta time, at night, and even when we would arrive home late from the movies after having eaten popcorn and chocolate-covered peanuts. We always ate at least one piece, just in case.

Now, every time I pass by the cheese section—one of my favorites—I keep on moving, acting as though something else has distracted me and I have not seen anything. I pass on by, but I do not go far, just a few steps, because the cold cuts neighborhood, which is the next one over, is also irresistible. I know very well, by memory actually, the name of these chilly meats, as well as their size, their packaging, their weight in kilos and grams, their pungent smell, the way the sausages are hung, as well as where all these products come from. Oh, and I know how much they cost. I go to this paradisiacal section so often that when I excitedly select a Genoa salami it greets me respectfully, as if it has been awaiting my arrival for some time. There are certain cold meats that are like that. The same thing happens when I visit the canned-foods section, with its sardines, peaches in syrup, tuna, tomato sauce, corned beef, palm hearts, etc. I never pass by without greeting them. Though their hermetic nature is radical, we exchange "hellos" and "goodbyes" in our own way. Their silence-dominated fate fills me with questions. Do they suffer from claustrophobia inside their metal containers? Do they fear can openers, or the idea of disorder? What do they do when not doing anything?

I went to a supermarket in Dallas once where the cheeses and watermelons lived on different continents. That huge place, called Whole Foods, was so enormous that when I got to the section containing herring I thought I had made it all the way to the capital of Finland. It was incredible. I was in Helsinki! Surrounded by so many cans of sardines, tuna, and cockle shellfish I felt as if I were walking on the Dead Sea, like a second Jesus Christ. The names of products keep their containers awake at night, and they keep them in line with their duty to exist, precisely as they are. I found so many transcendent things there together in that gastronomic neighborhood that it seemed like the United Nations of Food. The products, canned and bottled (though not bottled up in a meeting), came from all over the globe, including from countries where many people suffer from hunger. *Mondo Cane.* What little they have to eat they export.

Anchovies from Cameroon. Coffee from Ethiopia. Peppers from Côte d'Ivoire. Oysters from Senegal. Baby corn from China. Rice from India, the Philippines, and Thailand. Beans from Mexico. In short, portable food. It was not what I had gone there to buy, and yet, having found it there, it would now be possible to purchase some of it. And that is what I did. Suddenly, in the midst of that menagerie of jars and preserves lying in wait, I found some honey, Burleson's honey, a very popular brand. The label carried the following information: "Made with honey from Uruguay." I felt a chill like that experienced by someone who starts to feel less alone, and even a bit more in the company of another. I got excited, as excited as I did the first time I visited the supermarket where my grandfather worked, and I searched in vain for García Lorca behind the very green watermelons, and he was not there.